READINGS IN WORLD DEVELOPMENT: GROWTH AND DEVELOPMENT IN THE ASIA PACIFIC

READINGS IN WORLD DEVELOPMENT: GROWTH AND DEVELOPMENT IN THE ASIA PACIFIC

K.C. ROY
AND
S. CHATTERJEE
EDITOR

Nova Science Publishers, Inc.
New York

LIBRARY OF CONGRESS CATALOGING-IN-PUBLICATION DATA
Readings in world development : growth and development in the Asia Pacific / K.C. Roy and S. Chatterjee (editor).

p. cm.
Includes index.
ISBN 1-59454-947-8
1. Poverty--Asia. 2. Asia--Economic policy. 3. Asia--Economic conditions--1945- I. Roy, K. C. (Kartik Chandra), 1941- II. Chatterjee, Srikanta.
HC415.P6R429 2004
339.4'6095--dc22 2005036123

Published by Nova Science Publishers, Inc. ✣ New York

CONTENTS

LIST OF CONTRIBUTORS

K.C. Roy
Associate Professor
School of Economics
The University of Queensland
Brisbane QLD 4072
AUSTRALIA
k.roy@economics.uq.edu.au

Srikanta Chatterjee
Department of Applied and International Economics
Massey University
Palmerston North
NEW ZEALAND
s.chatterjee@massey.ac.nz

M.K. Dasgupta
202A, Picnic Garden Road
Kolkata
INDIA
anasuyadg@yahoo.com

D.B. Varadarajan
Professor & Head
Department of Environmental Economics
School of Economics
Madurai Kamaraj University
Madurai -625 021
SOUTH INDIA

S. Deb Kanango
Professor
Department of Social Work
Visva- Bharati
Sriniketan-731236
Dist-Birbhum
West Bengal, INDIA
ksh_ghosh@sancharnet.in/supriya_sadhu@rediffmail.com

D. Sinha
Reader
Dept of Social Work
Visva- Bharati
Sriniketan-731236
Dist-Birbhum
West Bengal, INDIA
debotosh@sancharnet.in

Sarbeshwar Chatterjee
370/1L, NSC Bose Road
Calcutta,700047
INDIA
c/o amitabhabasuin@yahoo.com

S. K. Roy
Reader
Goenka College of Commerce & Business Administration
210, B.B. Ganguly Street
Calcutta 700012
sujitkroy@lycos.com

R. James Ferguson
Assistant Director for the
Centre for East-West Cultural and Economic Studies
Bond University
Gold Coast QLD 4229
AUSTRALIA
james_ferguson@bond.edu.au

S. Ragothaman
Department of Economics
South Gujarat University
Surat 395 007
Gujarat, INDIA
subbiragurao@yahoo.com

L.R. Smith
Faculty of Business
Central Queensland University
PO Box 6421
CQ Mail Centre
North Rockhampton, QLD
AUSTRALIA
L.Smith@CQU.edu.au

A.N. Tien Le
IndoChina International Development & Investment Pty Ltd
Bentwood Tower
Suite 52
1 Jacobs Street
Bankstown
NSW, 2200
AUSTRALIA

Jamal Othman
Associate Professor
Faculty of Economics and Business
University Kebangsaan Malaysia
Bangi 43600
MALAYSIA
jortman@pkrisc.cc.ukm.my

Professor C. Siwar
Institute for Environment and Development (LESTARI)
Universiti Kebangsaan Malaysia
43600 UKM, Bangi
MALAYSIA
csiwar@pkrisc.cc.ukm.my

T. Sjah
Faculty of Agriculture
University of Mataram
Mataram 83115, INDONESIA
School of NRSM
University of Queensland,
Gatton Campus
QLD 4343
AUSTRALIA
s3233106@student.uq.edu.au

D. Cameron
School of NRSM
University of Queensland
Gatton Campus QLD 4343
AUSTRALIA

L. Russell
School of NRSM
University of Queensland
Gatton Campus Qld 4343
AUSTRALIA

T. Kiriti
Senior Lecturer,
Economics Department,
University of Nairobi,
Box 42793 Nairobi, Kenya.
tkiriti@yahoo.co.uk

PREFACE

K. C. Roy and S. Chatterjee

This book deals with important issues in poverty and development in poor countries with particular reference to Asian countries. But what is poverty? In simple language, to be poor is to be hungry, to lack shelter and clothing, to be sick and not cared for, to be illiterate and not schooled. But, living in poverty makes poor vulnerable to adverse events outside their control. They are often treated badly by the institutions of state and society and also excluded from voice and power in these institutions. What poverty means can be better appreciated from the following statements which appeared in a World Bank publication[1]:

> "Don't ask me what poverty is because you have met it outside my house. Look at my house and count the number of holes. Look at the utensils and the clothes I am wearing. Look at everything and write what you see. What you see is poverty."
>
> \- a statement by a poor man in Kenya.

> "Poverty is humiliation, the sense of being dependant on them and of being forced to accept rudeness, insults and indifference when we seek help."
>
> \- a statement by a woman in Latvia.

> "I beat my women regularly to keep them under control. They also remain good and like to be beaten."
>
> \- a statement by a village man in Bangladesh.

These statements reveal the nature of both economic and cultural poverty that the poor suffer from in many countries in the developing world and stress the urgency of measures needed to alleviate this poverty.

All chapters have been reviewed by an external referee before being included in this book. The book has been published by Nova Science, a well respected commercial publisher based in New York, USA.

---

[1] World Bank (2001), World Development Report 2000-2001, New York: Oxford University Press, P.3.

The editors wish to thank Nova Science Publishers in New York, USA, for agreeing to publish this book and to the University of Queensland in Australia and the Massey University in New Zealand for providing facilities to complete the manuscript. The editors also wish to thank all others who have been involved in the publication of the book in one way or another. The responsibility for all errors and omissions found in this book is due to the editors.

K.C. Roy
School of Economics
University of Queensland
Brisbane
Australia

S.Chatterjee
Department of Applied and
International Economics Massey University
Palmerston North
New Zealand

In: Readings in World Development
Editors: K.C. Roy and S. Chatterjee, pp. 1-10
ISBN 1-59454-947-8

Chapter 1

POVERTY AND DEVELOPMENT IN THE ASIA PACIFIC: AN OVERVIEW OF ISSUES

K. C. Roy and S. Chatterjee

Robert McManara (1972), in his capacity as the President of the World Bank, declared in his address to the UN conference on Trade and Development in 1972 that although the developing countries achieved rapid economic growth (in the 1960s), hundreds of millions of people remained not only poor in statistical terms but were also faced with day-to-day deprivations that degraded human dignity to levels which could not be adequately described by any statistics. Two thirds of children who lived beyond five years of age had their physical and mental growth stunted by malnutrition. There were 100 million more adult illiterates than there were twenty years ago. Education and employment were as scarce as squalor and stagnation common.

However, at the turn of the 20th century, after more than 25 years of growth promoting economic activities, the poverty, expressed as the 'number of people living below $US1 a day in the world', hovered around 1.2 billion (World Bank, 2001). However, the largest concentration of poverty was in South Asia and Sub-Sahara Africa where 522 and 291 million people lived below $US1 per day. Take the case of India, Pakistan and Bangladesh. The total population below poverty line in these three countries stood at over 472 million during 1999-2000 period (World Bank, 2001, 2004). This accounts for 43 percent of 1.1 billion people. But the average annual growth rate of population declined very marginally from 1.8 percent during 1990-1999 to 1.7 percent during 1990-2003 for India; from 2.5 percent during 1990-1999 to 2.4 percent during 1999-2003 for Pakistan and rose marginally from 1.6 percent during 1990-1999 to 1.7 percent during 1990-2003 for Bangladesh (World Bank, 2001, 2004). Thus, economic growth recorded by these developing countries during the last three decades of the 20th century seem to have failed to achieve a perceptible decline in the proportion of people in countries living below $US1 per day.

The effect of growth promoting economic policies on poverty reduction in these countries was, therefore, also curtailed by a very low rate of decline in population growth. While similar poverty levels existed in Sub-Saharan African countries, the East and South-East Asian countries achieved rapid reductions in poverty levels and population growth rate during the last two decades of the 20th century. Thus, a mixed picture of impressive and not so impressive performance in poverty reduction emerges in countries in the Asia Pacific region. While poverty is usually understood in terms of economic poverty, the term 'poverty' possesses several dimensions. Accordingly, tackling the problem requires first to find out the factors which contribute to the rise in different dimensions of poverty and then to design and apply measures to deal with different types of poverty. In the following sections, we will elaborate on these issues and also comment on why some countries have been more successful than others in poverty reduction in the Asia Pacific region.

Poverty and its Dimensions

Absolute poverty refers to an income level which is below the income that serves the poor people with bare essentials of food, clothing and shelter. Therefore, the extent of absolute poverty can be defined as the number of people who are unable to command sufficient resources to satisfy basic needs. They are counted as the total number living below a certain minimum level of income – an international poverty line which we have already referred to in the introductory section of this chapter. Such a definition of absolute poverty primarily highlights economic or material poverty. But there is also the non-economic or cultural or social dimension of poverty which the poor suffer from. Thus a broader definition of poor people would include all those who live without fundamental freedom of action and choice that the better off take for granted (Sen, 1999). Poverty, to those people who face extreme vulnerability to ill health, economic dislocation, natural disasters and to other risks, and who are often exposed to ill treatment by institutions of state and society, and are powerless to influence the key decisions affecting their lives, is therefore, the result of economic, political and social processes that interact with each other and quite often reinforce each other in ways that exacerbate the deprivation in which poor people live. These deprivations, powerlessness and voicelessness are outward manifestations of social poverty.

Social Poverty and Women

Women tend to suffer more from social poverty than men even with the same below-poverty level income in developing countries of both Asia and Africa. Women tend to have less freedom of action and choice than men. Intra-family allocations of resources between men and women, boys and girls, usually tend to be based on gender difference. Thus, allocation of resources per head to women and girls on food, clothing, education, health, nutrition, recreation and so on, tends to be less than that to men and boys. It is an accepted social perception that the status of women is inferior to that of men. Hence, since the allocation of the resources to women within the family is pre-determined by the society's perception of women's status, the allocation of resources to women and girls on the basis of their biological needs is not usually undertaken. In many poor rural families in South Asia, women are frequently beaten by their husbands on any pretext, and even in relatively well off families, women commit suicide or are murdered by their husbands and in-laws for the failure of their parents to make the full payment of dowry to the grooms family (Roy, Tisdell and

Blomqvist, 1996). On the other hand, female heads of rural households find that it is more difficult for them, due to gender based discrimination against them, to access labour and other inputs for carrying on their agriculture and other business operations (Vecchio and Roy, 1997). All these are dimensions of socio-cultural poverty. Women are powerless to take action against such violence committed against them and against social oppression they are subjected to. Vulnerability to such external and uncontrollable events exacerbates poor peoples' material poverty and weakens their bargaining position. However, vulnerability to external shocks also affects poor men.

Hence, one can say that poverty cannot be described purely in terms of material poverty such as lack of food, clothing and shelter, as poor people, particularly women, suffer from cultural poverty as well. To many women, this cultural poverty becomes far more unbearable than material poverty.

MEASUREMENT OF POVERTY

Unfortunately, the measurement of poverty in terms of poverty line income or expenditure does not include the cultural aspects of poverty. Ravallion, Datt and Van de Walle (1991), however, set an extreme poverty line which is accepted as the absolute minimum by international standards. It is based on a standard set in India and a poverty line which is higher than this absolute minimum, but, this still fails to include cultural poverty.

The World Bank, on the other hand, measures poverty and determines who are poor on the basis of the work done by Ahluwalia, Carter and Cheneny (1979) who defined extreme poverty line as the income needed to provide a person with food containing 2250 calories per day. Hence the World Bank's accepted definition of poor also does not take into account non-material poverty. Sen (1992) argued against using only Head Count Index (H) to measure poverty and deprivation because of its inability to capture different grades of poverty (Blackwood and Lynch, 1994) and stressed the need for combining head-count approach (H) with income-gap approach (I) which measures the additional income needed to bring the poor below the poverty line up to the level of poverty line and which is expressed in per capita terms. Therefore, being conscious of the need to include non-material aspects of poverty in measuring human welfare, Sen, in his welfare theory adopted "Capabilities Approach" which, in determining an individual's welfare level (i.e. whether the person is poor or non-poor), examines whether a person has the capability: to be properly fed and nourished; to prevent untimely death resulting from lack of food, nutrition, and health care; to move, speak and interact with people freely outside one's home without being ashamed; to be happy and free.

However, since it is difficult to assign certain values to these functions of welfare, Sen's concept of welfare with its intrinsic values remains somewhat impenetrable to sight for its use for determining a better method of measurement of poverty level. But, in absence of a comprehensive method of measurement of poverty, a true and clear picture of poverty level in developing countries will not emerge, for, a person above the poverty line and satisfying all material needs may still be living in a world of extreme unhappiness, powerlessness, helplessness and of fear and bondage. So, if poverty level is not estimated properly, true causes of poverty may not be found and the subsequent formulation and implementation of policies to reduce the level of absolute poverty may not achieve the desired result.

Sen's "Capabilities Approach" points us to institutions which make capabilities effective. Without conducive institutions, a person cannot exercise one's capabilities. But even with conducive institutions, if a person fails to exercise one's capabilities and stays below poverty line, even that person cannot be considered poor. Again being conscious of the fact that without effective freedom to take action, a person cannot exercise one's capabilities, Sen, in his later work (1999), placed strong emphasis on the need of a person to have substantive freedom to make one's capabilities work. Thus, to him, freedom at once is the means and the end of development.

CAUSES OF POVERTY

Quite frequently, economists and other social scientists cite the inability of the state to formulate and implement appropriate poverty alleviation policies as the reasons for the persistence of poverty. But, the failure of the state to formulate and effectively implement poverty alleviation policies results from institutional breakdown in the country. Therefore, in a world where political power is unequally distributed and often mimics the distribution of economic power, the way state institutions operate can be particularly unfavourable to the poor (World Bank, 2001). Poor people who are often the victims of corruption and arbitrariness on the part of the state, do not receive the benefits of public investment in education and health. Poverty outcomes are also greatly affected by social institutions such as social norms, values and customary practices that within the family, the community or the market, lead to the exclusion of the socially disadvantaged. Although it is difficult to change social institutions overnight to work for the poor, the leaders of political institutions, if honest and strong, can make social institutions work for the alleviation of poverty of the socially disadvantaged.

Mark Olson (1996) observed that everything that is happening in the world is consistent with rational human behaviour. Accordingly, poverty, hunger, war and unemployment are the result of institutions that provide the rational people with the incentives to behave in a corrupt and destructive rather than honest and destructive manner. Take the case of an African country such as Zimbabwe, where virtually no economic activity relating to production and distribution is taking place because the people who were producing goods and services were being driven out of their home by the state sponsored mafia. Such activities are expressions of rational human behaviour to earn quick income in a state where looting, confiscation and destruction of private property of producers go unpunished. Therefore, the rational behaviour of one group of politically powerful people, due to institutional breakdown, temporarily has provided these looters with economic gains but has kept the overwhelming majority of population in perpetual poverty in Zimbabwe. The reasons for the persistence of poverty in Somalia, Sierre Leone and Sudan can be explained in the same way. In South Asian countries too poverty exists because of the failure of state institutions to formulate poverty alleviation policies and to implement these effectively. For example, take the case of India. The federal government transfers substantial amounts of funds to provincial governments for implementing programmes for poverty alleviation in villages in respective provinces. But a substantial part of the money usually disappears into the pockets of politically powerful groups before it reaches the poor. Since the police force is corrupt and is controlled by the same corrupt political institution, viz government, the poor are helpless, and gain little from this money transferred by the federal government. Reasons for poverty in other countries of South Asia can also be found in similar institutional failures.

Furthermore, the capacity of the state to finance the poverty alleviation programme depends on economic growth. But the growth promoting economic policies cannot be formulated and implemented properly by the state when the state becomes its own vested interest group (North, 1981). Free market and outward oriented economic policy regime is known to maximize growth outcomes for a country by improving efficiency and minimizing corruption in all transactions. However, the state's vested interest groups are likely to oppose the implementation of the free market economic policy regime as they try to redistribute income towards themselves instead of trying to improve efficiency and raise national income, the benefit of which they will not receive (Olson, 1982). Thus, in a semi-closed economy, since the rent capturing power of the state's vested interest groups is likely to be higher than in an open economy, the rate of actual growth is likely to be lower than the country's potential growth and also is likely to be lower than the actual growth of an open and outward oriented economy. Thus, while the low economic growth provides handsome rent money to state's vested interest groups, it, combined with slow rate of reductions in population growth, prevents rapid reduction in the poverty level in the country. With low economic growth and virtually static population growth rates, the country's capacity to achieve high development outcomes is significantly undermined.

Hence, it can be argued that if India's potential growth is 10 percent, its actual growth which was close to 7 percent in 2004-05, falls short of its potential growth by 3 percent because of the absence of honest and strong state apparatus, rise of rent seeking behavior of state's vested groups and only partial implementation of open-market and outward oriented economic policies. But, India is a federal state with a democratic system of governance. Therefore, even with partial implementation of outward oriented economic policies in this country, the provinces in Southern, Western and Northern parts where institutional failures appear to be lower, have achieved higher growth, poverty alleviation and development outcomes than the provinces in Eastern parts where institutional failures are far greater.

On the other hand, in virtually all countries in East and South-East Asia, strong and autocratic state leaders aided by Confucian cultural conditioning implemented outward oriented economic policies which achieved high growth for the countries, which in turn helped the leaders to drastically reduce poverty levels and to achieve significantly higher development outcomes. Singapore and South Korea completely eliminated poverty. Institutional failures which were less in these countries than in South Asia also kept the size of rent collected through DUPE (Directly Unproductive Profit-Seeking Economic) activities smaller.

Poverty Alleviation Measures

Relative factor prices need to be altered to reflect the relative scarcity value of capital and labour. In a labour surplus and capital scarce country, the price of labour should be low and the price of capital should be high. As a result, employers would be keen to employ more labour and less capital in their enterprises. As employment of unskilled and semi-skilled labour (who generally suffers from poverty) would rise, their poverty level would fall. This measure was applied in South Korea, Taiwan and Hong Kong in the early 1950s and in China since 1980. Even in 2005, the price of labour has been kept at a very low level in China and Hong Kong compared with the price of labour in South Korea, Taiwan and Singapore. As a result, employment of unskilled and semi-skilled poor people in thousands of small and medium enterprises in China has risen and the poverty level has fallen dramatically. On the other hand, in India, a capital scarce and labour abundant country, the price of labour in all sectors (agriculture, industry, public and private sector, health, education) were raised by militant trade unions and their provincial governments, to levels which were considerably higher than those which would have prevailed under a free market equilibrium. As a result, public enterprises overstaffed with these highly unionised employees suffered huge losses and many private enterprises were forced to close down their operations. The result was low growth and marginal decline in poverty level.

Progressive redistribution of assets in favour of the poor is another measure which should be implemented. The ultimate cause of the unequal distribution of personal incomes in most developing countries is the unequal and highly concentrated patterns of asset ownership in these countries. Just by correcting factor prices, poverty cannot be eliminated if 20 percent of the population controls the overwhelming share of the country's assets which include land, physical capital, financial capital and human capital. Hence, surplus land has to be confiscated from the large land holders and to be distributed to the poor at a small price. This measure was adopted by both South Korea and Taiwan in the early 1950s. As a result, inequality in income distribution was reduced, economic growth increased and poverty level declined (Clark and Roy, 1997). In China, all assets belonged to the state, but in the early 1980s, the introduction of the "Household Responsibility System" in the rural sector allowed the rural families to acquire small plots of land from the state for cultivation and to keep a substantial part of the surplus generated from the production for their own consumption and saving (Clark and Roy, 1997). This measure reduced rural poverty considerably. In India's federal state, agriculture was placed under the jurisdiction of provinces. As a result, the land reform policy was implemented mainly in two provinces and not uniformly throughout the country. Therefore, the impact of land reform on poverty reduction in the country was marginal.

Use of a direct progressive tax system to force the rich to pay a progressively larger percentage of their personal and corporate incomes to help the government finance programmes of social sector development which benefits the poor is essential. But due to widespread tax evasion resulting from institutional failures, the amount of tax collected from the rich through the progressive income tax remains quite small in India.

Direct transfer payments and subsidies, targeted to the poor, if designed properly and implemented properly, can reduce the level of poverty. Sri Lanka has achieved remarkable success in achieving poverty reduction by adopting this measure. But, as economic growth stalled, such programmes became unsustainable. In India's federal state, the transfers and subsidies from the federal government have to pass through the respective provincial governments to the poor living in these states. However, due to wide spread corruption, only a small proportion of these funds reach the poor. In China, the communes have been highly successful in distributing benefits from public transfers and subsidies to the poor.

Finally, the development of a human capital base for the poor by improving their access to education, health, capital, technology and the market, thereby enhancing their capabilities, can achieve rapid reduction in poverty levels.

Since China and India are the two giants of Asia, a comparison of their relative performance in poverty alleviation, as presented in table 1.1, brings out a number of features which may provide valuable lessons for policy makers in developing countries.

It can be seen from the table that the percentage of population below the national poverty line in China declined to 4.6 percent in 1998 whereas that in India remained at 26.6 percent on average during 1990-2000 (column 3). The percentage of population below $1US per day declined to 13.6 percent in China in 2001 whereas it remained at 34.7 percent in India in 1999 (column 4). Along with remarkable success in poverty reduction, China also recorded significant improvement in human development in comparison with India. Columns 5 and 6 illustrate that in 2000, the life expectancy at birth and under 5 mortality rate per 1000 live births reached 71 and 38 whereas the respective figures for India were 63 and 90. Column 7 shows that the adult literary rate expressed as a percentage of population aged 15 and above in 2002 reached 91 in China and 61 in India. Such a remarkable achievement in poverty alleviation and human development by China has been aided by a phenomenal average annual economic growth rate of 9.5 percent during 1990-2003 (column 2). For India, during the same period, the economic growth rate was only 5.8 percent which accounted for only 61 percent of China's growth rate and population growth hovered around 1.7 percent. These achievements of China were facilitated by a number of non-economic factors and by economic policy regime which are illustrated in columns 8 to 12.

In China, the state is unitary and the government non-democratic and totalitarian. This has enabled the state to wield power to implement all policies effectively. Confucianism acted as a unifying force to bind the state and society together. The government, due to this cultural conditioning, also remained relatively honest and paid single minded attention to economic growth and development (Clark and Roy, 1999). Consequently, institutional failures remained relatively low. All these factors enabled the state to significantly dismantle restrictions in economic activities and to introduce international competition in the domestic economy. Such open economy policies also kept the institutional failures at a low level. In the case of India, the state is federal and the democratic governments at the centre and at provincial level are weak and are incapable of implementing policies effectively. Hinduism and Islam have never acted together as a unifying force to bind the state and society together. Institutional failures are higher than in China due to unfavourable political and cultural factors. Consequently, growth oriented economic policies have not been implemented properly and political compulsions have forced the central government to maintain a semi-open economy. The adverse impact of all these factors has been felt on the country's capacity to achieve the high economic growth, drastic reduction in population growth and in poverty level.

Table 1.1 China and India: Relative Performance in Growth and Poverty Alleviation Outcomes

Country	Rate of Econo-mic growth; average annual (1990-2002)	Rate of Population growth; average annual (1990-2002)	Percentage of population below national poverty line	Percentage of population below $1US per day	Life expectancy at birth, year 2002	Under 5 mortality rate (per 1000 live births) year 2000	Adult Literary rate (% of people 15 and above) year 2002	Type of State and govern-ment	State powers or policy implem-entation (Strong/ Weak)	Major culture and religion	Institut-ional failures: (High or Low)	Economic Policy regime: (Open/ Semi, Open/ Closed)
China	9.5	1.0	Year 1998 4.6	Year 2001 13.6	71	38	91	Unitary; non-democ-ratic and totali tarian	Strong	Confuc-Inism	Lower compared to India	Greatly open and outward oriented
India	5.8	1.7	Year 1990-00 26.6	Year 1999 34.7	63	90	61	Federal; Parlia-mentary democ-racy	Weak	Hindu-ism and Islam; wide variation in culture	Higher compareed with China	Semi open partially outward oriented

Data Source: World Bank (2004), World Development Report 2005, New York: Oxford University Press.

CONCLUDING REMARKS

The most important lesson that emerges from the analysis presented in this chapter is that growth, poverty alleviation and development are interdependent goals. For poverty alleviation and development two approaches are suggested:

1. Redistribution first and then growth
2. Growth first and redistribution later.

Sri Lanka used the first approach but growth faltered and several programmes of targeted transfer of income and food to the poor had to be cancelled. Therefore, the second approach is undoubtedly better than the first one as economic growth provides the government with the necessary income to implement policies to reduce the level of poverty and to enhance the level of social and human development. But the capacity of a country to effectively implement policies to achieve these goals depends on a strong and honest state leadership, dedicated state administrative apparatus and supportive cultural institutions. This chapter thus sets the scene for the discussions to follow in subsequent chapters.

A number of issues relevant to poverty and development in Asia-Pacific which arise, are: the role of international financial institutions in poverty alleviation in Asian countries; the inter relationship between energy, environment and poverty and the need for satisfying poor households' energy requirements from bio-mass for environmental preservation and poverty alleviation; citizen's participation in community development programmes; need for social sector development for poverty alleviation; the importance of social security in achieving social development in India; performance of India's manufacturing sector in post-economic reform period; the role of rural finance in agriculture development in Vietnam; the relationship between poverty and environment in Malaysia; the implications of policy failure for adverse externalities from the palm oil production in Malaysia and Indonesia; a better credit system to help improve farmers' income in Indonesia.; the impact of gender inequality on poverty level in Kenya; and issues of Indonesia's integration with other South East Asian countries through ASEAN and ASEAN Regional Forum for achieving its developmental goals. All these issues are discussed in this volume and are related directly or indirectly to poverty and development, which is the central theme of this book.

REFERNCES

Ahluwalia, M.S, Carter, N.G., Chenery, H.B. (1979), *"Growth and Poverty in Developing Countries"*, Journal of Development Economies, Vol. 6, pp. 299-341.

Blackwood, D.L. and Lynch R.G. (1994), *"The Measurement of Inequality and Poverty: A Policy Maker's Guide to Literature"*, World Development, Vol. 22, p.569.

McNamara, R.S. (1992), *Address to the UN Conference on Trade and Development*, Santiago, Chile, Washington DC: World Bank.

North, D. (1981), *Structure and Change in Economic History*, New York: W.W. Norton.

Olson, M. (1996), *"Big Bills left on the Sidewalk: Why Some Nations are Rich, Others Poor"*, Journal of Economics Perspectives 10 (2), p.22.

Olson, M. (1982), *The Rise and Decline of Nations*, New Haven, Conn: Yale University Press.

Roy, K.C, Tisdell, C.A and Blomquist, H.C. (Eds) (1996), *Economic Development and Women in the World Community*, CT, London: Praeger.

Ravallion, M, G Datt and Dominique Van de Walle (1991), *"Quantifying Absolute Poverty in the Developing World"*, Review of Income and Wealth, Vol. 37, pp. 345-361.

Sen, A.K. (1999), *Development as Freedom*, New York: Knof

Sen, A.K. (1992), *Inequality Re-examined*, Cambridge, Mass: Harvard University Press.

Vecchio, N. and Roy, K.C. (1997), *Poverty, Female Headed Household and Sustainable Development*, CT, London: Greenwood Publishing Company.

World Bank (2001), *World Development Report 2000-01*, New York: Oxford University Press.

World Bank (2004), *World Development Report 2005*, New York: Oxford University Press.

In: Readings in World Development
Editors: K.C. Roy and S. Chatterjee, pp. 11-20

ISBN 1-59454-947-8

Chapter 2

POVERTY ALLEVIATION AND DEVELOPMENT IN EAST AND SOUTH-EAST ASIA: SOME COMMENTS

Mrinal Kanti Dasgupta

ABSTRACT

One of the most important arguments put forward in favour of globalization is that it leads to better economic performance which can facilitate the reduction of poverty in developing countries. The role of international financial institutions assumes considerable importance in any poverty alleviation programme. It is now broadly agreed that development assistance should support integrated strategies that are formulated by the recipient countries themselves. However, the studies conducted by the World Bank, OECD and other agencies reveal that although developing countries such as India and Indonesia improved their economic performance during the 1990s, poverty remained firmly entrenched.

The impacts of reforms on poverty-stricken countries are diverse in nature. In the East Asia and Pacific Region, for example, the reduction is quite significant. However, the success of poverty reduction strategies in reducing the level of poverty depends on relations between population growth and economic development. If the development strategies are properly implemented, the reduction in rate of poverty level becomes obviously higher. Now, as a policy prescription there should be an integrated approach on the part of the developing countries, international financial institutions and the developed countries, such that they may together work more effectively to reduce the incidence of poverty. Action at the national level and local levels may not be enough for poverty reduction at a rapid rate and thus participation of international financial institutions is required in many areas. Some conditionalities imposed by international financial institutions on developing countries are not congenial for poverty reduction in the LDC's. They should enhance the ability of the poverty stricken countries by providing substantial debt relief.

INTRODUCTION

After economic liberalization, policies were implemented in many developing countries. A number of studies conducted by the World Bank and other agencies revealed that despite developing countries' improved economic performance during the 90's, poverty remained firmly entrenched in these countries including India and Indonesia.

When we examine the poverty reduction strategy adopted by various countries, we examine two things: (i) the various theoretical and empirical studies by a large number of eminent economists since the early 1970's and (ii) the poverty absorption capacity (P A C) of the people in different countries.

At the theoretical level, vast theoretical literature on the subject has been published since the beginning of the 1970's. Some notable contributions were made by a number of renowned Economists. In their studies they mainly dealt with the conceptual ideas of Poverty Indicator Statistics. The poverty indicator statistics include poverty measures, development progress indices, inequality measures, and so on. Theoretically, the national poverty line is measured in terms of food poverty line, as well as $US1 per day, poverty gap ratio and poverty severity index. Development Progress Indices (D.P.I) are indicated by Human Development Index (H.D.I), and Human Poverty Index (H.P.I.). Again income inequality within each country has been sought to be measured by Gini Coefficient and income ratio. These studies also dwell on absolute and relative poverty. However, relative poverty is used mainly in the inter country analysis of poverty. But within each country, it is important to take note of relative poverty as well as the endurance capacity which is defined here as poverty absorption capacity (P.A.C). In the L.D.C's of Eastern Asia, Pacific, South Asia, Latin America and Sub-Saharan Africa, P.A.C is very high. Due to a lack of basic education, the poverty stricken people in these countries are unaware of the fact that they are living below poverty line. They are not familiar with the concepts of opportunity, empowerment, and security. It is illiteracy and poor health that make them suffer from severe poverty stricken condition. In such cases, because of their lack of awareness of the existence of social support systems in their country, these poor people fail to take advantage of these facilities. Moreover, they do not seem to feel the need for coming out of the poverty line. The Asian Development Bank (ADB) outlines the objectives and issues that must be addressed if the goal of equitable growth is to be achieved. The three pillars of growth are good governance, social development, and sustainable growth. But PAC, among various groups of people, particularly in the LDC's of Asia and Pacific region, is so severe that growth in terms of income or any other indicator of development is quite meaningless to them. They still live with primitive ideas. They continue to earn their livelihood from nature and are satisfied with their mode of living. Among the tribal, such type of PAC is very high. Unless basic education and health care are imparted to such groups, PAC will not decline. Broader sets of actions are required to fight the problem of PAC across countries over time. For such situations where PAC is very high, immediate attention is needed for identifying the causes of the persistence of such PAC, and for application of measures to tackle this problem. One of the most important arguments put forward in favour of liberalization and globalization is that it contributes to better economic performance so that reduction of poverty will be achieved in the Pacific countries and South Asian countries. For poverty reduction, the following basic issues have been raised: (i) should governments of such countries pursue economic growth first and reduce poverty later? (ii) Does such growth benefit the people below poverty line? (iii) Should public investment, basic education and public health be raised proportionately to GDP? (iv) Should economic reform strategies through liberalization have employment focus? One can infer from these issues that poverty is not just a question of income. The poor also suffer from infant mortality, ill health, isolation, poor education, income inequality, gender inequality, and many others. However, the studies conducted by ADB, OECD, World Bank etc. on a number of Pacific, East Asian, South Asian, and Sub-Saharan countries, do not consider the problem of PAC. But, in those countries PAC's are very high among the tribal, as, for example, in India. Despite tremendous effort by government organizations and NGOs, the Jaroa community in Andamans and Nicobar islands never bothered to come to the main stream of life. The big question is: are they dissatisfied with their mode of living? In spite of the fear of extinction, like many other obsolete creatures, they continue to live with animal spirit. To call them poor or to bring them above poverty line – the term or the efforts become totally meaningless. Unless the developed world creates awareness among these type of people that they cannot continue to live in a primitive world, all the efforts made to alleviate poverty will be futile. Since it is difficult to estimate the rate of various groups of poor people in the developing world we will examine some indicators such as G.D.P, inflation rate, creation of employment opportunities, and reduction of inequalities in the market friendly reform period. We will try to examine the poverty situation in India, Indonesia, Pakistan, Nepal, Bhutan, Bangladesh, Afghanistan, and Sri Lanka etc. In this study, it is found that the impact of reforms on poverty level has not been fallible. In the East Asia and Pacific region, for example, poverty reduction is quite significant while in most of the South Asian nations including India, the picture is not at all satisfactory. India continues to languish at 115th rank on the UNDP's HDI which depicts the extent of human development in 162 countries in the WNDP Report of 2000-2002. In this connection, special attention should be given to tackle changes in rural poverty resulting from changes in weather, health, markets, investment and public policy, which affect all groups of the poor. Thus, macro economic stability along with the poor people's access to credit, education, health and entitlement to food are required to uplift their economic condition.

Involvement of International Financial Institutions in Poverty Alleviations

In the less developed countries, the orthodox doctrines of the theory of equilibrium and of free trade are not considered to be very relevant to their problems. It is often mentioned that in such countries, the 'laissez faire' approach in economic policies can do more harm than good because these countries experience a large balance of payment deficit and foreign exchange shortage. The world needs to understand that the perusal of economic growth alone couldn't solve the problems of lack of opportunity (including lack of access to market opportunities, assets, credit, jobs, school education, health care and so on), empowerment, security etc. This explains the L.D.C's search for assistance from various international institutions to reduce the level of poverty. As per World Development Report 2000-2001, 2.8 billion – almost half of the total 6 billion people, live on less than $ 2 a day and 1.2 billion – a fifth – live on less than $ 1 a day. However, as we have already mentioned, poverty is not just a question of income, as the poor suffer on multi – dimensional fronts, namely, infant mortality, ill health, isolation, poor education, income inequality, gender inequality and many others. On the infant mortality front in the poorest countries, 20% of the children do not reach their fifth birthday and as many as half of the children suffer from malnutrition. Regarding income inequality, it can be said that the distribution of global gains in GDP has been extraordinarily unequal. The average income in the richest 20 countries is 37 times the average in the poorest 20. To alleviate poverty, efforts from local, national and global levels are essential. The participation of industrial countries, international financial institutions and the governments of the L.D.C's, together in a global poverty alleviation effort can mitigate the problem to a great extent. When the governments of the respective L.D.C's try to take poverty reduction measures they often find a dilemma: should they pursue economic growth first and foremost with the help of international financial institutions and industrial countries through the reform measures, or should they focus on poverty reduction taking their assistance? Involvement of the international financial institutions through globalization is expected to raise the wealth of L.D.C's, thereby facilitating the reduction of poverty.

Several studies have been conducted on poverty and economic reforms. In those studies, a general argument is put forward that market friendly reforms have generally been associated with better economic performance. In such studies, in the post reform period, it is observed that they have achieved better results in terms of G.D.P., inflation rate and in the agricultural sector. However, in some south Asian nations such as India, Pakistan, Nepal, Bhutan, Bangladesh, Afghanistan, and Sri Lanka and in some other countries, the picture is not at all satisfactory as per UNDP Report. Pakistan, Nepal and Bhutan are placed at nos.127, 129 and 130 respectively. Sri Lanka is able to retain its position at 81. The report also highlights vast differences in the income levels in the world. Around 25 % of the world's population received 75% of the world's income. Poverty is still a major hurdle in development in South Asia and Sub-Saharan Africa, which lag far behind other regions. Thus, in this paper we will try to evaluate the program of international institutions for poverty reduction and economic management under economic reform in less developed countries.

Poverty Reduction During Reforms – A Trend Analysis

Studies based on country wise information reveal that the impact of reforms on poor people has been diverse. For example, case studies of Chile, China, Ghana, Uganda and Vietnam show that reforms have helped raise producer prices for small farmers. But, in countries like Cameroon, India, Bangladesh etc. after reform, market forces have reduced the implicit subsidies as well as erratic agricultural credit, and marketing activities have left many farmers worse off. A study on regional income and poverty indicates rates of reduction in various regions. In the following table, we have divided the regions into seven groups and have indicated the size of the population of the countries of the seven regions covered by at least one survey:

SL. NO.	NAME OF THE REGION	POPULATION COVERED BY AT LEAST ONE SURVEY (in percent)
1.	East Asia and Pacific including China (EAPIC)	90.8
2.	East Asia and Pacific excluding China (EAPEC)	71.1
3.	Europe and Central Asia (ECA)	81.7
4.	Latin America and Caribbean (LAC)	88.0
5.	Middle East and North America (MENA)	52.5
6.	South Asia (SA)	97.9
7.	Sub-Saharan Africa (SSA)	72.9

The above region wise survey was conducted by the World Bank to collect data on a number of people living on less than \$1 a day. The poverty line is estimated to be \$1.08 a day at 1993 purchasing power parity. The estimates are based on income or consumption data from the countries of each region for which at least one survey was available. From the World Bank's survey results, it was observed that people of all regions living on less than \$1 a day increased from 1183.2 million in 1987 to 1198.9 million in 1998 (including China).

The poverty reduction possibility is found from the trend analysis. Taking population below \$1 a day (both in absolute number and in percentage) as endogenous variable, depending on time for each region as well as total, parameters have been estimated using ordinary least square method in a two variable linear model (Y=a+bX) which is better fitted than the model in an exponential form ($Y=ab^X$). Thus, the Y's for each region are denoted as Y_1 (EAPIC), Y_2 (EAPEC), Y_3 (ECA), Y_4 (LAC), Y_5 (MENA), Y_6 (SA), Y_7 (SSA) and therefore for total including China, and excluding China are denoted by Y_8 (TIC) and Y_9 (TEC) respectively.

Against this background, the equations for actual population and for percentage of populations have been fitted by Ordinary Least Square (OLS) method using the data table (TABLE = 1 – Appendix). From 1990-1998 (N=9) problem like presence of autocorrelation is duly considered by providing D-W Statistic along with r^2 , $\bar{r}^2$, and F-statistic. Estimating all the 9 equations in case of actual as well as percentages the following results are obtained.

Actual

Y_2 (EAPEC) = 81.96 – 13.49T
SE = (4.634) (3.277)
t = (17.688) (-4.117)

$\bar{r}^2$ =0.85, r^2=0.79, D.W. = 2.71, F=16.95

3. Y_3 (ECA) = 14.86 + 6.25T

SE = (1.511) (1.068)

t =(17.688) (5.851)

$\bar{r}^2$ =0.92, r^2 = 0.89, D.W. = 1.80, F = 34.24

4. Y_4 (LAC) = 72.50 + 3.12T

SE = (1.400) (0.990)

t = (9.837) (5.851)

$\bar{r}^2$ = 0.76, r^2 = 0.69, D.W. = 3.11, F = 9.93

5. Y_5 (MENA) = 6.1 – 0.83T
SE = (0.648) (0.458)
t = (9.419) (-1.812)

$\bar{r}^2$ = 0.52, r^2 = 0.36, D.W. =1.61, F = 3.29

6. Y_6 (SA) = 505.66 + 13.18T
SE = (4.449) (3.146)
t = (113.645) (4.1891)

$\bar{r}^2$ = 0.85, r^2 = 0.80, D.W. =2.59, F = 17.55

7. Y_7 (SSA) =262.54 + 19.41T
SE = (4.605) (3.256)
t = (57.012) (5.961)

$\bar{r}^2$ = 0.92, r^2 = 0.89, D.W. =1.53, F = 35.53

8. Y_8 (TIC) = 1230.68 – 5.44T
SE = (28.38) (20.07)
t = (43.35) (-0.27)

$\bar{r}^2$ = 0.24, r^2 = 0.30, D.W.= 1.88, F = 0.07

9. Y_9 (TEC) = 943.56 +27.64T
SE = (5.676) (4.014)
t = (166.223) (6.886)

$\bar{r}^2 = 0.94$, $r^2 = 0.92$, D.W. = 1.52, F=47.4185

Percentages

1. Y_1 (EAPIC) = 21.92 – 3.53T
SE = (1.493) (1.055)
t = (14.686) (-3.345)

$\bar{r}^2 = 0.78$, $r^2 = 0.72$, D.W. = 2.486, F = 11.186

2. Y_2 (EAPEC) = 17.70 – 2.08T
SE = (0.919) (0.650)
t = (19.2695) (-3.2024)

$\bar{r}^2 = 0.77$, $r^2 = 0.70$, D.W. =1.47, F = 11.186

3. Y_3 (ECA) = 3.2 +1.33T
SE = (0.340)(0.240)
t = (9.420) (5.539)

$\bar{r}^2 = 0.91$, $r^2 = 0.88$, D.W.= 1.717, F = 30.657

Y_4 (LAC) = 15.72 – 0.06T
SE = (0.317) (0.225)
t = (49.513) (-0.267)

$\bar{r}^2 = 0.23$, $r^2 = 0.302$, D.W. = 3.069, F= 0.071

Y_5 (MENA) =2.46 – 0.54T
SE = (0.32) (0.32)
t = (7.687) (-2.386)

$\bar{r}^2$=0.65, r^2=0.54, D.W. = 1.597, F= 5.695

Y_6 (SA) = 42.72 – 1.15 T
SE = (0.237) (0.167)
t = (180.203) (-6.860)

$\bar{r}^2$=0.94, r^2 =0.92, D.W. = 3.191, F= 46.06

Y_7 (SSA) = 42.72 – 1.15 T
SE = (0.237) (0.168)
t = (180.203) (-6.860)

$\bar{r}^2 = 0.94$, $r^2 = 0.92$, D.W. =3.191, F= 47.06

Y_8 (TIC) = 1.31T
SE = (0.563) (0.398)
t = (47.604) (-3.293)

$\bar{r}^2$=0.78, $r^2 = 0.71$, D.W. = 2.129, F= 10.845

Y_9 (TEC) = 27.5 – 0.57T
SE = (0.078) (0.055)
t = (353.067) (10.349)

$\bar{r}^2$= 0.97, $r^2 = 0.96$, D.W.= 1.40, F= 107.11

From the estimated equations the values of the parameters a and b reveal the trend of poverty reduction of the seven regions. The statistical significance of the estimated values can be judged from the values of S.E., t and r^2. In the regions EAPIC and EAPEC, the negative values of b (both in case of actual and percentages) indicate that with the active participation of international institutions, poverty reduction is possible significantly during the reform period. However, in the regions ECA and LAC, a number of people living below poverty line increases significantly which can be understood by analyzing the estimated values. Further, in case of MENA, the negative trend is fairly significant, though the r^2 values are low. The S.E.'s and t-values corroborate the hypothesis of poverty reduction. In the case of SA and SSA, the results are significantly positive, i.e. poverty rises during the reform period. But the total including China (TIC) and total excluding China (TEC) give different results. In the case of TIC, the trend is thought negative, yet the estimators are not at all significant for the actual. However, in the case of TEC, the trend is positive and it is also significant both for the actual and the percentages.

From the foregoing facts it is found that uniform results are not obtained for all regions. Thus, the impact of the Programme of Poverty Reduction and Growth Facility (PRGF) supported by IMF has not been uniform. But, the program has important implications for low-income countries. Again, the above analysis and results could not show any reflection on PAC of those countries.

CONCLUSION

In many developing countries the improvements that have occurred over time should be sustainable. Otherwise, it is easy to overlook the lack of progress in many countries where millions of people live below the poverty line without the basic provision of health, education, gender equality and other human rights. In 1996, the organization for Economic

Co-operation and Development (OFCD) published a report in which it laid out the following goals of development:

1. Reduction of the proportion of people living in extreme poverty by half between 1990 and 2015;
2. One hundred percent of enrolment of children in primary schools by 2015;
3. Achieving progress towards gender equality and the empowerment of women by eliminating gender disparities in primary and secondary education by 2005;
4. Reduction in infant child mortality rates by two thirds between 1990-2015;
5. Reduction in maternal mortality ratios by three fourths between 1990-2015;
6. Provision of reproductive health services to all who need them by 2015;
7. Implementation of national strategies for sustainable development by 2005, so as to reverse the loss of environmental resources by 2015.

It is suggested that along with economic growth, investment in basic social services, especially for the poor, be made and for this to happen, the international financial institutions will have to be an active part. As the improvement of the LDC's are occurring very slowly, the responsibility of high-income countries cannot be neglected. Debt relief for the most heavily indebted poor countries will free resources that can be used to support national poverty reduction strategies. But, the international financial institutions with their strict conditions make the terms of trade unfavorable for the LDC's and there lies the limitations of many programmes. An integrated approach is required so that the developing countries, international financial institutions and developed countries work together more effectively to reduce the incidence of poverty.

To reduce PAC and to enable the poorest of the poor to enjoy the livelihood of the mainstream population, it is necessary to work out the participatory approach in implementing development programmes. Previously, government and NGO's, with the help of various international financial institutions, adopted various poverty reduction strategies including the provision of debt relief. But, when PAC is very high, then the method adopted by government and NGO's during the 1990's under the caption of 'Participatory Poverty Assessments' (PPAs) could not enlighten the group regarding their condition. A PPA is a tool that allows various agencies that work for poverty reduction to consult with the poor directly and to transmit their ideas to policy makers, thereby enabling the poor to influence policy. When they are involved in their own poverty alleviation programmes, the possibility of success rises. Through PPA, they could feel how vulnerable they are towards various aspects of poverty.

The experiment of PPA has already started in many LDC's of Asia and Africa. The various international institutions, with the help of the government extension workers, local and international, NGO's, academic institutions and many others activated the PPAs in many countries. The outcome of many PPAs has been an increase in face-to-face interactions between diverse groups such as NGO's, local Community and local and central government, and a better understanding between civil society and state. From experience, it has been observed that including the poor in a PPA leads to better design of programmes and solutions to their problems. Thus, attacking the PAC directly by PPA may improve the lot of the poor. Above all, sustained efforts should be made to identify the groups with high PAC and educate them to understand that PAC is a curse for human civilization.

REFERENCES

Asian Development Bank, (1996), *Asian Development Outlook*, New York: Oxford University Press.

Chadha, G.K., (1994), *Employment, Earnings and Poverty: A Study of Rural India and Indonesia*, New Delhi: Sage Publication.

Chambers Robert, (1983), *Putting the Last First*, London: Intermediate Technology Publications.

Gaiha, R, (1993) *Design of Poverty Alleviation*, Rome: F.A.O.

Sen, A.K., (1999), *Development as Freedom,* New York: KNOPF

Tendulkar, S.D., (1998), *Indian Economic Policy and Poverty: An Assessment,* New Delhi: Oxford University Press

World Bank (2000), *World Development Report (2000-2001)*, New York: Oxford University Press.

APPENDIX:

Table 2.1.People living on less than $ 1 a day (million)

No.	Name of the regions	1990	1991	1992	1993	1994	1995	1996	1997	1998
1.	East Asia & Pacific (including China)	452.4 (27.6)	441.6 (26.9)	433.2 (26.4)	431.9 (25.2)	332.6 (23.1)	306.5 (22.9)	265.1 (14.9)	260.4 (14.8)	278.3 (15.3)
2.	East Asia & Pacific (excluding China)	92.0 (18.5)	89.2 (17.4)	85.3 (16.5)	83.5 (15.9)	75.4 (13.6)	63.6 (11.1)	55.1 (10.0)	54.0 (9.9)	65.1 (11.3)
3.	Europe & Central Asia	7.1 (1.6)	13.2 (2.8)	15.3 (3.5)	18.3 (4.0)	20.4 (4.4)	21.9 (4.8)	23.8 (5.1)	24.11 (5.2)	24.0 (5.1)
4.	Latin America & Caribbean	73.8 (16.8)	74.6 (17.0)	75.0 (17.1)	70.8 (15.3)	74.0 (15.4)	74.9 (15.4)	76.0 (15.6)	77.3 (15.6)	78.2 (15.6)
5.	Middle East & North Africa	5.7 (2.4)	5.5 (2.3)	5.2 (2.2)	5.0 (1.9)	5.3 (2.1)	5.1 (2.0)	5.0 (1.8)	5.3 (2.1)	5.5 (1.9)
6.	South Asia	495.1 (44.0)	499.2 (43.8)	501.0 (43.1)	505.1 (42.4)	519.4 (42.4)	525.3 (42.3)	531.7 (42.3)	532.2 (40.4)	522.0 (40.4)
7.	Sub-Saharan Africa	242.3 (47.7)	252.1 (47.9)	262.4 (49.0)	273.3 (49.2)	281.4 (49.2)	284.2 (48.7)	289.0 (48.5)	290.0 (46.8)	290.9 (46.3)
8.	Total (Including China)	1276.4 (29.0)	1286.0 (28.6)	1292.4 (28.4)	1304.3 (28.1)	1233.1 (26.8)	1217.9 (25.4)	1190.6 (24.5)	1189.6 (24.3)	1198.9 (24.0)
9.	Total (Excluding China)	916.0 (28.1)	953.6 (28.0)	944.5 (27.8)	955.9 (27.7)	975.9 (27.4)	975.0 (27.1)	980.5 (27.0)	983.2 (26.6)	985.7 (26.2)

In: Readings in World Development
Editors: K.C. Roy and S. Chatterjee, pp. 21-28
ISBN 1-59454-947-8

Chapter 3

ENERGY, ENVIRONMENT AND POVERTY NEXUS IN DEVELOPING COUNTRIES

Dhulasi Birundha Varadarajan and K. Arockia Raj

INTRODUCTION

A growing consciousness of the intertwined issues of environment and development and the particular role of energy in the nexus of these issues have been realised at present. As a result of this awareness, voices of concern in support of Environmentally Sound and Sustainable Development (ESSD) are now increasingly heard. The great challenge now is to move from the voicing of concerns to accelerated action and change. The list of environmental issues that are relevant to any discussion of ESSD strategies is long and diverse. Implementing development strategies which include the alleviation of poverty as a central focus must address both the direct and indirect linkages between these environmental issues and poverty.

THE DIMENSIONS OF POVERTY

The concept of poverty refers to an individual's (or family's) lack of access, associated primarily with inadequate income, to basic human needs such as food, shelter, clothing, safe water, sanitation, health care and education.

Operationally, however, poverty standards are typically expressed in single dimensions, the monetary resources that would enable an individual to consume either a fixed bundle of basic goods and services (absolute poverty) or some fraction of the bundle of goods and services that some reference group is able to or actually does, consume (relative poverty).

It has been estimated that, as of 1993, roughly 1.3 billion people in developing countries – 30 percent of their total population – consume less than one dollar per day worth of goods and services. Statistics on the inability of people in developing countries to satisfy basic human needs corroborate the enormous scale of poverty and highlight its breadth and complexity. For example, an estimated 20 percent of people in developing countries do not have access to health services; 30 percent lack access to safe water and 61 percent lack access to sanitation.

Poverty and Environment

The linkages between poverty and the environment are far too complex. An argument is generally made that poor people have a tendency of overusing resources like land, forests and water, thereby degrading them. It was even said one time that poverty is the greatest polluter. There is some evidence to say that the poor are more dependent upon such natural resources. The number of poor being large in several countries, the total environmental damage may look too high. Even then, it is the type of property rights (such as open access, or neglected state properties) that can be a major cause of environmental degradation.

The neglect of the environment in development economics is ironic, because people in poor countries are in great part agrarian and pastoral. Rural people account for about 65 per cent of the population of what the World Bank classifies as low income countries. The proportion of the total labour force in agriculture is a bit in excess of this. The share of agriculture in gross domestic product in these countries is 30 percent. These figures should be contrasted with those from industrial market economies, which are 6 percent and 2 percent, respectively, for the latter two indices (Partha Das Gupta, 1996).

Poor countries are in large measures biomass based subsistence economies, in that the rural poor eke out a living from products obtained directly from their local environment. For example, in its informative study of life in a micro water shed of the Alaknanda river in the Central Himalayas in India, the Indian Centre for Science and Environment reports that, of the total number of hours worked by the villagers sampled, 30 percent was devoted to cultivation, 20 percent to fodder collection, and about 25 percent spread evenly between fuel collection, animal care and grazing. Some 20 percent of time was spent on household chores, of which cooking took up the greatest portion and the remaining 5 percent involved other activities such as marketing.

In Central and West Africa, it has been shown how vital forest products are to the lives of rural people. In many instances, natural resources are of direct value to us as needs for sustaining our lives or as consumption goods (e.g., breathable air, drinkable water and fisheries), in others they are of indirect value, sometimes they are both. The value may be utilitarian (e.g., the resource may be a source of food, or a key stone species in an ecosystem), it may be aesthetic (e.g., a landscape) or it may be intrinsic (e.g., it could be a living animal), indeed, it may be all these things at once. Resource stocks are measured in different ways depending on their character: in mass units (e.g., biomass units for forest, cow-dung and crop residues in number e.g., size of animal herd); in indices of quality e.g., water and air-quality indicators in volume units (e.g., acre-feet for aquifers) and so forth.

Problems of poverty and environmental degradation in developing countries are closely linked (WCED, 1987). The majority of poor people live in rural areas and derive most of their income from soil and forest resources (World Bank, 1990). It has been claimed that poverty may lead to short-planning horizons, which may prevent poor farm households from investing in conservation to protect their natural base. Yet, there have been very few empirical studies of the planning horizon or Rates of Time Preferences (RTPS) among rural poor.

Environmental degradation such as eroding soil, receding forests and vanishing water supplies, is a cause of accentuated poverty among the rural poor in poor countries. There is truth in this. But there is also much accumulated evidence that poverty itself can be a cause of environmental degradation.

This reverse causality arises because some environmental resources (e.g., ponds and rivers) are essential for survival in normal times, while others are a source of supplementary income in times of active economic stress. This mutual influence can offer a pathway along which poverty, environmental degradation and even high fertility feed upon one another in a synergistic manner over time. Indeed, an erosion of the environmental resource base can make certain categories of people destitute even while the economy's GNP increases.

Poverty Environment and Development

Based on the studies after Kuznetz, it can now be said that there is a clear inverse relationship between increase in poverty and economic growth. The relationship between economic development and environmental degradation is quite mixed, between U-shaped, inverted U-shaped, or S-shaped etc. The major issues in the poverty environment and developments are:

An increase in poverty within the community results in increased environmental degradation. Conversely, a reduction in poverty will increase environmental degradation. Other things being equal, an environment inhabited by the poor will be more degraded and become degraded than one inhabited by the rich.

There have been important social changes (policies, external events) that have resulted in concurrent increases in poverty and environmental degradation in a number of developing countries.

Deterioration of the ambient environment hurts the poor more than the rich. But, Jaganathan (1989) looked at rates of deforestation and the level of poverty in West Java and land use and poverty in Nigeria and found little evidence that poverty was a driving force in the deforestation or in the damaging changes in land use.

Policies that change the environment can hurt the poor more than the rich and vice versa. In this regard, Linde Rahr (1998) analyses the effects of income and gender on tree planting. He found that tree planting increases with the increase in female numbers of household members and also increases with the increase in male income.

CPRs as Source of Livelihood

Common property resources also provide the rural poor with partial protection in times of unusual economic stress. For landless people they may be the only non-human assets at their disposal. A number of resources, such as fuel, wood and water for home use, berries and nuts, medicinal herbs, resin and gums are the responsibility of women and children.

The extent of common-property resources as a proportion of total assets in a community varies considerably across ecological zones. In India, they appear to be most prominent in arid regions, mountain regions, and un-irrigated areas. They are least prominent in humid regions and river valleys. The links between under nourishment, destitution and an erosion of the rural common property resource base are close (Das Gupta, 1993, 1996). Jodha (1986) used data from over eighty villages in twelve, districts from six dry tropical states in India to estimate that, among poor families, the proportion of income based directly on the local commons is for the most part in the range 15-25 percent (Jodha, 1995). In his work on the dry lands of India, Jodha (1986) noted a decline in the geographical area covering common property resources ranging from 26 to 63 percent over a twenty-year period. This was in part due to the privatization of land, a good deal of which in his sample had been awarded to the rural non-poor.

The impact of these forms of privatization on the poorest of the poor is confirmed by economic theory. They suggest that privatization of village commons and forest lands, while hallowed at the altar of economic efficiency, can have disastrous distributional consequences, disenfranchising entire classes of people from economic citizenship.

Energy Poverty Nexus

Energy services are a crucial input to the primary development challenge of providing adequate food, shelter, clothing, water, sanitation medical care, schooling and access to information. Energy therefore is one dimension or determinant of poverty and development, but it is vital.

Energy supports the provision of basic needs such as cooking food, a comfortable living, temperature, high living, the use of appliances, pumping of piped water or sewerage, essential health care, educational aids, communication. Energy also fuels productive activities, including agriculture, commerce, manufacturing, industry and mining. Conversely, a lack of access to energy contributes to economic decline. The energy dimension of poverty – energy poverty – may be defined as the absence of sufficient choice in accessing adequate, affordable, reliable, quality, safe and environmentally benign energy services to support economic and human development.

Biomass Consumption

The reality is that biomass energy is the fuel for the poor. Biomass fuels are used by 3 billion, or half of the Global population, to cook their food everyday. Biomass is contributing as a source of energy in the development and developing world. South Asia, with a population of over 1.2 billion, is largely dependent on biomass energy for meeting the energy needs in member countries. Contribution of such traditional biomass energy in the total energy consumption varies from 33 percent in India to 92 percent in Nepal (Pradeep Chaturvedi, 2000). The WEC projections of biomass energy use are given in Table 3.1, which shows increasing dependence of biomass energy use.

FAO's forestry department recently established a Wood Energy Information System (WEIS) which collects the existing data through the implementation of Regional studies (Wood Energy Today for Tomorrow (WETT), 1977). Table 3.2 explains the wood fuel consumption from 147 countries arranged in line with the FAO classification already used in other documents, such as the state of the world forests. The total production of wood in 1995 reached approx 3900 million cum, out of which 2300 million cum have been used for wood fuels (Table 3.2). This means that approximately 60 percent of the world's total wood removals from forest and non-forest land have been used for energy purposes. FAO's Regional Wood Energy Development Programme for Asia operating in 16 developing countries in Asia, collected data for their member countries and projected that two-thirds of wood fuels come from non-forest resources (1997).

World production of fuel wood for energy use in 1995 is estimated to be about 1.9 billion cum or 1.4 billion tonnes (FAO, 1998). An estimated additional amount equivalent to some 0.3 billion tonnes of wood is recovered and recycled for energy use. The total of 1.7 billion tonnes of fuel wood is equivalent to 550 million tonnes of oil. Compared to 9 giga tonnes of oil equivalent of primary energy supply in 1990, it stands at 6.7 percent. Most of it (76 percent) is used in developing countries. The balance of 24 percent fuel wood used in developed countries represents only 2 percent of their total energy consumption; 44 percent of the total wood fuel consumed in the world is used in Asian countries.

Energy Carriers

Roughly 2 billion people depend mainly on traditional fuels for cooking. Households use fuel in a variety of activities, including cooking, water heating and lighting. Different energy carriers can be used for each of these activities. These carriers form what is commonly referred to as an energy ladder for that activity. It is well known that people living in poverty tend to rely on a significantly different set of energy carriers than the rich.

Each rung corresponds to the dominant fuel used by a particular income group, and occupy different rungs (Hozier and Dowd, 1987; Reddy and Reddy, 1994). Wood, dung and other biomass fuels represent the lowest rung on the energy ladder for cooking. Charcoal and coal (when available) and kerosene represent higher steps up the ladder to the highest rungs, electricity and LPG.

Environmental Aspects of Biomass Consumption

The ordering of fuels on the energy ladder also tends to correspond to the efficiency of the associated systems and their cleanliness. For example, the cooking stove efficiencies of firewood, kerosene and gas are roughly 15, 50 and 65 percent respectively.

The emission of wood energy systems normally depend on the type and scale of the system and its operation. Conversion related emissions become lower when the scale of conversion unit increases. The most important emissions that can occur are carbon monoxide Polycylo-Aromatic-Carbon Hydrogens (PACs), Nitrogen Oxide (NO_X) particles. Thermal efficiencies in small scale household wood heaters can be around 50 percent but are much lower in less efficient designs.

It appears that the patterns of energy consumption of people living in poverty tend to increase their misery and aggravate their poverty (Leach, 1992; Das Gupta, 1993) for the following reasons: the use of biomass compromises the health of household members, especially when it is burned indoors without a proper stove to help control the generation of smoke outside. Thus, in addition to its relatively high cost, the use of biomass fuel may also promote higher medical care expenditure and diminish the ability of the poor to work productively.

Traditionally, biomass energy has been associated with environmental degradation and health hazards. Biomass for direct combustion is widely discussed. Production of bio-ethanol for transport vehicles is an emerging application where biomass can substantially avoid carbon emissions. Bio fuel production is regarded as a carbon sink; the total amount of carbon stored per hectare under the bio-energy crop is greater than the level of stored carbon in the vegetation previously on that land.

In India, the National Project on Biogas Development (NPBD, 1981-82) aimed at setting up 12 million biogas plants based on cattle dung, and 2.7 million biogas plants have been set up till March 1998. In the year 1997-98, the improved cooking stove on average saved about 400 kg of fuel wood equivalent per year. Fuel wood based biomass gasifier systems, with capacitities of up to 500 Kw, have been developed indigenously and are manufactured in the country. The biomass based cogeneration programme of 25-30 MW has been attracting the interest of a number of small and medium industries from other countries.

CONCLUSION

To conclude, the challenges of finding more sustainable growth paths and dealing with the nexus of poverty, energy and environment are too great and the intellectual and financial resources available are too scarce for multiple agendas and insensitive or ill-conceived positions.

A consideration of characteristics associated with sustainable development should include: development strategies to provide all people, especially the poor, with livelihoods which are relatively non-polluting, non-resource degrading and less intensive with respect to purchased inputs.

Solving the many problems of the poverty – environment nexus will require many changes, including the empowerment of poor people. Only when poor people have the requisite energy and other natural resources as well as other factors of income and wealth generation, will they be able to and want to act to conserve these resources.

Poor people must have access and control over not just energy and other natural resources, but the other factors of production critical to sustainable development, namely management capacity, to implement this know-how.

Sustainable development means information and management intensive strategies. It is better to educate the rural mass about other matters – namely, the complexities of these intertwined problems of poverty, other natural resource management and the environment, and the challenges in dealing with these problems in societies without well-developed markets, regulatory entities and physical and institutional infrastructure.

Avoid natural resource degradation or depletion except where the economic calculus allowing such depletion explicitly considers the spatial and intertemporal costs and externalities of such depletion. Externalities and use of the common problems are ubiquitous in the developing countries as traditional mechanisms and regulations for common resource management. They often collapse under demographic, commercial and climatic forces.

Thus, if poor people are to have the option of this development path in the midst of many changes, tremendous political, social and financial shifts will be needed. Whether such changes are likely is questionable.

Table 3.1WEC Projection of Bio-Mass Energy use 1998
Role of Bio-mass in Future Global Energy Use (EJ)

Scenario	Year	2025	2050	2100
Shell	1996	85	200-220	-
IPCC	1996	72	280	320
Green Peace	1993	114	181	-
Johnsson et al	1993	145	206	-
WEC	1993	59	94-157	132-215
Dessus et al	1992	135	-	-
Lashof and Tirpak	1991	10	215	-

Scenario	Year	2025	2050	2100
Shell	1996	85	200-220	-
IPCC	1996	72	280	320
Green Peace	1993	114	181	-
Johnsson et al	1993	145	206	-
WEC	1993	59	94-157	132-215
Dessus et al	1992	135	-	-
Lashof and Tirpak	1991	10	215	-

Source: Hall and Screase – WEC's, World Resource Handbook (1998)

Table 3.2Total Wood Fuel Consumption by Regions 1995

Regions	1000 cum	PJ	Ratio wood Fuel / All Energy	Ratio Wood Fuel / All Wood Uses
Development Countries	1763262	17633	0.15	0.80
Developed Countries	536754	5368	0.02	0.31
World	2300016	23000	0.07	0.59

Source: FAO State, United Nations Energy Year Book 1997, Wood Energy Today for Tomorrow Studies (FAO 1997).

REFERENCES

Jaganathan, V.N. (1989), *Poverty, Public Policies and the Environment*, Environment Working Paper No.24, Washington DC: The World Bank.

Jodha, N.S. (1986), *Common Property Resources and the rural poor*, Economic and Political Weekly, 21.

Jodha, N.S. (1995), *Common Property Resources and the Environmental context*: Role of biophysical versus social stress, Economic and Political Weekly, 30, 3278-3283.

Linde – Rahr (1998), *Rural Deforestation: Gender Effects on Private Investments in Vietnam*, Working paper, Department of Economics: G. Teborg University.

WCED (1987), *Our Common Future*, Oxford University Press, New York.

World Bank (1990), *World Development Report*, The World Bank: Washington DC.

In: Readings in World Development
Editors: K.C. Roy and S. Chatterjee, pp. 29-37
ISBN 1-59454-947-8

Chapter 4

COMMUNITY DEVELOPMENT AND CITIZENS' PARTICIPATION IN GOVERNANCE

Sukla Deb Kanango

The century preceding the current millennium had been witness to much turmoil which had shaken the human civilization in a big way. It had been witness to the two world wars, and to many others, minor or major, over the years. It reaped the benefits of industrial revolution; in many respects it also became the victim of the wrath of this revolution. It had been witness to mankind's valiant fight against imperialism and for the right to self-determination. It had seen the gradual demise of the colonial era and wider recognition by the world community of the need for self-rule. The transition had been far from smooth, often stained with bloodshed and the sacrifice of millions of innocent lives.

However, from within these tumultuous situations there had also been the ringing of some same voices which had stood through and made it possible for mankind to find a space for themselves, and to strive to make this world a liveable place. This, as is natural, has been a continuous process.

BROAD WORLD SCENARIO IN SOCIO-ECONOMIC RECONSTRUCTION

The consequences of the upheaval during the first half of the twentieth century had been that the old world changed, and it changed drastically. Social disintegration of various kinds took part, and various kinds of alignment and realignment of power bases started taking place.

Historically however, one factor remained constant, that is, the power that be decided the destiny of its people. If the ruler wanted to go to war, the citizens had to go along with it. It happened in the past, it is happening now. This changing scenario of the twentieth century necessitated for common people a struggle to come out of such dislocation to find a meaningful space for themselves.

Scenarios in the third world countries bear special significance here because these countries' struggle had been on different fronts. It had to come out of the shackles of imperialistic power and following the independence, whatever they strived to do, it had to address the mass of people, not one or two individuals, nor one or two communities. The post-colonial era in third world countries witnessed individual efforts of socio-economic reconstruction at various levels, but it had to become a programme of intervention of the kind whose focus would be a larger number of people and in this respect, in many countries, the state took the initiative and provided practically total support, like what happened in some countries, such as India.

The discussion in this paper will be on the issue of people's participation in development endeavour and how the deliberations have shifted the focus from participation in community development to participation in governance. The discussion will dwell mainly on the experiences in India while keeping the focus on the issue as is deliberated globally.

Community and Community Development

Development endeavour in post-colonial eras in third world countries is characterized by what is commonly known as community development—development of communities based in small geographical areas so that the efforts can be more intensive and its impact intensely felt. Such localized efforts were to be attempted all over the country covering the mass of people so that the country as a whole would move ahead towards growth and progress. The state here assumes the lead role as it only has the command over resources required for such a massive endeavour.

It will be relevant here to delve briefly into the concept of community and community development. A community is not signified by the locality to which people belong, nor by the particular pattern of activity in which they are engaged, nor by the type of social relationships they indulge in, but the sentiment—the degree to which the members "experience both a sense of solidarity and a sense of significance within it". Shared beliefs, values and attitudes are important phenomena in community, in other words, where people are 'experientially'. If we have community in the first place, then only the question of striving for community development comes.

It is the contention of the writer that while community development certainly conveys specific meaning as a concept, it is also a philosophy. It is a philosophy because it has a vision of the human society where co-existence and harmony are perceived as the goals which can give true meaning to the welfare of human society. It is a philosophy for it attempts to show how the goal can be achieved through the means which rests on a fundamental truth—truth that individuals have potentials and that opportunity should be there to put these potentials to use in their collective endeavour, only which can ensure true development of a community.

Whether in developed or in developing countries, unfortunately, somehow over the ages, we developed a system which destroyed the very essence which signifies a community. Ruling over this fact, Rabindranath Tagore wrote that thousands of years of history of this country testify to communitarian life of Indian people[1]. Provisions from education to drinking water were looked after by the people themselves. People never looked upon the king or someone from outside to do these. But, whenever society would like to get such works of

[1] Tagore, Rabindranath, Bharatbarsiyo Samaj, an essay in Atmasakti published in Tagore's writings (Rabindra Rachanabali) Vol.II, 1986, p.626

community import done by the state, the state would, in other words, make the society not only averse to self-help but incapacitate the society both morally and physically. It would only be at their peril that society would look upon the state and the government for meeting their needs (Tagore, 1904). It is noteworthy here that community development assumes true meaning when community has its heart in it and strives to maintain it and sustain it on the strength of its confidence in itself. Its shared beliefs, values and attitudes provide it the strength.

As the state is a major player in the community development endeavour in third world countries like India, it draws one invariably to the discussion centering state vis-à-vis peoples' role in it.

STATE AND COMMUNITY DEVELOPMENT

To achieve the goal of community development is difficult, but the encouraging sign is the efforts of different people, big or small, the world over directed towards it. While many groups and individuals have taken upon themselves the daunting task of community development, there are countries where the state has not remained far behind and has put its whole hearted effort to the task. India is one of them. Sri S.K.Dey[2], the architect of the community development programme in India mentioned that democracy would not survive if it could not find a living answer to the basic question of meeting the elementary needs of life: "Community Development in India is an all out quest for this answer". (Dey, 1962)

Poverty and large scale deprivation, the germs that necessitate community development to eliminate them, require enormous resources. Only the state has command over such resources to meet this challenge. However, this contention throws up certain issues as is discussed below.

PUBLIC VERSUS PRIVATE EFFORTS IN COMMUNITY DEVELOPMENT —SOME METHODOLOGICAL ISSUES: THE CASE OF INDIA

Before it became a programme of Government for India, community development work was initiated by individuals and groups in different parts of the country in response to the large scale dislocation at social and economic levels that took place, particularly in the rural areas of the country in the early part of the twentieth century. Rabindranath Tagore, the poet philosopher himself was one of them. His experiment in community development work at Sriniketan (where the writer is presently working) provided the model to the national progamme as well as to many other such endeavours in different parts of the country. Some of these endeavours left their deep imprint on the psyche of the nation.

To begin with, although the state was the major player in the community development programme in India, at present, with the change in the world economic scenario, increasing responsibilities are entrusted to people's institutions and organizations for the same. With

[2] Dey, S.K. in Foreward to the first edition of 'A Guide to Community Development (Revised)' issued by the Ministry of Community Development and Cooperation, Government of India, 1962

shifts towards open market policy and the increasing thrust on efficiency and productivity, it is believed this can be ensured in an atmosphere of voluntarism. Even for implementation of various programmes of community development the state is looking towards voluntary bodies for their involvement. Thus, one can see community development endeavours at two levels—state initiated and citizens' groups initiated.

These two, however, have different implications so far as approaches are concerned. State initiated community development programmes are perceived as services. As users of the services, community exerts a significant influence on these either by accepting or rejecting the services. This is a major challenge before the state.

Where community development work is initiated by voluntary organizations, the approach generally is people's (beneficiaries) involvement in the organization of the programme. However, this may not be true in all cases but it is imperative that whatever programme is initiated, there has to be takers of benefits of these services and therefore, these have to be made acceptable to them. In other words, the issue of acceptance or rejection of programmes is settled at the initial stage itself by voluntary organizations; this is not the case with the state's approach.

Differences in the perception about methodology among the voluntary sector also led to the developmental pursuits in different ways among them which, briefly stated, are like this: (a) one group of voluntary organizations are operating their own projects, the goals being to improve the conditions of communities at local level. They operate at micro-region; (b) the second group of voluntary organizations consists of the ones who strive to facilitate popular participation in development endeavours by helping the disadvantaged to articulate their needs, working in remote areas, mobilizing indigenous resources—both men and material, working with local level officials to change their perception and even their mode of functioning. In fact, they play quite a decisive role by advocating change/correction and improving government's service delivery or even policy formulation. Because of this advocacy role, they succeed in focusing on areas which are increasingly becoming a major concern of all development endeavours, whether governmental or non-governmental. For example, human rights, rights of the various disadvantaged/marginalized groups, women's rights, preventing environmental degradation, transparency and accountability in administration (govt.), peoples' participation and empowerment etc.; (c) The third group of voluntary organizations are the ones established by the corporate sector at the insistence of popular contention that they are not only to reap the profit but also to give something in return to the society. These resulted in many of the corporate houses, through floating of registered societies, adopting some rural and/or tribal areas for developmental work. They are engaged mostly in activities for socio-economic regeneration and empowerment of the disadvantaged sections through education and training. Their approach obviously differs significantly from the second category mentioned above. They are also comparatively very recent entrants in the field and they adopt a patronizing approach, although their goal is laudable.

FROM COMMUNITY DEVELOPMENT TO PARTICIPATION IN GOVERNANCE, THE ASCENSION

The issue of peoples' participation in governance has come in two ways in a country like India. Firstly, the state initiated development endeavours failed to derive the desired results or bring marked change (positive) in the living conditions for the majority of the people. It remains a state's urge to mobilize people. Secondly, the scenario in the post-colonial era in India is like this (and in so many others)—it represents "the striking experience of a traditionally political society steering its way through both the inherited phenomena of caste and communities and the modern structure of institutions and interests essentially through a dynamic and on the whole autonomous political process….." (Kothari, 1998)[3]. In this, the state became the main instrument using both top down and bottom up approaches.

In the process, many intermediate groups also came to play and introduced new ways of addressing the whole issue. The consequence of this was that on the one hand, there was this old and plural society and on the other, the urge to build a nation by bridging the centre-periphery dichotomy. The need of the hour was to build a linkage between a modern state 'which had a vision of unified society and widely dispersed, both traditional and newly emerging, peripheries'. There is now increasing demand on the part of the masses for decentralization, federalization of governance of the country and their participation in the governance of their region. However, the state is still doubtful of 'how much' of its power and authority can be devolved and shared with the people. People, on the other hand, see no way out but participation in governance through which they can only gain command over resources and formulation of major policies which affect their lives.

PEOPLES' PARTICIPATION: DEVELOPMENT-GOVERNANCE INTERFACE

Peoples' participation, therefore, needs to be considered in two different contexts: (i) participation in developmental activities initiated by government and others, and (ii) participation in governance, again mainly in the context of development pursuits. The latter however, is much more encompassing in the sense that it does not remain confined to the issue of development programmes only but addresses a host of other issues related to it, e.g. the way policies are formulated, the way policies are diluted, bureaucratic activism (well placed or misplaced) or inactivism, administrative machination-desirable or undesirable etc.

Contextual differences apart, the two often merge into each other and it is difficult to draw a line of clear demarcation between them, as may be seen in the popular arguments put for and against peoples' participation. Let us take the argument against peoples' participation first. These are broadly: (a) costs of development projects increases as negotiations with people delay the initiation of the project; (b) increased manpower is required to mobilize peoples' support; (c) instances are not few when people oppose projects when consulted initially or their support sought; (d) unpredictable participatory methodologies; (e)

[3] Kothari, Rajni: Fifty years of Democracy: an Overview of Development, A Magazine on National Scenario, published from New Delhi, April,'98, p.14

involvement of inexperienced and undesirable people in the project – it may be those who have nothing to do with the projects get involved instead of those whose participation matters (Peter Oakley).[4]

The arguments put forward in favour of peoples' participation invariably touch upon how government gains by promoting this, despite political costs. The arguments are: (a) real needs, priorities and capabilities of people can be gauged; also it gives proper feedback about the impact of governmental programmes; (b) programmes can be adapted to local conditions which put the scarce resources to more efficient uses; (c) reduces cost of implementation by gaining access to people through their organizations like clubs, co-operatives and others; (d) tap information about indigenous technology which are not only suitable to the local conditions but even more economical and effective than the imported technology; (e) mobilization of local resources augment or substitute government resources; (f) improved utilization and maintenance of government facilities (Uphoff, 1986). These gains are possible only when there is legitimacy. Peoples' participation gets legitimacy when they are allowed to do so by the government. Conversely, legitimacy of governmental programmes comes when it derives the authority from the people - its legitimacy depends on peoples' acceptance, or rejection, of its programmes or projects.

Participation in the context of programmes and projects may mean that once these are completed, peoples' participation ends. Participation in the development context is a process which 'unfolds' over the passage of time and leads ultimately to the empowerment of people when they are able to take decisions, intervene in situations directly or even make the government take the decisions of their import. Therefore, the goal of development can not end with achievements of goals of a particular project, and participation is not an input like other inputs in the project. Government functions merely as an instrument; real governance lies with the people.

Citizens' Participation in Governance: What Would it Really Mean?

Participation depends on the environment that facilitates it. The quality of people's participation in governance therefore, differs according to the system of governance in the respective countries. Discussion here would refer to democratic systems of governance.

Democratic systems of governance, theoretically, may be called peoples' government, but it does not call for individuals to have access to political power. It is a representative body where the representatives only enjoy the power if they are the party in power (Sarukkai, 1998).[5] By casting a vote, an individual undoubtedly exercises his power, but it practically ends at that because once in power, his representatives do not generally speak in his voice.

Apparently, democratic systems of governance gives wider choices to people in terms of choosing one from among many aspiring candidates contesting elections. While selecting a candidate, the voter generally performs a balancing act between quality and cost. For

---

[4] Oakley, Peter: Understanding participation in projects with people. Mimeo, undated, p.14-15.
Uphoff: 1986, p.425-426 quoted in Peter Oakley's Memeo undated

[5] Sarukkai, S.: 'Democracy as Consumerism' in Denoument, a magazine on national scenario, April,'98, p.21
Kumar, Arun: 'A case of strengthening Democracy in India', in Politics India, Vol.II, No.7, January, 1998, p.25

example, among the many aspirants, he may go for a person from his caste or from his neighbourhood or the one who espouses his political ideology, not because of the efficiency of the person or his personality but because he may benefit personally. This is an intrinsic part of the democratic process.

"No democracy can be a full blown one from the beginning. It has to evolve its own form depending on the genius of the people, their ideas and visions. A democracy is always in the process of being created; it has to be given content through the experience of the people" (Arun Kumar, 1998). It will be sheer wild imagination if we think that each and every individual can be directly involved in governance; it will always remain a representative one, but how to make that truly representative of the people's wish in their functioning is the main issue.

Citizen's participation in governance in a country like India has two dimensions: one, participation by the articulate, educated and socio-economically well placed sections of the society; two, participation by the marginalized, socially destitute, inarticulate sections of the society. While the former, a sizeable section of whom are very much actively involved in governance and the rest among them, in spite of not being so (rather indifferent), take care of themselves well, it is the marginalized group that become more pertinent to this question of participation in governance.

Marginalization of non-elites in terms of their participation in governance has been "the result of ignorance and loss of the consensus". The ignorance was on the part of both; the elitist nature of governance thought by excluding this section, the persons in power could be better placed, while the ignorance of the marginalized section deprived them of their entitlements. The loss of consensus among the ruling elite about the fact that governance could lead to real partnership among the different sections of the society resulted in getting increasing numbers of people gradually excluded from the mainstream. Rising aspirations and expectations among the people on the one hand, and failure of the government to fulfil these on the other, have resulted in growing alienation among larger sections of the people. This also resulted in the call for self rule by the marginalized groups.

In this scenario, it is rather difficult to say with certainty what form and character such participation in governance should have. But having committed to the contention that participation in governance is the answer to many of the ills that afflict governance, one has to seek and find ways. Without being prescriptive, participation could be thought of in the following way: a framework of governance that would ensure space for these alienated sections of society. The question is basically political—distributive justice is what is first of all required—admitting the demands of 'class, gender, generation' and recognizing the plurality of culture of the country which bring with it the associated differences. That would mean empowering the citizens through a right to information; decentralization of administration which gives the people a sense of partnership in governance and in turn also make them responsible citizens; administrative procedure needs to be simplified so that people can follow it easily. In a sense, transparency in administration is needed to regain peoples' faith in it. Mutual trust only facilitates the sense of give and take. Directly or indirectly, people exercise their influence on the government; so that they can do it with responsibility requires the development of institutions and practices which will give the people a sense of involvement and a sense of participation.

CHECKS AND BALANCES IN GOVERNANCE: THE CASE OF INDIA

Partisan politics is an inherent element of a democratic system of governance. The parties are not always drastically different in their ideology and mode of functioning. In fact, for a common man, it is often rather difficult to differentiate one from the other. Some, of course, have strong political ideology and pursue their agenda accordingly. Often, partisan politics degenerate into personal politics, the cause of much of the malaise that affects the democratic system of governance. Under the circumstances, one tends to think: can't democratic government be run on non-party basis? The justification for partisan politics seems to be the following: governance is not the job of one or two persons but of a group of persons. The group needs an identity and it is the political ideology that provides the identity.

In the absence of a multiparty system, it is not possible to put a check on the individual agenda of an individual party or an individual member. In reality however, how far is this check realizable? With less success or more success this seems to be realizable, as is happening in India. The elections fought in the recent past returned no single political party in majority and this demonstrated the cutting edge of democracy whereby the citizens are expressing their wishes and aspirations in the form that, within the unified whole, the cultural and social plurality of the Indian masses has to be recognized and accommodated. It is also the warning that they cannot be bypassed.

Governance at the grassroot level is considered as another automatic check on the higher ups in the political and administrative ladder. Local self-governance is regarded as a very important mechanism through which citizen's participation in governance can be truly ensured and India is one of the firm believers in this. The beginning of the 90s saw two landmark legislations in the form of the Constitution (Seventy-third) Amendment Act, 1992 and the Constitution (Seventy-fourth) Amendment Act, 1992. These local self-government bodies in rural areas called Panchayats, and Municipality in urban areas, became constitutional entities—they became statutory bodies, the status which they did not enjoy till then. Mahatma Gandhi advocated the creation of people's power alongside the power of the state and panchayatiraj institutions were regarded by him as the main instrument of self-rule by people. Jayprakash Narayan, freedom fighter and a noted Gandhian, talked of people controlling power in spite of their not being in power (Govt.) and thereby deciding their destiny. He was of the view that democracy must be built on ancient Indian tradition "and the new policy must be founded on the principle of self-government….." (Mathias and Raj, 1998).

The Constitutional Amendments do not perceive the panchayati raj institutions or urban municipalities as administrative units or development agencies but as self-governing units at the local level. The amendment is a giant leap forward for it opened the doors of reversal of the political system. Until now, all decisions were flowing from the top and it was top heavy. But now the country was going to be managed by lakhs of people's representatives in place of few thousands that did till now.??

This positive action however, is regarded as having limitations which do not make the local self-government autonomous in the true sense. It is argued that the powers to discharge their responsibilities are derived from state legislature which decides what power and authority can be devolved to this level. These local self-governments have been given the powers of delegated legislations like budgets, by-laws, rules and regulations attached to their functional responsibilities. Two areas which are said to have been advertently, or inadvertently, left outside their purview are judicial systems and police functioning. Had these been included, they would have made the power and authority of these bodies meaningful.

Functional decentralization, financial decentralization and popular participation in the provision and monitoring of the local affairs have been aimed at by the Constitutional Amendment. Provision in these regards has undoubtedly been made, but the citizen-government interface remains (to some extent by nature) ambiguous. Therefore, the way this needs to be taken care of is by clarity of the power and functions of the elected representatives and "their interface with the public and citizens interest groups". Transparency of rules and procedures are of crucial importance for promotion of effective and efficient local government. Situations that are unfolding are creating some hope that the government, national or local, will ultimately have to come down to the level of intimate contact with people and workout a positive working relationship with the citizens. If it chooses to remain indifferent it will be at the cost of its own existence.

CONCLUSION

Community development efforts are going on in different parts of the world. A common urge seems to have been gaining ground among the people of many countries to have freedom in their living, freedom to express themselves, freedom to decide the kind of life they would like to lead, freedom to decide how they should administer themselves. In the process of their struggle for this freedom, some are encountered with insurmountable obstacles; some begin losing hope as the struggle seems to be a continuous affair without having any end in sight. Living within a democracy and achieving true democracy seems to be a distant dream in many countries of the world. However, in spite of all these, the urge is what seems to keep people moving ahead. Citizens' participation in governance is argued to have already been there wherever democratic system of government is functioning. The ultimate issue is the quality of such participation. It has been demonstrated that such government will remain a representative one; the average citizen cannot be in power but they should have control over the power that is vested in their representatives. The mechanism that can assure this will differ according to the socio-political cultural contexts in a particular country. The struggle has been going on and it is hoped that it will create and develop the system of its own which will conform to the cultural ethos of the particular people.

In: Readings in World Development
Editors: K.C. Roy and S. Chatterjee, pp. 39-52
ISBN 1-59454-947-8

Chapter 5

SOCIAL SECTOR DEVELOPMENT IN INDIA IN THE NEW MILLENNIUM WITH SPECIAL REFERENCE TO POVERTY ALLEVIATION

Debotosh Sinha

ABSTRACT

The social sector occupies a pivotal place in development. The founding fathers of the Indian Constitution also recognized its primacy in the life of people. Economic growth coupled with Social Justice has been the avowed objective of our planning process since the inception of planning in India in 1951. The major developmental programmes in social sector in the new millennium are directed towards poverty alleviation, including a major thrust on rural poverty. Agriculture and rural development, ensuring social justice in the field of education, health and family welfare, housing, water supply, sanitation and employment generation, welfare of the weaker sections, are also the objectives of social sector development.

What the author would like to highlight in this paper is that after a brief introduction of social sector development and its allied dimensions, as well as the importance of social sector development in poverty alleviation, the concept of poverty, its causes, incidence and magnitude in India will be explained. Rural poverty, various strategic poverty alleviation programmes by the Government of India from time to time, till to date, under different policies and programmes, the manifestation and outcomes of such programmes and lastly, what needs to be done more to encounter with the problem of poverty, will be critically analysed.

INTRODUCTION

The term social sector is often used to refer to education, health and nutrition sectors. According to K. Seeta Prabhu (2001), Head of the Human Development Resource Centre at the UNDP, India Country Office, the term has not been formally defined and thus has come to acquire several connotations. One of the definitions of social sector is related to human development, as against human resource development.

There are two distinct schools of thought that could govern public policy with respect to social sectors. The first is the neo-classical viewpoint which is reflected in the concept of human resource, the theories of human capital and the more recent theories of endogenous growth. The alternative approach is that of human?? which has been defined by UNDP.

The UNDP defines Human Development Approach as the process of enlarging people's choices. The concept encompasses empowerment, sustainability and security. In this approach, people occupy center stage and measures such as education, health and nutrition are emphasized for their intrinsic value and their role in enhancing the basic capabilities of people. The emergence of the concept of human development can be traced to efforts by economists such as Amartya Sen (1995) who defines standard of living in terms of functioning and capabilities rather than in terms of commodity possessions. This approach emphasizes acquisition of education, health and nutrition, which is considered as an essential human right.

The difference between what Streeten (1994) terms 'human resource developers' and the 'humanitarians' is that the former considers human beings as 'means' to an end whereas the latter, in true neo-Kantian tradition, considers human beings as ends in themselves. In fact, to the 'humanitarians', the human resource approach which acts towards people with a view to turning them into better human capital, which in turn contributes to greater human prosperity, is offensive. The difference between the terms is not merely of semantic importance but reflects very different philosophical approaches to the issue and could shape public policy in decidedly different ways.

Social sector development has been the raison-d'etre (V.S Gupta, 2002) of planning in India. The Directive Principles of the state policy, enshrined in the Constitution, form the social premise of planning in the country. The founder Chairman of the Planning Commission, set up in 1950, was Pandit Jawaharlal Nehru, who had identified the major task before the nation as "the ending of poverty and ignorance and disease and inequality of opportunity". Right from the beginning of the first five year plan (1951-56) the prime objectives of the planning process has been the enhancement of the social sector development, but it has only been towards the end of the Tenth Year Plan (2002-2007) that they were largely addressed.

Let's have a brief glimpse of the objectives of the earlier plans and also to see how the paradigms are shifting from one plan to another.

The First Plan (1951-56) laid emphasis on agriculture, irrigation, power and transport so as to provide an infrastructure for rapid industrial expansion in the future. The Second Plan (1956-61) aimed at achieving rapid industrialization of the economy and bringing about greater equality in income and wealth for the establishment of a socialistic pattern of society in India. The Third Plan (1961-66) aimed at securing a marked advance towards self-sustaining growth. It listed a set of five objectives namely: increase in annual income by 5 percent; self-sufficiency in agriculture; growth of basic industries; maximum use of manpower resources; and decentralization of economic power. Agriculture was given the top priority and about 35 percent of the outlay was allocated to this sector. The Fourth Plan (1969-74) aimed at accelerating the tempo of development and reducing fluctuations in agricultural production as well. The Fifth Plan (1974-79) gave emphasis on self-reliance and to adopt measures for raising consumption standards of people living below the poverty line.

Removal of poverty was the foremost objective of the Sixth Plan (1980-85). Stress was laid on economic growth, elimination of unemployment, raising the lifestyles of the weaker sections of society, improving the public distribution system and control of the increasing population. The Seventh Plan (1985-90) emphasized policies and programmes, which aimed at rapid growth in food grain production, increased employment opportunities, self-reliance and social justice. Incidence of poverty was also touched upon. The Eighth Plan (1992-97) recognized the need for a re-orientation of planning. The plan period emphasized: (a) human development as the main focus of planning; (b) a large economic space for private sector. The Ninth Plan (1997-2002) was launched in the fiftieth year of India's independence. The specific objectives were: (a) priority to agriculture and rural development with a view to generating adequate productive employment and eradication of poverty; (b) accelerating the growth rate of economy with stable prices; (c) ensuring food and nutritional security for the vulnerable sections of society; (d) providing basic minimum services of safe drinking water, primary health care facilities, universal primary education, shelter and connectivity to all in a time bound manner; (e) containing the growth rate of population which would help in poverty reduction; (f) ensuring environmental sustainability of development process through social mobilization and participation of people at all levels; (g) empowerment of women and socially disadvantaged groups as agents of socio economic change and development; (h) promoting and developing Panchayati Raj Institutions (PRIs), cooperatives and self- help groups; (i) strengthening efforts to build self-reliance.

India embarked on its Tenth Plan from 1st April 2002. The aim is to set a higher growth rate of the economy at 8 percent during the period 2002-07. That there has been a paradigm shift in attempting to tackle problems of social sector development is clear from the following enunciation relating to objectives of the Tenth plan:

> 'Economic growth can not be the only objective for national planning and indeed over the years, development objectives are being defined not just in terms of increases in GDP or per capita income but broader in terms of enhancement of human well-being. This includes not only an adequate level of consumption of food and other types of consumer goods but also access to basic social services, especially education, health, availability of drinking water and basic sanitation. It also includes expansion of economic and social opportunities for all individuals and groups, reduction in disparities, and greater participation in decision- making. The Tenth Plan must set suitable targets in these areas to ensure significant progress towards improvement in the quality of life of all our people' (Planning Commission, 2002-2007).

At this juncture we would try to analyze what the scenarios are in the three core areas of social sector development in the new millennium: health, nutrition, and education.

HEALTH

Despite concerted efforts, India continues to record high levels of morbidity, especially among infants, children, the elderly and women. The burden of major morbidity falls on the vulnerable section of the population, including wage labourers, minorities and the low-income groups. In the new millennium, the basic thrust in the health sector is the radical reform in both health care and medical education system to ensure that the advance in medicine and the vast infrastructure for health care created over the past five decades were made accessible to the masses at affordable cost.

This was to be achieved through improving access to the utilization of Health, Family Welfare and Nutrition Services with special focus on under served and under privileged segments of the population. There will have to be continued commitment to provide essential primary health care, emergency life saving services, services under the National Disease Control programmes and the National Family Welfare programmes free of cost to individuals based on their needs and not on their ability to pay. At the same time, suitable strategies have to be evolved, tested and implemented for levying and collecting user charges from people above poverty line and utilizing funds obtained for improving the quality of health care services.

It has also been looked into and much discussed in the Indian planning arena that the reorganization and restructuring of existing health care infrastructure, at primary, secondary and tertiary levels, so that they have the responsibility of serving populations residing in a well defined geographical area and have appropriate referral linkages with each other. At the same time, it is essential that there is appropriate delegation of power to PRIs so that there is local accountability of the public health care providers.

Nutrition

The major nutrition-related public health problems currently are chronic energy deficiency and micro- nutrient deficiencies, such as anemia due to iron and folic acid deficiency. Nutritional problems need to be tackled across a broad front. There needs to be a continued increase in food grain production to meet the needs of the growing population. The increase should be more in the case of coarse grain production to meet the energy requirements of Below Poverty Line families at lower cost. Efforts have to be made to check the sluggish trend in per capita availability of pulses, and increase pulse production, improve affordability of pulses and increase consumption. Similarly, increased availability of vegetables at affordable cost throughout the year in urban and rural areas is desirable to address nutritional needs of the population.

Education

In terms of human development objectives, education is an end in itself, not just a means to an end. Education is a basic human right and without education, development can be neither broad based nor sustained.

However, from all accounts, India's report card in terms of educational attainment has been highly unsatisfactory. In this context, our performance in the field of education is one of the most disappointing aspects of our development strategy. Out of approximately 200 million children in the age group 6-14 years, only 120 million are in schools and net attendance in the primary level is only 66 percent of enrolment. Education for all is the primary objective in this millennium. The Sarva Shiksha Abhiyan (universalization of education), which has been launched to achieve this objective, indicates a strong reiteration of the country's resolve to give the highest priority to achieve this goal during this century.

Ensuring universalizing access to primary education and improvement of basic school infrastructure are the calls of this millennium. In order to ensure proper control over schools for imparting quality education, the states should be encouraged to implement 73rd and 74th Amendments of the Constitution, which facilitate the transfer of management of primary and upper schools to local bodies. Planning, supervision and management of education would have to be through local bodies at district, block and village levels. Efforts should also be made for social mobilization of local communities for adult literacy campaigns and for promotion of primary education.

The university and higher education sector have also been strongly emphasized. Although the number of universities has expanded, and many of the universities continue to maintain high standards of education, it is a matter of serious concern that the expansion in quantity has been accompanied by a fall in quality. Both technical and management education are managed strategically in order to provide broad based, multi-disciplinary education incorporating composite skills and knowledge to meet the challenges posed by globalization.

CONCEPT OF POVERTY

Poverty, according to the Human Development Report, 1997, is the denial of opportunities "to lead a long, healthy, creative life and to enjoy a decent standard of living, freedom, dignity, self-respect and the respect of others".

Income, however, is only one measure of poverty. Another approach is the basic needs approach, according to which poverty should not be viewed at merely in terms of private income but should include access to basic needs like health, education, employment and other essential services which the community usually provides to the citizens.

There are important limitations in measuring poverty in terms of either income or consumption levels. These approaches do not pay attention to the assets on which most poor people rely for their livelihoods. These assets can include their access to natural and financial resources, their health and capacity to work. Another drawback of the traditional approaches is that these do not focus on the social relations which lead to the process of impoverishment. For instance, the lack of political influence of the poor and their being subjected to discrimination are issues which are relevant while studying the nature and causes of their poverty.

The new approach is known as the "sustainable livelihoods" approach. This addresses issues such as the capabilities, assets, and labour required for a means of living. A livelihood is stated to be sustainable if one can cope with and recover from stresses and shocks, and maintain or enhance its assets both now and in the future.

The other important aspect which must be discussed briefly is to see another dimension of the concept of poverty. Poverty line is traditionally based on some minimum nutritional level in terms of calorie consumption. The amounts required to buy the minimum calorific requirements is quantified in terms of money. Households which fall below this level are considered to be below the poverty line.

There are wide variations among the estimates of poverty line. The 8th Plan (1992-97) had fixed it at Rs11,000 per annum. The planning Commission estimated that the population below the poverty line was 51.5percent in 1972-73 and came down to 18.95 in 1993-94 (Rural 54.1 and 21.7 and Urban 41.2 and 11.6 respectively).

According to the NSS (National Sample Survey, 55th round, 2003) estimates, there has been a sharp decline in the percentage of people below the poverty line in recent times. During 2002-2003 the percentage has declined to 26.10. In absolute terms, the population below the poverty line has declined to 260 million, after remaining stationary at around 300 million for almost 30 years (table 5.1).

Table 5.1: State wise (selected) percentage of persons below poverty line 1993-1994 and 2002-2003

State	Rural %	Urban %	Total %	Rural %	Urban %	Total %
	1993-1994			2002-2003		
Andhra Pradesh	15.92	38.33	22.19	11.06	26.63	15.77
Assam	45.01	7.73	40.86	40.04	7.47	36.09
Bihar	58.21	34.50	54.96	44.30	32.91	42.60
Gujrat	22.18	27.89	24.21	13.17	15.59	14.07
Haryana	28.02	16.38	25.05	8.27	9.99	8.74
Karnataka	29.88	40.14	33.16	17.38	25.25	20.04
Kerala	25.75	24.55	25.43	9.38	20.27	12.72
Madhya Pradesh	40.64	48.38	42.52	37.06	38.44	37.43
Orrisa	49.72	41.64	48.56	48.01	42.83	47.15
Punjab	11.95	11.35	11.77	6.35	5.75	6.16
Rajasthan	26.46	30.49	27.41	13.74	19.85	15.28
Tamil Nadu	32.48	39.77	35.03	20.55	22.11	21.12
Uttar Pradesh	42.28	35.39	40.85	31.22	30.89	31.15
West Bengal	40.80	22.41	35.66	31.85	14.86	27.02
Maharashtra	37.93	35.15	36.86	23.72	26.81	25.02
All India	37.27	32.36	35.97	27.1	23.6	26.1

Causes of Poverty

- Indian poverty is predominantly rural and the reasons are in most cases agrarian. Output in the farm sector has remained stagnant for far too long, whereas the number of people eking out a living in this sector has steadily gone up.
- The Government's employment generation schemes have not made much dent due to bureaucratic apathy and total lack of imagination of the planners. Moreover, uniformity of approach throughout the nation has led to avoidable wastage.
- Per capita income has not grown much due to rising population canceling out the gains of economic growth.
- Political expediency has led to the neglect of the endemically poor yet voiceless sections like the widowed, separated, and deserted women, households headed by women, the disabled, and the destitute who can not undertake any productive endeavour.

- Growth has accelerated distortion in income distribution. Ironically, the process of development itself throws out of the economic system a vast number of people who are already unemployed. Instances of tribal people being displaced to make way for large hydro-electric projects, or of farmers being dispossessed of their land to build industrial sheds, are not uncommon.

SOCIAL SECTOR DEVELOPMENT AND POVERTY ALLEVIATION

The basic objective of social sector development is the eradication of poverty and creating gainful employment opportunities for the unemployed and the under-employed so that all have at least a decent minimum level of living.

Poverty can be seen at three levels, i.e., the individual or the family level, the community level, and the social level (Yashwant Sinha, 2001). At the individual and family level, to be out of poverty, a person must be able to earn and arrange for at least two wholesome and nutritious meals a day. At the community level, people do not have a sense of deprivation if drinking water, electricity, roads, health and educational facilities etc. are provided for everyone's use. At the social level, people are better off if they get the social respect that has been denied to some classes of people (including women) by the society for a long time.

Promotion of rapid economic growth has been viewed as central to the objective of poverty alleviation. For eradication of poverty, the strategy is to (a) accelerate economic growth with stable prices; (b) focus on direct attack against poverty; and (c) accord top priority to government expenditure in social sectors.

In the context of the poverty reduction in the Indian situation, greater attention has been provided to the development of social infrastructure. Thus, it has been ensured that greater numbers of children should be sent to school for education, awareness and better future skill formation. It has also been felt to provide a wider prevention and curative health cover to the most vulnerable and poorer sections of the society, especially women and children belonging to this strata. The efforts have been made to facilitate the women in general in our society in order to eliminate the gender bias prevailing presently. The government is seized of these problems and has initiated and implemented several policy measures whereby social infrastructure could be expanded and its services utilized by the disadvantaged sections of the society and, in turn, the phenomena of poverty will be dealt with more strongly.

The government has initiated, sustained, and refined many programmes since independence to help the poor attain self-sufficiency in food production. Probably the most important initiative has been the supply of basic commodities, particularly food at controlled process, available throughout the country. The poor spend about 80% of their income on food while the rest of the population spends more than 60 % (D.Das,1999).

India has had a number of anti poverty programmes since the early 1960s. These include, among others, the National Rural Employment Programme and the Rural Landless Guarantee Programme, Food for Work Programme etc with a view to address the plight of the hard-core rural poor by expanding employment opportunities and building the rural infrastructure as a means of encouraging rapid economic growth.

While higher economic growth is definitely the key variable in combating poverty, pure growth is not enough for poverty reduction in the short run. It is being increasingly realized that poverty reduction is not possible without structural soundness and balance between various sectors. Growth policies have been combined with social sector development. Expenditure on basic education, health care and essential infrastructure has been raised along with a simultaneous reduction in wasteful, non-asset generating outlays.

I would like to mention here that the share of the central government expenditure in the social sectors, aiming at the poverty reduction, as compared to the central government expenditure in all the sectors, increased from 7.7 percent in 1991-92 to 10.8 percent in 1999-2000. In absolute terms the expenditure of the central government on social services has increased from Rs.15026 crore in 1994-95 to RS. 36270 crore in 2000-01 showing an increase of about 141 percent over this period.

The current Indian strategies to deal with the problem of poverty are two pronged in this new millennium – employment generation and agriculture and rural development. Of course health, education and nutrition are the integral component of the above three areas.

Employment Generation

The latest comprehensive data on employment situations in the country is available from the results of the 50-th Round survey on employment conducted by the National Sample Survey organization (NSSO). As per the information available from the survey, the average annual growth rate of overall employment (in both organized and unorganized sectors) declined continuously from 2.75 percent in the period 1972-78 to 1.77 percent in 1983-88, but increased to 2.37 percent in 1987-1994 (**table 5.2**).

Table 5.2 Growth of Employment (in percent)

Period	Growth rate of Overall Employment	Growth rate of employment in the organized sector	
		Public	Private
1972-73 to 1977-78	2.75	-	-
1977-78 to 1983	2.36	2.99	1.41
1983 to 1987-88	1.77	2.17	0.43
1987-88 to 1993-94	2.37	1.00	1.18

Source : Planning Commission

As per the Ninth Five Year Plan (1997-2002) labour force growth is expected to be at its peak in the Ninth Plan period. Attainment of near full employment by the year 2007 may not be an unreasonable target provided that the conditions are created for further acceleration in the growth rate and the intensity of labour absorption is not substantially reduced both sectorally and in terms of the sectoral structure of growth. It is estimated that that full employment by 2007 is contingent upon acceleration in growth of employment in post Ninth-Plan period to 2.8 percent compared to a realized growth of 2.37 percent (1978-94) and projected at 2.44 percent in the Ninth-Plan. The projection of labour force and work opportunities created during the Ninth-Plan would lead to a reduction in the average rate of employment during the Ninth-Plan as compared to the Eighth- Plan (table 5.3)

Table 5.3 Labour Force and Employment in Eighth and Ninth Plan Periods

	8th Plan (1992-97)	9th Plan (1997-2002)
Labour Force	3742	4234
Employment	3672	4164
Unemployment	70	70
Unemployment (Per cent)	(1.87)	(1.66)

Source: Planning Commission

The government has decided to set up the Second National Commission on Labour with a view to providing protection to millions of labour. Finally, it is important to reiterate the Government's firm resolve to evolve and implement policies that would create increased opportunities for employment generation. Our employment policy is based on equity and social justice and provides direction for gainful employment.

AGRICULTURE AND RURAL DEVELOPMENT

Poverty is predominantly a rural phenomenon; urban poverty is only a spill over of the rural poor who migrate to urban areas in search of some source of livelihood. Therefore, the emphasis has been on removing rural poverty through a three pronged approach:

a) Agricultural Development
b) Promote rural self-employment by helping the beneficiary to own some productive asset through a mixture of subsidized bank credit and outright subsidy.
c) Provide direct wage employment to the unemployed/ under employed by utilizing the labour to create and maintain community assets like irrigation tanks, roads, and so on.

Some of the major initiatives in the above direction have been discussed below.

We believe that agriculture is essential for alleviating poverty, generating income and employment, bringing about food security and sustaining a buoyant domestic market for industry and services. It is necessary to strengthen the rural economy. A number of initiatives have been taken in the last few budgets and plan periods to facilitate rapid growth of this vital sector of the economy.

1. Credit flow to Agriculture and Rural Infrastructure Development Fund (RIDF).
2. Micro finance has been given a big thrust for speedier alleviation of poverty (Self-Help Group).
3. Creation of Micro Finance Development Fund.
4. Strengthening of Cooperative Credit System.
5. Farmers' Credit Cards coverage to be enlarged.
6. Major steps towards convergence of and decentralization in agriculture development.
7. Setting up of National Commission on Land Use Policy.
8. Special schemes for North-East Region.

9. Tariff adjustment in sensitive agricultural products.

The Rural Development Minister dwelt upon the various development schemes very emphatically in 2003, with the essence of poverty alleviation through rural transformation, including Swajaldhara (safe and potable drinking water), Haryali (wasteland development programme), Pradhan Mantri Gram Sadak Yojana (improving rural road connectivity) and Swarnajayanti Gram Swarozagar Yojana (holistic self-employment scheme). The hallmark of these programmes is to make the Panchayat Institutions (Local Self Government) the backbone of India's development.

Displaced Concerns, Misplaced Priorities

Despite the strong articulation of a multidimensional view of human poverty, India has been overwhelmingly concerned with income poverty. The focus on income poverty began in the 1960s when a Working Group of eminent economists was set up by the Government of India to assess the extent of poverty in the country. This Group used a nationally desirable minimum level of consumption expenditure to define India's poverty line and based it on a standard balance diet prescribed by the Nutrition Advisory committee. Based on such a measure, the Group found that "half the population lives in abject poverty". The report discussed the consequences as well. Such widespread poverty is a challenge which no society in modern times can afford to ignore for long. It must be eradicated on humanitarian grounds and as a condition for orderly progress.

The Report of the Working Group was influential in many respects. It set the trend for defining and measuring income poverty. Subsequent studies on poverty in India continued to use either income or consumption as the basis for defining and measuring poverty. The attention of policy makers shifted to a narrow conception of poverty as income deprivation. The Planning Commission declared "The stage has now come when we should sharply focus our efforts on providing an assured minimum income to every citizen of the country within a reasonable period of time. Progressively this minimum should be raised as development goes apace". To this day, India's income poverty line is the monetary equivalent of a minimum daily calorie intake: 2400 calories per person in rural areas and 2100 calories per person in urban areas.

The proportion of income poor in India has fluctuated widely in the past but the trend is downwards. Economic growth has the potential to reduce income poverty. Several factors mediate the conversion of economic growth into income poverty reduction. Kerala, for instance, ensured maximum reductions in income poverty despite slow economic growth through political activism and a rapid expansion of equal opportunities. Improvements in infrastructure and access to assets also play an important role in income poverty reduction.

Clearly, growth is important but the conversion of higher incomes into income poverty reduction is contingent upon several factors: effective public policy interventions, the redistribution of assets, the equitable expansion of physical and social infrastructure, an even and rapid spread of health, education and employment opportunities, and the assurance of people's participation.

POVERTY REDUCTION: NOT BY INCOME ALONE

The overwhelming attention paid to measuring and monitoring income poverty has resulted in a gross neglect of other serious forms of human deprivation. Some of these deprivations are loud and visible: child labour, illiteracy, damaged environments. Others are largely silent but visible: caste discrimination, discrimination against women and girls, and child prostitution. Many other forms of deprivations are, to this day, silent and invisible. These include issues of womens health, domestic violence, child malnutrition. These deprivations are not related to income poverty levels in any predictable manner. Haryana is one of the richest and fastest growing states in terms of per capita income. Yet, infant mortality at 68 per 1,000 live births is four times higher than income-poorer Kerala. And women in Haryana suffer systematic deprivation that gives them one of the lowest female-to-male ratios in the country-865 per1000 males.

Income levels often fail to capture deprivations along other dimensions of human life. Rural Andhra Pradesh and Madhya Pradesh, for example, suffer from similar levels of educational deprivation- an illiteracy rate of 64%-but the proportion income poor is 29% in Andhra Pradesh and it is 45% in Madhya Pradesh. Again, the extent of urban literacy is the same in Punjab and Orissa (28%), and yet the proportion of urban income poor is 11% in Punjab, and in Orissa, it is 41%. Similarly, Kerala, Tamil Nadu and Andhra Pradesh, which report the lowest levels of child malnutrition, do so despite having relatively low levels of per capita incomes. Madhya Pradesh and Maharashtra report the same levels of child malnutrition even though Maharashtra's per capita income is more than double that of Madhya Pradesh. Gujrat, among the high-income states, reports the highest levels of child malnutrition.

All this is not to say that income does not matter. It does, but people often value other things in life much more than income. Even to the very poor, self-respect and a good reputation mean a lot. They often articulate their immediate needs as a good education for their children, access to good health care facilities, and a safe environment. They detest exploitation and discrimination. To most people, to be treated with dignity and respect matters much more than incomes.

POVERTY ERADICATION BY 2005 AND BEYOND (FUTURE PROMISES)

In 1996, the United Front national Government announced a definite poverty goal for the country: poverty eradication by the year 2005 and beyond. What does this mean? According to the Prime Minister: "Programmes for generation of employment, creation of assets, imparting of productive skills and raising the incomes of the very poor people would all be strengthened and provided with larger funds. At the same time, there is need to review these programmes, sharpen their focus, improve their delivery system and involve the poor in their implementation. Effective steps will be taken to ensure that the benefits reach the needy people".

According to the Government of India, success in alleviating poverty will be contingent upon three factors:

1. a GDP growth rate of at least 6% per annum over the next 10 years.

2. provisioning of at least 7 basic minimum services:
   a) universal access to safe drinking water.
   b) 100% coverage of primary health care centers.
   c) universalization of primary education.
   d) public housing assurance to all shelter less deserving families.
   e) extension of mid-day meal school throughout all primary schools.
   f) road connectivity to all villages and habitations.
   g) streamlining the public distribution system targeted to families below the income poverty line.
3. ensuring that the income poor and the socially disadvantaged group receive special attention and priority.

Other planned initiatives include a universal employment assurance programme that will guarantee 100 days of employment for every unemployed person, and to achieve universal literacy. Agricultural growth will be stepped up by improving productivity in regions with a high concentration of poverty.

If we look at **table 5.4**, we see that China, Indonesia, Thailand and South Korea have all achieved and sustained higher levels of per capita incomes than India because they have done much better in terms of expanding human capabilities. These countries recognized the strong complementarily between income expansion and social development. If human poverty has to be eradicated, India must, as a priority, invest in its people-in their health and education.

Table 5.4 : Comparative data on human development: India and selected countries

	Life Expectancy		Adult Literacy		Real GDP per capita	
	1960	1993	1960	1993	1960	1993
India	44.0	60.7	34	51	617	1,240
Botswana	45.5	65.2	41	68	474	5,220
Indonesia	41.2	63.0	54	83	490	3,270
China	47.1	68.6	-	80	723	2,330
Thailand	52.3	69.2	60	82	985	6,350
South Korea	53.9	71.3	88	98	690	9,710

Source : Human Development Report 1996

Secondly, India needs to strike a balance in its development. This balance is not on the economic front alone: between receipts and expenditure, between imports and exports, between savings and investments. A balance is needed between economic growth and an expansion of social opportunities. A balance is needed between the assurance of economic rights and political rights. A balance is needed between expansion of physical infrastructure and basic social infrastructure. The priority has to shift basic education, to preventive and promotive health care. At the same time, several imbalances need to be corrected: between men and women, between rural and urban masses, between socially disadvantaged communities and the rest of the society.

Thirdly, there is the issue of resources. Clearly, more financial resources are required if all children have to attend school, if all villages must have access to a primary health care centers, if all communities must have access to safe water, if all pregnant mothers have to be assured of safe motherhood. Additional resources could be mobilized by improving tax-to-GDP ratio and ensuring a growth rate of 6-8% per annum; by eliminating subsidies to the rich by cutting losses of public enterprise; and by reducing defense spending.

Fourthly, the State, instead of abdicating its responsibility for expanding social opportunities, needs to play a more proactive role than it has in the past. If something has not been done, it usually reflects unwillingness rather than an inability to act. For example, the state has shown dynamism in reducing controls, liberalizing the economy, and opening up the economy. The recent Constitutional amendment to ensure women's participation in local governments displays an extremely progressive and proactive face. On the other hand, the State's effort at abolishing child labour, preventing child prostitution, and until recently, addressing the problem of AIDs reveals shocking recalcitrance. Similarly, its unwillingness to make primary education compulsory, despite the affirmation in the Constitution of India, reveals inexplicable reluctance. For many of these matters, sustained advocacy, open debates, concerted pressure and public action are urgently needed to provoke a positive response from the State.

Fifthly, opportunities must be created and expanded for women to participate more fully in economic and political decision-making. The human development experience from Kerala and Manipur suggest that society's well-being improves when women enjoy greater freedoms: economic, social and political. But, ensuring greater freedom for women is not easy. Unfortunately, many see it as usurping of power from men with no net gains. The overall gain to society increases many times when men and women contribute equally. However, to achieve this, changes are required in the way people think and behave, in the way society perceives the role and contribution of women.

Finally, economic growth has to be participatory. It must be planned and managed locally by people whose lives it affects. Communities must participate actively to shape programmes, ensure that opportunities are expanded, and that the benefits are shared equitably. For this, structures of local self-governance must be strengthened, and people's participation has to become a way of public life.

CONCLUSION

Is there any hope for optimism? Yes. First, the official stated policies for poverty eradication reflect human development priorities. Second, following the post-1991 reforms, economic conditions are more favourable. Third, democratic participation is opening up. This is not just through local governments but through people's organizations, and in particular women's groups that are frequently organized around credit, economic activities and social empowerment. At the same time, there are some causes for concern. The focus on reducing fiscal deficits is forcing major cuts in social sector spending. The pressure to pursue state minimalism is leading to an abdication of state responsibilities as the pressure to privatize is beginning to affect people's access to basic health and education.

What does India need to do? Mahatmam Gandhi had once remarked: "India's salvation consists in unlearning what she has learned during the past fifty years. Similar changes are now required in thinking, in living, and in cultivating a genuine public spirit. India needs to get its development priorities right. We need to undo and unlearn. At the same time, we also need to learn and act". If human poverty has to be eradicated, attention must shift from income poverty to the poverty and inequality of opportunities: economic, social and political. India needs sustained public action to be guided by strong human development priorities.

REFERENCES

Ahuja R, (1997), *Social Problems in India*, New Delhi: Rawat Publications.

Bagachee, S, (1987), "*Poverty Alleviation Programmes in Seventh Plan: An Appraisal"*, Economic and Political Weekly, January 24.

Das, D, (1999), *Social Sector Development-Experience and Challenges*, New Delhi: Deep and Deep Publishers.

Dreze, J, and Sen, A, (1995), *Indian Economic Development and Social Opprtunity*, New Delhi: Oxford University Press.

Ghate, P, (1984), *Direct Attacks on Rural Poverty*, New Delhi: Concept.

Government of India, (2002), *India 2002,* New Delhi: Publication Division, Ministry of Information and Broadcasting.

Government of India, (2001), *Approach Paper to the Tenth Five Year Plan (2002-2007)*, New Delhi: Planning Commission.

Gupta, V.S, "*Social Sector Development and the Tenth Five Year Plan"*, Employment News, (6-12 April,2002).

K.Prabhu, S, (2001), *Economic Reform and Social Sector Development*, New Delhi: Sage Publications.

Streen, P, (1994), *Human Development-Means and Ends*, AEA Papers and Proceedings, 4 (2),pp-232-37.

In: Readings in World Development
Editors: K.C. Roy and S. Chatterjee, pp. 53-58
ISBN 1-59454-947-8

Chapter 6

Social Security and Development in India

Sarbeswar Chatterjee and Sujit Kumar Roy

The dictionary meaning of 'Social Security' is: the principle or practice or a programme of public provision (as through social insurance and assistance) for the economic security and social welfare of the individual and his family. By now, Social Security has transcended its original meaning particularly when 'Social Welfare' has been added to the term or concept of 'Social Security'.

In 1884, Germany introduced the first system of compulsory national insurance against sickness. Shortly afterwards Denmark, New Zealand and Australia introduced non-contributory old age pension. In Britain a series of similar welfare reforms was enacted by the Liberal Government between 1906 and 1914. However, the most significant developments took place in the 1930s and 1940s with, for example, the New Deal in U.S.A., the People's Home in Sweden, the post-war welfare reforms in Britain, France and Germany. Most of these reforms centred upon the goal of full male employment supported by family allowances and insurance benefits for sickness, unemployment and old age.

William Beveridge (1942) pointed out that his plan was only part of a general programme of social policy. It is one part only of an attack on five giant evils: upon the physical want with which it is directly concerned; upon Disease which often causes that want and brings many other troubles in its train; upon Ignorance which no democracy can afford among its citizens; upon the Squalor which arises mainly through haphazard distribution of industry and population; and upon Idleness which destroys wealth and corrupts men, whether they are well or not, when they are idle. The same year (1942), Dr. L. Marsh's report on Canadian Social Security gave three contingencies to be covered by Social Security: 1. Interruptions of earnings, due to unemployment, sickness, permanent disability, old age, premature death; 2. Occasions requiring expenditure which strains the family budget, such as medical care and funeral costs; 3. Insufficiency of income to meet the cost of child maintenance. The obvious reason for including medical care within Social Security is that, with the exception of Britain, medical care is partly or wholly linked with social insurance. The main exponent of Philosophic approach, Pierre Laroque (1966), President of the National Social Security Fund in France, regarded increasing acceptance of Social Security as a stage in general social development. Social Security represents a guarantee by the whole community to all its members of the maintenance of their standard of living or at least tolerable living conditions, by means of a redistribution of incomes based on national solidarity. Fundamentally there is no difference among them and the difference is only a matter of semantics and not of substance – no known definition has excluded the benefits listed by the Beveridge Report. But, the general agreement on the desirability of Social Security has not been matched by a corresponding agreement on the definition of Social Security. This lack of agreement has led Mr. Altmeyer (1966) to make a special plea for the use of the term in a 'restricted' rather than an 'expansive' sense. Similarly I.L.O., having given up the idea of a definition that would be internationally acceptable, formulated three criteria that had to be satisfied before a scheme or service could be considered part of the National Social Security System. These were:

1. The objective of the system must be to grant curative or preventive medical care, or to maintain income in case of involuntary loss of earnings or of an important part of earnings, or to grant supplementary incomes to persons having family responsibilities.
2. The system must have been set up by legislation which attributes specified individual rights to, or which imposes specified obligations on, a public, semipublic or autonomous body.
3. The system should be administered by a public, semipublic or autonomous body.

The paper proposes a reappraisal of the approach to Social Security, especially in view of its role in Development.

Welfare has also been difficult in defining. There is not and cannot be a single, total or complete theory of welfare. Some theories provide insights into political economy, some into political ecology, and some into cultural expressions of identity, inclusion or exclusion. Theories offer prospects and limitations for understanding social welfare and encourage critical perspectives on the world. They do not store up the 'true' answers to the world's problems but, instead, enable different questions to be posed about the world and the problems and potentials it contains.

Definitions apart, we should not find any difficulty, with our existing knowledge and ideas, in finding out the relation between Social Security and Development which also has numerous definitions – there are more than seventy definitions currently in circulation (Holmberg and Sandbrook, 1992). Among the high income democracies, nations spending the most (% of GDP, 1980) include Sweden (31.2 per cent), the Netherlands (27.6 per cent), Denmark (26.2 per cent), and France (25.5 per cent); Japan, Italy, Australia and U.S.A. are exceptions possibly due to their individual characteristics in Social Security Systems.

Furthermore, countries with 'universal benefit systems' have been much more successful than countries with strongly targeted systems in moving people out of poverty simply because very few poor individuals are then left outside the group of beneficiaries. For instance, in several countries in north-western and northern Europe with universal benefits, about 70 to 80 per cent of the pre-transfer poor seem to have been lifted from poverty by various welfare–state arrangements; examples are Belgium, Denmark, the Netherlands, Norway and Sweden. By contrast, again, Canada, Australia and United States have much less corresponding figures; a study in detail of these countries' systems would probably reveal the causal connections.

For the success of its economic reforms, China recently feels the implication of beefing up Social Security System (International Journal of Economic Development, 1(4), 1999: pp. 365-368).

But, the above position is qualified by the income inequality that has become an increasingly important public policy issue in industrialized countries in recent years. Although macroeconomic conditions have been favourable in many of these countries, the distribution of income within and across countries has remained uneven. In fact, in several countries, income inequality has risen. As a result, policymakers have become concerned that large segments of the population are not reaping the benefits of economic growth. In the United States and the United Kingdom, the Gini Coefficient increased by between 1 and 2 per cent a year between the late 1970s and the mid-1990s. The rise was smaller, but still positive in Germany, although wage inequality has not risen in continental Europe. Nevertheless, inequality did increase in 12 out of 14 countries in the 1996 Organisation for Economic Cooperation and Development (OECD) Study. And, as Kevin Murphy pointed out, the growth of inequality is a pervasive phenomenon, not just a story of the very rich or the underclass.

Against this backdrop and even after about 68 years since the Social Security Act, 1935, passed by the Roosevelt administration in U.S.A. (where the term Social Security had been used for the first time), American Statistics are busy with measuring poverty rates, how much lower the average earnings of blacks are than those of whites, the historical background of the predicament of the poor; whereas, it should have been busy with finding how many persons have been economically, physically, mentally, morally, educationally and socially lifted up to contribute to the process of development. Attitude towards the Social Security System vis-à-vis development should change from what it is now. Despite enormously increased expenditure on Social Welfare from 1965 on, progress against poverty ceased at that point. In the face of steadily improving economic conditions, the period 1965 to 1980 was marked by increases in poverty, family breakdown, crime and voluntary unemployment (Murray, 1984).

Coming back to Beveridge again, it is said to be possible to tinker at the edges of the unequal society, ensuring that, by and large, such inequality does not result in mass starvation, disease or premature death. Indeed, it is possible, over time, to use Social Policy as a tool to maintain 'relative' inequality whilst simultaneously abolishing 'absolute' poverty. So long as this social policy would continue, problems of above nature would persist. In the 1990s, after more than three decades of 'development', many developing countries have debt burdens which outweigh their Gross National Product several times over. Nine of the 'top ten' most indebted countries globally are in Africa. Income inequalities across the world have also increased rather than decreased with the passage of each United National Development Decade; in 1993, the richest 20 per cent of the world's population had a greater share of global income than they did in 1960. The ratio of richest to poorest within countries across the globe has increased from 30:1 to over 60:1 during the same period (UNDP, 1993).

If we perceive the concept of Social Security in its proper perspective we can get rid of this social and economic imbroglio. Social Security is not just giving doles and fringe benefits to sustain. It should be used as a tool, enabling every member of the society to participate in and integrate into the major institutions of society; otherwise constant hostility, suspicion and apathy will jeopardize the process of development. In many societies a segment of population, particularly minorities, whether discriminated or not, feels isolated and cannot participate fully in the mainstream activities of the Society; this is detrimental to development. Socialisation is the proper remedy here. Social Security is not to be seen in an isolated way as it is done now. Planners, politicians, executives and academicians should, by now, look at Social Security as an index of development; it is development itself. Development, as one Prime Minister of India said, must have a human face. It is not only the face; it is the body and soul of development. When Assar Lindbeck suggests policies to increase "human capital" of the disadvantaged, he means Social Security System to be productive in helping total development, to be our desired goal.

South East Asian countries did succeed in having a positive impact on the Social Sector because the "initial conditions" were favourable. The favourable initial conditions included fair egalitarian land distribution, availability of infrastructural facilities, especially in the rural areas, and investment in health and education. These facilities, along with a high rate of growth and political commitment to protect the Vulnerable Sections of Society, enabled the South East Asian countries to utilize economic reforms to improve the lot of the poorer sections.

By contrast, the Indian Social Security and Welfare System are in rudimentary form. Its basic disadvantage is that while the system is trying to adopt the image of advanced countries' Security Schemes through monetary help and insurance, its expected beneficiaries are the majority of the population and not the minority of it like those of advanced countries. In India, the Social Security Schemes are executed through different agencies, apart from the Central and State Governments, LICI (Life Insurance Corporation of India), General Insurance Companies, N.G.O.s. Their schemes range from maintaining crèche for children to providing life insurance protection to the rural and urban poor (persons below poverty line and marginally above poverty line). Unemployed youth, women and children, and the handicapped are included in the schemes. Barishtha Pension Bima Yojana gives higher interest rates to the pensioners through LIC. Janashree Bima Yojana provides life insurance protection to the rural and urban poor (persons below poverty line and marginally above poverty line). Loans to the youth in the Self-Help Scheme are granted by the Central Government, Shiksha Sahayag Yojana, to help students. Central Welfare Board under the Department of Women and Child Development, Ministry of HRD, Government of India, is implementing various schemes through voluntary organisations and N.G.O.s. Recently the Central Government announced that the cabinet had cleared the health insurance and pension schemes for the unorganised sector of labour. The Government of West Bengal has, amongst many others, the Old Age, Widow and Disability pensions.

The Social Security System in India is scanty in two senses: One, in terms of percentage of Government expenditure; and two, in terms of the amount of help that the beneficiaries receive. One, please take note of the following table and, two, for example, widows are given Rs. 500/- per month, while the income of marginally poor is regarded as Rs. 1,000/- per month. Under the Shiksha Sahayog Yojana the students (XI-XII) are paid Rs. 100/- p.m. while a book for them may cost far more than Rs. 100/-.

The scheme is not total in the sense that it cannot, for financial constraints obviously, reach all persons of the target group. The recent figures of persons getting Old Age, Widow and Disability Pensions in the state of West Bengal are 3,900, 2,163 and 646 only respectively. LIC paid only 185 scholarships in Kolkata in 2002-2003.

Central Govt. – Social Security and Welfare (% of share to respective total expenditure)	
1990-91	0.31
1991-92	0.34
1992-93	0.37
1993-94	0.34
1994-95	0.37
1995-96	0.62
1996-97	0.65
1997-98	0.60
1998-99	0.57
1999-00	0.52
2000-01	0.52
2001-02	0.47
2002-03	0.23
2003-04	0.25

The scheme is scattered through different agencies and hence through different buildings and places. People seeking help are bewildered in locating the offices particularly when, surprisingly West Bengal Government's Old Age, Widow and Disability pensions are administered by the Department of Vagrancy!

The implemental aspects of the schemes are not very much practically oriented: Group Insurance Scheme under Janashree Bima Yojana is being difficult for implementation owing to the incapacity in forming groups; the Village Workers' Social Security Scheme has come to a stand still as West Bengal Government is not able to pay the matching grant.

Apart from the schemes mentioned above, there are numerous other schemes. The problem in India is not the problem of forming schemes and keeping record of them, it is the problem of ground reality that drives us to question once again, is this system at all working to any useful purpose? In India, the old age is scared of chill penury, so to say – old age pension is not only insufficient, but also it reaches very few of them. Everyone is aware that a sizeable portion of a pensioner's budget is allocated to medicine and medical care. If a fifth generation antibiotic tablet costs more than Rs. 50/-, if the hospital admission, even in emergency, is not guaranteed, if the medicines are not all genuine (according to WHO's recent report 20% worth of medicines in India are fake. WHO experts have said three injections out of every four in India and other countries in South Asia are made with unsterilised needles, exposing countless people to hepatitis, HIV and other infections – The Statesman, Kolkata, 7 Nov., 2003), if the health service is inadequate (Dr. Devi Shetty said, if a hospital is built for 1,000 people and there are 10,000 people visiting it regularly, how can it function properly? – The Statesman, Kolkata, 10 Nov., 2003) what is the use of a health insurance scheme? Health Service comes first, only next comes health insurance. Similarly, in Janashree Bima Yojana insurance benefit is only obtainable after death – for productive purpose, benefit during lifetime (even after 60) is more important than the posthumous one. The youth are in constant consternation of unemployment and the middle-aged are shaky in fear of losing employment any time under, what is called euphemistically Voluntary Retirement Scheme (V.R.S.). To top it all, people in India are really insecure owing to inordinate delay in settling the disputes in Law Courts, where crores of cases are pending.

Insecurity apart, the delay hinders productivity and development. The Indian Scenario further buttresses the basic proposal in this paper that a reappraisal of the Social Security Scheme, to fulfil its purpose, is necessary; instead of being stragglers we want the target group to be the Vanguard of Civilisation.

REFERENCES

A Review by C.T. Kurien of book: Seeta, K (2001), *Economic Reform and Social Sector Development: A Study of two Indian States*, New Delhi: Sage Publications.

Centre for monitoring Indian Economics Pvt. Ltd., (CMIE), (2003), Economic Intelligence Service, Nov., Mumbai.

Encyclopaedia of Sociology, (1992), *Social Security Systems,* Macmillan, Vol. 4.

Frontline, Volume 18, Issue 24, Nov. 24 – Dec. 07, 2001.

George, V, (1968), *Social Security : Beveridge and After*, London: Routledge and Kegan Paul.

Income Inequality : Issues and Policy Options – a Symposium sponsored by The Federal Reserve Bank of Kansas City, (1998), Jackson Hole, Wyoming, August, 27-29.

O'Brian, M and Penna, S, (1998), *Theorising Welfare – Enlightenment and Modern Society*, New Delhi: Sage Publication.

Webster's New Collegiate Dictionary, (1981), Springfield, Mass, U.S.A.: G. and C. Meniam Co.

In: Readings in World Development
Editors: K.C. Roy and S. Chatterjee, pp. 59-70
ISBN 1-59454-947-8

Chapter 7

PERFORMANCE OF MANUFACTURING AND SERVICES SECTOR IN INDIA IN POST - REFORMS PERIOD: ISSUES AND EXPERIENCES

Subadra Ragothaman

INTRODUCTION

The development path of the economy, world over, has been characterized by a shift from agriculture led economy to an industrial economy and finally to a service led economy. Despite the dominance of the service sector in the developed countries, there are strong inter-relationships between the manufacturing sector and the rest of the economy. The multiplier effects of a rise or fall in industrial production are significant. Many service sector jobs depend on manufacturing activities. The service sector and manufacturing sector have close linkages.

We have attempted to analyse the performance of Indian economy in the post- reform period in order to find out the characteristics of our development path. The dominance of service sector vis-a-vis the manufacturing in recent times is also analysed.

During the late 1990s, the India's manufacturing sector witnessed strange foreboding moments. The manufacturing sector, once ranked amongst the eight largest in the world, was creaking to a painful slowdown. The Indian manufacturing sector was forced to rise from the slumber of decades of protectionism. Persistent investment slowdowns in the key manufacturing sectors, alarming slump in profitability and closure of several industrial units, seemed to signify erosion of business confidence.

The manufacturing competence is an important factor in the strategy for enhancing India's global competitiveness. Indian's lower wage structures, an already established base of a range of manufacturing industries in the small, medium and large scale of operations, basic materials industries such as steel, other metals, coal, petroleum and petro-chemicals and importantly an abundant availability of technical manpower, are the ingredients which show that manufacturing sector has a strong growth potential.

The analysis of major developments since reforms in India will help us in finding out the linkages between the manufacturing and service sector in the Indian economy. The reform period can be taken up for analysis in two phases. During the first phase, i.e. during 1992-93 to 1996-97, India could witness an improved growth performance led by a marked acceleration in the industrial growth. The growth momentum however slackened in the latter phase of reforms, i.e. 1997-98 to 2002-03 with the slowdown exacerbated by the global recessionary conditions. However, the important fact is that the services sector provided some resilience to the overall growth process. The pronounced deceleration in manufacturing activities during the second phase of the reform period posed a major challenge for sustaining the growth momentum.

This paper is presented in five sections. Section one is on the general growth prospects of Indian economy in the post reforms period. The performance of manufacturing sector is analysed in section II and that of services sector in section III. The linkages between these two sectors are examined in section IV. The conclusions and suggestions are presented in Section V.

SECTION I

The impact of economic reforms in India on growth of the economy is taken up for an in-depth study in this section. It may be mentioned at the outset that the prime mover for the post-reform growth experience happens to be the development of service sector in India.

The programme of macroeconomic stabilization and the structural reforms introduced since 1991 brought about an improved growth performance during the first phase of the reform period, i.e. from 1992-93 to 1996-97. The overall growth in this period was led by a marked acceleration in the industrial growth.

The economic performance during the reform period reflected an improvement in real Gross Domestic Product (GDP) (Table 1.1). The growth process responded favourably to the initial productivity gains arising from deregulation of trade, industry and finance. The overall growth during the reform period was marked by higher services sector growth (8.0 per cent) as compared with 6.7 percent during the 1980s, while agriculture and industry witnessed some deceleration.

We can clearly note the declining trend in the manufacturing / industrial sector and the picking up of the service sector. The coefficient of variations in the agricultural and industrial sector is also cause for concern. The coefficient of variations in the agricultural and industrial sector was very high at 130.2 and 53.5 respectively, where as in the services sector it was only 22.7. The deceleration of economic activity raised some concerns about the feasibility of rapidly moving the economy to a higher growth path in the medium term.

However, the performance of the economy in external sectors gives positive signals and stresses the need to accelerate the reforms process. The competence in the manufacturing sector is an important ingredient in the strategy for enhancing India's global competitiveness.

Five years of continued slow growth in the manufacturing sector was matched by high rates of growth in the service sector. This contributed to the fancy notions of India having leapfrogged over the industrial stage of development into a post-industrial knowledge and services economy. The focus of this presentation is to negate this notion so that we will not take wrong policy decisions.

Table – 7.1Sectoral Trend Growth Rates of Real GDP Percent

Sector		Decade				
		Preceding Reforms		Year	Reforms	
		1981-82 to 1990-91		1991-92	1992-93 to 2002-03	
		Growth	CV %	Growth	Growth	CV %
		1	2	3	4	5
1	Agriculture of Allied Activities	3.1	150.7	-1.5	2.5	130.2
2	Industry	7.6	24.1	-1.2	6.2	53.5
	Mining and Quarrying	7.5	59.3	3.7	4.2	84.7
	Manufacturing	7.4	28.9	-3.6	6.6	62.0
	Electricity, Gas and Water supply	9.4	21.2	10.4	6.0	46.4
3	Services	6.7	18	4.5	8.0	22.7
	Construction	4.8	102.5	2.1	6.0	51.0
	Trade, Hotels and Communication	5.9	18.9	2.5	8.6	22.0
	Financing, Insurance, Real Estate and Business Services	10.1	16.3	12	7.8	40.2
	Community, Social and Personal services	6.6	30.9	2.6	8.0	44.7
4	GDP at Factor cost	5.6	39.1	1.3	6.1	23.0

Note: (1) Trend growth rates have been calculated using semi-logarithmic regression.
(2) CV refers to coefficient of variation of growth source computed on the basis of data from the CSO.

SECTION 2

Performance of Manufacturing Sector

Manufacturing plays a significant role in countries' economies. In India, as a developing economy, the importance of manufacturing cannot be under-emphasized. India's manufacturing sector had registered healthy growth right from 1950s to 1990s. In fact, growth in manufacturing has consistently outstripped the overall growth in GDP, indicating the increasing significance of manufacturing in the overall economy as can be seen from the table 7.1.

The manufacturing sector in India, which is extremely large in absolute terms given the size of the Indian economy, accounted for about 15 to 20 percent of GDP, which is rather low, compared to other developing nations like Brazil, Mexico, Argentina and Korea.

The Indian manufacturing sector is quite diversified with capital and intermediate goods constituting 21.6 percent and 36.8 percent of total value added in manufacturing in 1980-81. But the decline in the performance of capital goods can be seen from its relative weight, which was only 9.26 as compared to 35.57 of basic goods and 26.51 for intermediate goods. Tables 7.2 and 7.3 explain the relative contribution of different sectors to the growth of manufacturing sector in India.

Table 7.2Rates of growth of India's GDP and Manufacturing 1950 to 1998 (at constant 1993-94 prices)

Time Period	Manufacturing	GDP at factor cost
1950s	6.4%	3.7%
1960s	4.2%	3.1%
1970s	5.0%	3.9%
1980s	7.3%	5.5%
1990s	9.3%	6.7%

Source: National accounts statistics from EPW Research Foundation.

Table: 7.3 Use-based classification of Industrial Production (Base: 1993-94=100)

Industry Group	Weight	Index 2001-02 P	Index 2000-01	Growth Rate (per cent) 2001-02	2000-01	1999-00	1998-99	1997-98
1	2	3	4	5	6	7	8	9
Basic Goods	35.57	152.5	148.5	2.7 (31.9)	3.6 (24.0)	5.5 (27.7)	1.6 (13.9)	6.9 (34.9)
Capital Goods	9.26	160.6	166.2	-3.4 (-11.6)	1.8 (3.5)	6.9 (10.2)	12.6 (28.1)	5.8 (7.8)
Intermediate Goods	26.51	180.1	177.4	1.6 (16.1)	4.7 (27.2)	8.8 (37.7)	6.1 (42.3)	8.0 (33.0)
Consumer Goods	28.66	175.1	165.2	6.0 (63.7)	8.0 (45.4)	5.7 (24.4)	2.2 (15.8)	5.5 (24.2)
a) Consumer Durables	5.36	253.7	227.6	11.5 (31.4)	14.5 (20.1)	14.1 (13.7)	5.6 (8.7)	7.8 (7.3)
b) Consumer Non-durables	23.30	157.0	150.8	4.1 (32.4)	5.8 (25.1)	3.2 (10.6)	1.2 (6.6)	4.8 (16.8)
IIP - General	100.00	167.0	162.5	2.8	4.9	6.7	4.1	6.7

Note: Figures in bracket are relative contribution computed as the ratio of the change in index of the respective industry group to the change in the overall index.

Table 7.4 Relative contribution of Sectors to Industrial Production

Sector	1981-82 to 1990-91 (Average) Percent	1992-93 to 1998-99 (Average) Percent
Basic Goods	43.6	35.8
Capital Goods	25.0	7.1
Intermediate Goods	14.6	35.2
General Index	100.0	100.0

The institutional milieu of Indian manufacturing also displays an interesting diversity. The most remarkable aspect is the importance of production by traditional and small scale enterprises. The so called unregistered non-factory sector, consisting predominantly of cottage and village industries utilizing traditional techniques and employing household labour to a significant extent, contributed about a third of total value added in manufacturing in 1978-79 (CSO 1981).

Small scale industries continue to be an important segment of Indian industry in terms of output and employment. In the post-reform periods, the SSI segment faced increasing competition from domestic and foreign producers due to de-reservation and import liberalization of many items.

Then there are manufacturing units operated by the state, i.e., the public sector units. Value added by public sector manufacturing units contributed about 16 percent of total GDP in the manufacturing sector. The remaining part of the manufacturing sector is of course the private sector steered largely by domestic entrepreneurship.

These records of the manufacturing sector clearly show its criticality for the Indian economy. With India's lower wage structures, an already established base of a range of manufacturing industries in the small, medium and large scales of operations, basic materials and importantly an abundant availability of technical manpower, the economy had many ingredients necessary to show that India is emerging as a future manufacturing hub of the world.

The manufacturing sector has a significant role to play in India's prosperity and growth. Manufacturing value added grew at a rate of 7.4 percent during the period 1980-90. The share of manufacturing in India's GDP had gone up from 16 percent to 19 percent in 1995. However, when compared to other key developing countries, India's performance is quite low. For example, against the growth rate of 7.4 percent for India, the GVA growth rate of China was 10.7 percent, that of Korea 12.1 percent, and other Asian countries 7.5 percent. Even as a percentage of GDP, Indian manufacturing at 19 percent falls far below China (37 %), Brazil (23%) and other SE Asian countries (ranging from 22 to 34 %).

Manufactured goods constitute 75 percent of India's exports (excluding services) for 2001-02, out of total exports of $43.7 billion, manufactured goods constituted more than $33 billion. Most of the goods exported are low value, low tech items. High tech constitutes only 11 percent of India's exports as compared to 67 percent for Malaysia, 21 percent for China and 18 percent for Brazil.

The comparative growth rates recorded in the 1980s and the 1990s (Table 7.5) clearly brings out the fact that industrial slowdown is widespread covering all broad sectors such as manufacturing, electricity and mining, and all use based groups.

The manufacturing sector had witnessed a number of reforms such as delicensing, restructuring through mergers, competition from external units, reforms in the stock market influencing the availability of finance, partial labour reforms and disinvestments policies. These reforms brought out changes in the overall environment and organizational structure in this sector. With a time lag in 1993-94, industrial production remained high and responded positively in the following two years. A peak growth rate of 13 per cent was reached in 1995-96. The boom, however, ended after 1995-96 and the growth rate remained sluggish since then.

The slowdown of the capital goods sector after the reforms was partly due to import expansion after the reduction in tariff rates. The manufacturing growth in the post reforms period has clearly been led by the intermediate goods sector and by the consumer goods.

Mergers and Acquisitions are on the rise in the industrial sector. During 2001-02 there were 1050 acquisitions involving an amount of Rs. 35,360 crore as compared to 1183 acquisitions involving an amount of Rs. 33,649 crore during the previous year.

Table 7.5Comparative Growth Rates in the Industrial Sector 1980-2000

Parameter	Avg.Annual * Growth rate 1980-81 to 1991-92	Avg.Annual Growth rate 1992-93 to 2000
General	7.8	6.00
Manufacturing	7.6	6.3
Mining	8.4	3.3
Electricity	9.0	6.6
Use based classification		
Basic goods	7.4	6.1
Capital goods	9.4	5.9
Intermediate goods	4.9	9.1
Consumer goods	6.0	6.3
GDP manufacturing at 1993-94 prices		
Total	6.1	7.4
Registered	6.8	8.1
Unregistered	5.0	6.2

* Simple Average Annual Growth Rates.
Source: Economic Survey 2000-01

However, seventeen major industry groups showed negative growth in food products, cotton textiles, Jute etc.

All these show that Indian manufacturing is at a crossroads today. It faces great challenges, as well as great opportunities. India has the potential to emerge as a global manufacturing hub.

SECTION 3

The Rise of the Service Sector in India

The emergence of the so-called service or post-industrial society has been seen as the cause of changes in the income distribution in the developed, industrialised countries. Simon Kuznets observed a relationship between inequality and economic development in a country with two sectors, namely a traditional agricultural sector and a small modern industrial sector that can be described as an inverted U[9]. The so-called 'Kuznets curve' seemed to have appeared with the rise of the post-industrial society variously described as de-industrialisation, service society or the third industrial revolution.

The de-industrialization and the growth of the service sector have been related to the slowdown of the economic growth. In a study of the U.S., Baumol and Wolf concluded that the employment shift to service sector implied in fact a shift to a sector with a lower productivity level. This can be seen as the reason for the resulting income-inequality.

Ekstedt showed the heterogeneity in the service sector. He is using the distinction between "knowledge companies" and "service companies." The former has a better educated labour force.

Bringing this analysis in the context of the rise of the service sector in India, we find that though employment in the service sector has shown an upward trend, (Table 3.1) the rate of growth is extremely slow.

Table 7.6 Employment by sectors (All India)

Sector	1972-73	1977-78	1983-84	1987-88	1993-94
Agriculture	73.9	71	68.6	65	64.7
Mining and quarrying	0.4	0.4	0.6	0.7	0.7
Manufacturing	8.8	10.2	10.7	11.1	10.5
Electricity, gas and water	0.2	0.3	0.3	0.3	0.4
construction	1.9	1.7	2.2	3.8	3.2
Trade	5.1	6.1	6.2	7.2	7.4
Transport	1.8	2.1	2.5	2.6	2.8
Services	7.9	8.1	8.9	9.3	10.3
All	100	100	100	100	100

The employment potential in the knowledge based service sector is limited in the Indian context where the majority of the Indian population faces the problem of access to higher education. However, the upward trend in the share of the IT sector in total GDP has risen from 2.8 per cent in 2000-01 to 2.9 percent in the next year, which raises our hopes.

Services have been India's most dynamic sector in recent years registering rapid growth. At a time when the manufacturing sector has been reeling under stagnant growth during the last few years, it is the record contribution of the service sector that has been saving India through its contribution to the GDP. This sector has not been much affected by the recession. With a growing rate of 8-10 per cent it has been contributing around 49 per cent of the GDP. The annual average growth of 7.7 per cent was attained during the period 1997-2002. As per the revised estimates, the growth of real GDP from the services sector rose to 6.2 percent in 2001-02, risen up from 5.0 percent during 2000-01 but well below that of 9.4 percent during 1999-2000. Thus, service sector has also been facing a slight deceleration of growth in recent years.

The share of services was estimated to be 54.1 percent of GDP in 2001-02 as against 53.7 percent in 2000-01. On an annual basis, the services sector has exhibited a strong trend component, which has provided an element of stability to the growth process. In the recent period, the performance of the services sector has been considerably influenced by financing, insurance, real estate and business services.

The rising contribution of skill intensive services with high value additions such as information and technology to the overall output in the economy has been a significant feature in the structural transformation of the Indian economy.

In India's health services, super speciality hospitals specializing in both modern and traditional Indian medical systems supported by the state-of-the-art-equipment, are attracting patients from across the world. This constitutes a significant segment of India's services sector.

By virtue of having the second largest scientific and technical manpower in the world, India has been providing various consultancy and other services globally.

Service intensity is found to be high for Indian industries. One of the indicators of direct contribution of services to the manufacturing in India is financial intermediation services indirectly measured (FISIM). The FISIM used up in the manufacturing gross value added increased from 5.7 percent in 1990-91 to 7.6 percent in 1999-2000. All these show the interdependence of growth of service and manufacturing sector on each other.

The development of the manufacturing and services sectors in the post-reform period described in these sections point out that there are many issues in both the sectors that need to be addressed. India cannot afford to ignore the importance of the strengthening manufacturing sector. There is little evidence of any systematic "de-industrialization" in India. The challenge for India is the pursuit of trade liberalization, hand in hand with concerted effort to expand the domestic manufacturing sector.

In sum, it can be said that India has a global competitive advantage in many areas of the service economy and should invest intelligently to device its benefits. At the same time, we cannot afford to ignore the manufacturing sector because of the strong linkages between these two sectors in India.

SECTION 4

Manufacturing and Service Sector Linkages

The development experience of many countries shows that the sectoral inter-linkages and the extent of synergies and feedback between industrial and services sectors underpin the dynamics of growth. Increasing global integration and competitive pressures have expanded the demand for technology intensive and knowledge based services. This has led to the application of improved management techniques in the production process, speeding up production, marketing and the reaping of economies of scale. The externalization of a large number of services, which are important inputs in production, and distribution of goods is reflected in a rise in 'outsourcing' of services and an evolution of subsidiaries of production enterprises selling services to both the parent enterprise and other enterprises. There exists close linkages between manufacturing and service sectors.

Apart from providing inputs, services contribute to the outward shift of the industrial sector's production frontier by enhancing productivity growth. The US labour productivity growth in the 1990s has been achieved mainly due to the rapid diffusion of information and communication technologies. Social infrastructure services such as education, health and other services are also considered as critical for improving labour productivity in manufacturing.

In the Indian context, producer services such as trade, transport and communication, financing, insurance, real estate and business services account for 70 percent of the total services. This reflects the strong inter-linkages between the services and goods producing sectors of the economy.

The empirical estimate of income elasticity of producer services at 1.2 reveals that a major part of demand for services comes from the income generated in other sectors of the economy. The demand for producer and government services has strong multiplier effects on real GDP. With regard to the producer services and manufacturing output, the causality is bi-directional.

It is true that of late, the growth in the service sector has engineered the growth of the GDP. The recessionary trend, which has become a global phenomenon, needs to be analysed by taking the GDP and its components.

Here we have attempted to find out such linkages in India, by first finding the relationship between GDP-agriculture and GDP-manufacturing and GDP-service since 1991 (the post reforms period). Such an exercise is carried out both at current level as well as with one year lag. The one year lag period is because it is assumed that the economy takes time to adjust to changes.

The results are presented in the following table.

Table 7.7 GDP as a function of Sectoral Contribution to Output

In Rs. Crores	Intercept	Slope	Correlation coefficient
1993-94 prices			
Agriculture GDP	-881799	6.4**	0.976
Manufacturing GDP	48331	3.86**	0.994
Service GDP	240148	2.26	0.999
Lag Agriculture GDP	-836624	6.445	0.939
Lag Manufacture GDP	91758	3.90	0.988
Lag service	266277	2.37	0.994

** significant at 1% level

The limited nature of this exercise cautions us in arriving at long drawn conclusions. Nevertheless, it clearly shows that the manufacturing sector, agriculture and service sector contributes to the GDP in the above mentioned order. The service sector comes in last, which means that the growth in the service sector has the least possibility of contribution to the growth of the GDP. The GDP responds very significantly to the growth in agriculture; the manufacturing sector also has significant influence on the growth of GDP. All these point out that reform in these two sectors should be taken forward so that these sectors perform well and support the growth of service sectors.

We also find from the above analysis that the manufacturing and the services sectors depend on each other for their growth. The correlation between the two is measured for the 10 year post reforms periods, which are explained here below:

Inter Relationship Of Manufacturing – Service Sector In India (1991-2000)

(1) Service sector (dependant) on Manufacturing sector

SER = -82701.98 + 1.6938 ME $R^2 = 0.98$

(-4.44) (22.077)

(2) Manufacturing (dependant) on Service sector

ME = 52252.796 + 0.5796 SER $R^2 = 0.98$

(6.024) (22.077)

(3) Service sector (dependant) on Manufacturing sector (with one year lag)

$$SER = -68412.14 + 1.732\, ME_{-1} \qquad R^2 = 0.98$$
$$(-3.64) \quad (21.66)$$

(4) Manufacturing (dependant) on Service sector (with one year lag)

$$ME = 60987.59 + 0.5994\, SER_{-1} \qquad R^2 = 0.97$$
$$(5.338) \quad (16.539)$$

Note: Figures in parenthesis are t-value

The above records show that for one unit increase in the service sector there will be 0.58 unit increase in manufacturing sector where as if manufacturing sector grows by one unit, there will be 1.69 unit increase in service sector. Similar results were recorded even if take one year lag. Based on this we can say that service led growth may not be the best option for Indian economy, though its relevance is no less important.

We find that a growth propelled by the service sector is the slowest growth possible among the agriculture, manufacturing, and the service sector. Any expansion in the manufacturing will produce a growth effects, which is larger than the growth effect produced by the services sector.

Conclusion

Manufacturing plays a significant role in economies of many countries. As countries become more prosperous, consumers spend more on value-added goods and services, and the role of manufacturing and services in the country's economy increases. In highly developed countries, services will be the dominant sector, since much of manufacturing in these countries is outsourced.

As a developing economy, the importance of manufacturing in India cannot be under-emphasized. Indian manufacturing constitutes nearly one fifth of the economy. It employs nearly 1.8 million people in the organized sector alone, and contributes more than 75 percent of India's exports.

While Indian manufacturing has been growing in absolute terms, it is in great danger of getting marginalized in the world market by the South East Asian countries and China. Hence, efforts at promoting growth in Indian manufacturing must also be aimed at making it more competitive in world markets.

The post-reforms period in India has brought in structural changes in the manufacturing sector in the form of mergers, a new awakening from protectionism to face global challenges and a vibrant service sector. From the analysis carried out in the previous sections it is evident that manufacturing is a key building block of the Indian economy, since growth in this sector will have a complimentary effect on the service sector as well. Therefore, any future growth in the Indian economy will greatly depend on the growth of manufacturing.

However, the forces between which India's manufacturing sector have been caught are: sustained weak economy, low demand, excess capacity, global competition, and an unfavorable external environment, ranging from labour laws to poor infrastructure.

Though the prime mover for the post reforms growth experienced was the service sector, it is evident that growth cannot be sustained only through contributions of the services sector. The close linkages between the service sector and the manufacturing sector in India show the need to design policy measures, which help to promote growth in both the sectors simultaneously.

In fact, the government can do well in framing suitable measures so that they attend to the issues that are affecting the manufacturing sectors. A major issue with the manufacturing sector in India is the issue of labour laws. We are yet to evolve a suitable exit policy. Use of technology in manufacturing sectors is not satisfactory in India. India was ranked 42 among the top 53 manufacturing countries when it came to global competitiveness. This indicates that the manufacturing organizations were not able to exploit technology by aligning planning and production processes in an integrated manner. The policy measures should aim at improving technology. Until now, we have given a very low emphasis on quality and the production catered to only the domestic market. But, in the WTO era, catering only to the domestic market is uneconomical.

Industrial performance in recent times is dominated by the behaviour of manufacturing. In 2002-03 it was the distinct improvement in manufacturing which led the industrial recovery. The sectoral growth of the index of industrial production showed tremendous growth in 2002-03. The growth of manufacturing was highest in September 2002. This was mainly due to a growth of export demand in a wide range of industry mining; quarrying also required good growth, and in this period, the growth of electricity remained more or less unchanged.

A large number of infrastructure industries achieved their target set for 2002-03 which was not the case in the previous year. However, the performance remained below target in power, finished steel, crude petroleum fertilizers and petroleum refinery products.

Despite various efforts and the setting up of the specialized Infrastructure Development Finance Company (I D F C) in 1997, private sector participation in infrastructure financing has not been satisfactory. There is lack of commercialization due to inadequate reforms in the area of user charges, cross subsidization, and a lack of structure financing options to mitigate the risks involve.

We need to move further in this direction to strengthen the infrastructure industries which are basic for the growth of the manufacturing sector. On the whole, the growth of the industrial sector needs to be strengthened and supported by favourable reforms so that both the manufacturing and service sector will push the economy towards a high level of development.

REFERENCES

Ahluwalia, I.J, and Little, I.M.D, (1998), *India's Economics Reform and Development: Essays for Manmohan Singh*, New Delhi: Oxford University Press.

Alderson, A.S, (2002), *"Globalization and the great U-turn: Income inequality trends in 16 OECD countries"*, American Journal of Sociology, Number 5.

Andersen, I I M Lucknow, I I T Madras, (2003), *India's Manufacturing Sector: Policy Framework*, New Delhi: Academic Foundation.

Bhowmik, R, (2000), *"Role of Services Sector in Indian Economy : An Input – Out put Approach"*, Arth Vijnana, Vol. XLII, No. 2.

Nayyar, D, (1996), *Economic Liberalisation in India: "Analysis, Experience and Lessons, in R. C. Dutt Lectures"*, New Delhi: Orient Longman.

Government of India, (1999), *Department of Statistics, Ministry of Planning, Statistical Abstract of India,* New Delhi

Government of India, (2000), *Ministry of Statistics and Programme Implementation*, National Account Statistics, New Delhi.

Goldar, B.N, (2002), *TFP Growth in Indian Manufacturing in 1980s,* Economic and Political Weekly, Volume: 37 Sept 14: pp.4966-68.

Jain, L.C, (1993), *Turnaround in Industrial Growth, Hasty Claims for Liberalisation,* Economic and Political Weekly, 27-28, July 3-10; M2 – M11.

Kuznets, S, (1955), *"Economic Growth and Income Inequality",* The American Economic Review, vol 45, Number 1.

Nelson, R and Pack, H, (1999), *"The Asian Miracle and Modern Growth Theory"* , The Economic Journal, 109 : 416-36.

Porter, M E, (1990), *'The Competitive Advantage of Nations'*, New York: The Free Press.

Pradhan, B K, Sachoo, A and Saluja, M.R, (1999), *"A Social Accounting matrix for India, 1994-95"*, Economic and Political Weekly, Vol. XXXIV, No. 48.

In: Readings in World Development
Editors: K.C. Roy and S. Chatterjee, pp. 71-85
ISBN 1-59454-947-8

Chapter 8

DEVELOPMENT OF AGRICULTURE AND RURAL FINANCE IN VIETNAM

Lawson R. Smith and Alfonso Ninh Tien Le

ABSTRACT

This paper examines aspects of the development and increasing liberalization of Vietnam's hitherto socialist-oriented agriculture sector, the role of rural financial markets in that transformation process and integration into a multi-sectoral economy. The progressive abandonment of collectivization and liberalization of agriculture which pre-dated Vietnam's 1986 *doi moi* reform thrust has engendered significant, sustained productivity gains as evidenced from the country's change in status from periodic rice importer to the world's second largest rice exporter. Moreover, these gains were achieved despite rural financial markets being repressed and segmented, the failure to mobilize rural household savings, adverse terms of trade, poor inter-sectoral linkages and loss-prone financial institutions. To be sure, continuing growth in agricultural output, productivity gains, value-adding and full integration into the multi-sector economy will only be possible if a similar great leap forward is engineered in Vietnam's rural financial markets.

INTRODUCTION

This appraisal of agrarian reform in the Socialist Republic of Vietnam since 1980 relies upon contemporary agricultural economic theory that, consistent with the 18th century Physiocrats (Cleveland 1999), recognizes the unique, vital contribution of agriculture to economic modernization and growth (Timmer 1990). The contemporary approach is in contradistinction to that of economists, from Ricardo to Lewis, for whom agriculture either impeded growth or was 'reduced to a mere reservoir of labor' (Martinussen 1997, p.130) thereby overlooking its Rostovian leading sector and total factor productivity (TFP) growth potential. This, in terms of the induced development model is, 'the capacity to generate an ecologically adapted and economically viable agricultural technology in each country' (Ruttan and Hayami 1990, p.109), coherent with an optimal industry structure - 'endogenously determined by that economy's endowment structure' (Lin 2002, p.277). State-led agricultural development has a long history in Asia. Irrigated rice production, coupled with river and canal transport, enabled hydraulic agro managerial societies to flourish in ancient China and the over-rivalrous Indo-Gangetic plain (Wittfogel 1957; Lal 1988) besides Cambodia during the legendary 7th-14th century Angkor Wat civilization (Sinath 2001). A one percent annual growth rate in agrarian output was in fact, 'feasible in many pre-industrial societies' (Hayami and Ruttan 1985, p.41). In the 19th century, unused land in the southeast Asian continental zone comprising the Irrawaddy delta in Myanmar, Chao Phraya Delta in Siam and Mekong Delta in Vietnam, was a resource responsive to colonial influence, free trade, rising demand for cheap food and innovations in ocean transport. This previously unused land:

> ... became the basis for vent-for-surplus growth. Deltas were converted into paddy fields for commercial rice production ... [that was] ... reinforced by comparative advantage within the region, which was largely determined by ecological conditions. (Hayami 2001, pp.170, 181)

Moreover, Hayami's (2001, p.195) general conjecture is particularly applicable to Vietnam given its troubled 20th century geopolitical experience and late mid-1970s unification: that, 'the agrarian structure of a nation and the value system in its society have been created along a unique historical trajectory, under unique ecological conditions.'

Under French colonial rule up until 1954, land use and the agrarian structure - dominated by delta rice monoculture, enabling sizeable exports - was somewhat polarized and oppressive. Landless peasants and landlordism were an instrument of economic policy – that, 'the resources of Vietnam should be exploited for the benefit of France and the empire' (Kratoska and Batson 1992, p.277). Following the departure of the French and the division of the country in 1954, in a phase marked in the north by 'over-enthusiastic land reforms' (Owen 1992, p.474) there was a transfer of 800,000 hectares to two million households. Then, consistent with the classic socialist system (Kornai 1992) it was in effect reassigned to agricultural collectives or cooperatives. The impact of this natural property rights experiment – regrettably then forgotten - in the north on rice productivity was predictable, rising from 278 kgs per capita in 1955 to 367 kgs with privatization then falling to 297 kgs per capita with recollectivisation in 1959-60 (ILO 2000, sec.II, p.1). While in the south, although inequities continued, "land to the tiller" reform measures were implemented in the 1960s. Consequently, on reunification there was stiff resistance to collectivisation in the Mekong delta with the upshot that, 'by the time the country decollectivised 13 years later, less than 10 percent of all the region's farmers had been organized into collectives' (Ravillion and van de Valle 2003, p.4).

In fact, during 1979 shortly after reunification, in three of monsoon Asia's low wage, subsistence rice-based economies - Cambodia, Laos and Vietnam (collectively, Indochina) - land reform began as part of the transition from 'the centrally planned economy to a market-oriented rural development', and eventual establishment of what Zhou (1996, p.1) inaccurately refers to as, 'nominal state - but de facto private - land ownership'.

To be sure, in 1979 the social system of production in relation to land in the biomass-based economy of Vietnam, which provided a precarious subsistence livelihood for some 80 percent of the population, was not coalesced in a coherent configuration or system (see Hollingsworth and Boyer 1997, Chapter 1). Elements of Polanyi's (2001) four non-market and informal institutions - reciprocity, self-sufficiency, autarkic householding, barter and redistribution - were observable as forms of economic coordination, integration and livelihood in addition to the market mechanism and collectivization. This was somewhat reminiscent of the 'multisymbiotic' socioeconomic structure of ancient China with its three distinct economic types - customary, market and command - in which, 'at least 60 percent of the total products (70-80 percent being recognised as the norm) were not subject to market sale' (Deng 2003, p.480).

AGRICULTURE'S LOW EQUILIBRIUM TRAP

In the pre-reform era, Vietnam's agrarian sector was in the throes of a classic low subsistence level equilibrium trap. Most land was held by collective and production groups which experienced high X-inefficiency - that is, 'the resources available to the firm are not utilized as well as they could be' (Liebenstein 1989, p.1364). Consequently, agrarian output was well inside the production-possibility frontier. The whole sector was typified by inertia and a low rate of technological change, a low ability and incentive to learn. Furthermore, general post-war demoralization coupled with further collectivization, led in 1980 to rice production falling to a low at only 20 million tons (or 215 kgs per capita), requiring rice imports of one million tons. Net rice imports continued until 1985 (Le 2004). Dissatisfaction with the incentive structure - in which output was diverted to support the cooperative cadre - was widespread, leading to a correlation of poor effort and poor reward. This led – as in Russia (Brooks 1990) – to a diversion of resources to household plots, which though comprising only 5 percent of land, household plots generated 40-60 percent of total output and 60-70 percent of household income during this period (ILO 2000 Sec. II, p.1).

Vietnam's low rice output during this era was quite inconsistent with its ecologically-based comparative advantage in rice production. A comparison of output in 1979 and 1995 is salutary. In 1979, rice output was a low 20 million tons from 8 million hectares (2.5 tons per ha) – an intensity index of 1.13. Then, resultant upon cumulative reform measures, in 1995, rice output reached almost 25 million tons from 10.5 million hectares – with an intensity index of 1.43 (ILO 2000 Sec. III, p.4) - and reached 34 million tons in 2002. This sizeable increase in production was obtained by intensifying land use in a land scarce, labour surplus economy: levels of double and triple cropping increased sharply and cultivated land increased from 6.9 to 7.6 million hectares by the mid-1990s. The Cobb-Douglas agrarian production function for 1976-1995, in which total output in tons (ignoring sugar) is a factor of the following factor shares, explains why output could rise sharply by one-third over 1980-86 as under-employed households intensified labour input and land use in response to reforms that altered incentive structures. Also, during 1980-86, the cooperatives still supplied key inputs (seed, fertilizer and irrigation etc), consequently production was not finance constrained in that first critical phase of land reform (ILO 2000, Appendix 1):

Labor (L) 0.4; Land (A) 0.3; Livestock (S) 0.1; Fertilizer (F) 0.1; and Machines (M) 0.1.

There are four identifiable phases in the process of agricultural transformation: rising productivity per worker; increased surplus being tapped by taxes, factor flows and adverse terms of trade to fund the non-agricultural sector; the progressive integration of agriculture via better infrastructure and market-equilibrium linkages, into the macro economy – this requires re-investment in agriculture; and its full integration into a multi-sectoral economy (Timmer 1990, p.61). Selecting the right, well-sequenced policy elements is problematic given agriculture's three unique features: 'the peculiarities of the agricultural production function, the importance of home consumption for output in the sector, and the role of the agriculture as a resource reservoir. These features are more evident in traditional societies' (Timmer 1990, p.61).

Productivity gains in a dominant agrarian sector can have large aggregate GDP effects (Winters et al. 1997, pp.8-9), as evidenced in the case of Vietnam. Moreover, in agriculture, 'decision making is conditioned primarily by the nature of incentives to work rather than the pace and design of the work itself' (Timmer 1990, p.59). In Vietnam, with factor and price reform, the terms of trade for agriculture improved over 1986-88 (0.8 to 1.2) and then declined 3.1 percent per year to 1995 (0.8) despite rapid diversification away from food production to industrial crops and animal husbandry. This was due to the adverse combination of higher fertiliser costs, inefficient rice marketing (the quota system) and an over-valued exchange rate which taxed rice exports (ILO 2000 Sec. IV, p.4).

The Importance of Property Rights in Vietnam's Agrarian Transformation

Good economic performance is reliant upon well defined private property rights (North 1981, 1996) since they dictate individual and group incentives. Moreover, 'the system of property rights describes the distribution of power in society' (Eggertsson 1996, p.14). A well articulated, efficient land rights system is vital for developing countries where land is the major asset of a rural-based populace and agriculture a sizeable share of national income (Do and Iyer 2003; Deininger 2003). In Vietnam's transition to market-socialism, the transfer of land from collectives to households units has been fundamental in minimising poverty and maintaining an egalitarian livelihood system. Land reform tenure arrangements, as in China, have had to ensure economic opportunities for all households. For the 1960-2000 period, countries with more egalitarian land distribution and land tenure systems attained higher economic growth – Vietnam included (Deininger 2003)- consistent with: the lack of economies of scale in agriculture with simple technology; and the higher cost of supervising wage labour so that the family farm is the most efficient unit of production, then fixed-rent tenancies and sharecropping (Binswanger and Deininger 1997, p.11).

It is total factor productivity gains that drive economic growth and development rather than factor accumulation (Easterly and Levine 2001). Institutions and property rights are vital. While human capital and technology are the proximate causes of growth, the real ultimate external levers include private property rights. Efficient economic transactions require well defined, secure property rights with embodied incentive effects. This is evidenced by the fact that over 1975-1995, property rights had a positive effect worldwide on economic efficiency and income levels, with Heitger (2003, p.25) finding that, 'a doubling of the property rights index more than doubles per capita income.'

In his analysis of the *liberal concept of full individual ownership rights* in both modern socialist and capitalist economies, Honore (1961, p.107) describes the 'standard incidents of ownership' in terms of, 'those legal rights, duties and other incidents which apply, in the ordinary case, to the person who has the greatest interest in a thing admitted by a mature legal system.' He then identifies eleven standard incidents of ownership, 'to be united in a single person' and cogently argues that if a legal system did not allow this, 'we would conclude that it did not know the liberal concept of ownership' (Honore 1961, p.112). The 11 standard incidents – a composite of rights and duties - collectively amount to ownership:

Ownership, comprises the right to possess, the right to use, the right to manage, the right to the income of the thing, the right to the capital, the right to security, the rights or incidents of transmissibility and absence of term, the prohibition of harmful use, liability to execution, and the incidents of residuary: this makes eleven leading incidents. (Honore 1961, p.113)

Most relevant in a transitional economy are: 0the rights of security and duration (i.e. absence of a term); the right to ownership indefinitely and immunity from expropriation; and unlimited duration allowing transfer to successors in title, not being determinate, that is expiring at a future date. Lesser ownership interests are of course recognised by mature legal systems including easements, short term leases, licences, life interests and bailment.

Rural property rights in Vietnam on the dissolution of collective ownership and transfer to household units of production were in a state of flux, being indeterminate, insecure and protean at best. This reflected in part an over-extensive weak government, with no clear division between executive, legislative and judicial subsystems and ill-defined real property rights. Although, as noted above, in the southern Mekong delta region following reunification in 1975, less than 10 percent of farmers were organised into collectives (Ravillion and van de Valle 2003, p.4). In general, family units during this early transitional period had little more than bare possessory, usage and usufructuary rights to real property-based livelihood – i.e. insecure rights to the first 4 of the 11 standard incidents of ownership. Moreover, there was no dispute resolution system independent of the communal governance system – as dominated by functionaries of the Vietnam Communist Party (VCP) - to arbitrate on disputes vis-à-vis the disparate modes of acquisition and loss. Households were therefore subject to the sovereign risk of the uncompensated for compulsory transfer of their family plots via byzantine, overtly political, unaccountable and opaque decision-making processes of local VCP instrumentalities.

This period nonetheless witnessed the initial basic recognition of private economic freedoms and property rights that evolved over time into full(er) ownership rights, recognised and entrenched in Articles 21 and 22 of the 1992 Constitution, revised in 2001. With reference to Block 2 of Kornai's (2000, p.29) Model of the Socialist and Capitalist Systems, what was eventually achieved was nothing less than a shift from the dominant position of state and quasi-state ownership to a dominant position of private property in the agrarian sector of the economy, with the upshot that the state sector's role in agriculture is now under 3 percent of total output (Malesky et al. 1998, p.23). Land is probably Vietnam's most valuable asset, with a hectare of irrigated and non-irrigated land now worth about US$ 5,500 and US$ 2,000 respectively, (World Bank 2004a, p.68).

Rural land reform in southeast Asia's transitional economies has typically proceeded by, first, creating short term (3-15 years) non-transferable leases to households. Then subsequently, as the efficiency gains from such improved incentive structures were fully exploited and the enhanced property rights became politically acceptable, leases of longer duration were granted, bundled together with ever more of the 11 standard incidents of ownership, including rights of renewal and mortgage. Arguably, a 50 year agrarian lease with rights of renewal and immunity from expropriation for village land redistribution purposes, is now perhaps the greatest rural ownership right recognised under Vietnam law.

Zhou (1996) misleadingly denotes this as 'nominal public but *de facto* private land ownership', whereas it is arguably neither. Article 1 of the *Land Law 1993* declares that all land is formally owned by the State, whilst Articles 21 and 22 of the 1992 Constitution recognise and guarantee private economic freedoms and property rights. In its recognition of dual, concurrent state and private ownership rights vis-à-vis land, Vietnam law arguably now does little more than replicate what was achieved in the ancient era in India. In Kautilya's *Arthasastra*, as Gopal (1935, p.62) opined:

> 'Land belonged to both the state and the cultivator, and both of them were only conditional owners. The state was entitled to land revenue, and so long as it was paid could not lawfully eject the cultivator ... In other words, it [property] was a sort of perpetual lease held on the annual performance of an obligation'.

There were four key related elements of post-1979 economic reforms in Vietnam: land rights; introduction of the market mechanism; price liberalisation; and dissolution of the collectives and production groups (ILO 2000 Sec. III, p.2). From 1979, evident failure of the collectives led to informal contract renegotiations with households which it was agreed could retain surplus output above an agreed quota in exchange for access to more land and other inputs.

These informal ad hoc arrangements were sanctioned in 1980 by Decree 100 in which land was transferred to the operational control of households as the main economic unit, subject to a quota production regime and retention of the surplus. Key inputs (irrigation, seed, fertilizer, land preparation and marketing) were to be supplied by local cooperatives. This improved incentive structure had the desired effect with output rising one-third by 1986. It then stagnated due to higher input prices, increasing quotas and cadre demands, in addition to poor production, management and coordination by the cooperatives. Consequently, Decree 10/1988 abolished the quota system giving households control and cash flow rights. Leases for 10-15 years were granted based on pre-1975 use with tacit renewal rights. Price controls were lifted and markets liberalised. The role of cooperatives was reduced to irrigation supply, with production equipment and livestock being transferred to households. The state then made up for the loss of land rent/income in kind from its domainal holdings by an imposition in 1989 of a land tax on income at a rate of 10 percent. Then, five years later in 1993, the Land Act and Land Use Certificate System implemented a further round of reforms, driven by the necessity of better formalizing and administering the 1988 land reform measures. An array of "five rights" were granted to households. In essence, the remaining five of the eleven standard incidents of ownership were recognized and bundled together with existing lease and usufructuary rights. In doing so, the Government created efficiency and equity enhancing rural land and financial markets. The five rights being the rights to transfer, exchange, inherit, rent and mortgage land. Relatedly, a system of Land Use Certificates (LUCs) was inaugurated in order to facilitate the establishment, verification and certification of leases. Property rights were extended over 1998-2001 to allow subleasing and use of land in foreign joint venture operations (Do and Iyer 2003, pp.6-9; van Thuyet 1995, pp.5-8). Overall, good progress was made in the issuance of LUCs to households. This achieved a coverage by year end 2003 of '90 percent of agricultural land, 75 percent of rural residential land, 25 percent of forest land, 20 percent of urban industrial land and only 15 percent of urban residential land' (World Bank 2004a, p.68). The markedly low level of urban LUC issuance and inability to access land held by state-owned enterprises has impeded the establishment of urban residential mortgage markets and land-reliant business ventures (van Thuyet 1995, p.8-11; World Bank 2004a, pp.680-673).

Studies indicate that these land reforms have had a strongly positive effect on economic development, equity and household welfare, with southern farmers benefiting the most (Do and Iyer 2003; Deininger and Jin 2003; Benjamin and Brandt 2002). More secure land rights are associated with a larger total area being devoted to perennials, more irrigation investment, a massive increase in total rice output and broad poverty reduction from about 60 percent to under 40 percent over the 1992-97 period. Also, the active land rental market established has not seen landlessness increase, but on the contrary has had a positive overall equity effect, 'by transferring land to those with more limited endowments' (Deininger and Jin 2003, p.14). And, there was no evidence of poor, but efficient producers having to sell their land. But, better access to rural credit markets was necessary to enable households suffering, for example, an unexpected shock to avoid having to sell land as an adjustment mechanism. These research findings somewhat disprove Zhou's (1996, p.13) assertion that private land markets are inefficient and 'make new landlessness possible'. Even in the paradigmatic case of China, research indicates that, 'land markets seem to be better than bureaucrats in transferring land to poor and more efficient producers ... implying that such land markets contribute to higher productivity' (Deininger and Jin 2002, p.3). Moreover, better land tenure allows the poor more flexible land rights usage including subleasing their land to others, allowing them to work elsewhere, thereby improving their living standards (Deininger 2003, p.40).

Rural Financial Markets

That there is a positive correlation between financial development and economic growth is undisputed. The issue is rather, 'whether financial markets and institutions appear on demand. If they do not, then the underdevelopment of financial markets and institutions would prevent an immediate response to industrial needs and retard the growth of a country' (Rajan and Zingales 2001, p.468). The ability of de novo firms to retain their earning and obtain external finance is more critical at the initial stage of their emergence than their subsequent expansion. The role of finance in the semi-monetised classic socialist system in which the state-owned banking subsystem was subordinated to central planning and control, was necessarily limited. Money was not the general medium of exchange. There were in effect two socio-economic spheres (the private and public sectors) operating under hard versus soft budget constraints. In the public socialist sphere, money, profit and prices are, 'mere extras in bureaucratic coordination' (Kornai 1992, p.148).

In Vietnam's transitional economy, as elsewhere, rural financial markets have required promotion in order to address four objectives: to promote growth by mobilizing resources; to boost efficient resource allocation; to enhance income distribution and reduce poverty; and to establish viable financial institutions. At the household level there are hard annual cash income constraints. Agrarian income and expenditure are seasonal and without access to external finance, households face limited, suboptimal choices in relation to investment, production and consumption (Duong and Izumida 2002, pp.319-20). Consequently, there was – and continues to be - a high demand from de novo autonomous household units for finance to expand production and escape from the vicious circle of low capital formation, investment, productivity and income. Vietnam experienced a low historic savings rate – at below 20 percent but improving to 33 percent over 1998-2002 (World Bank 2004a, p.56) - and still operates as a cash economy. Concomitantly, there is a continuing shortage of inter-firm credit that constricts the growth of small/medium rural enterprises, since state-owned enterprises still have privileged access to available funds, rural savings have not been mobilised to any degree, and foreign investment inflows have been inadequate (Smith and Le 2003).

The unique features of the agrarian sector of an economy are also a major impediment to development of Vietnam's rural financial markets, and include: higher transaction costs and systematic risks, greater cash flow variance, and the variable ability of households in production and risk-bearing, apart from being naturally more risk-averse (Klein et al.1999, pp.4-17). In Vietnam, repressed rural banking services have faced higher transaction costs due to distance and dispersed clients, seasonal credit demands and the mismatch between sources of finance, loans and assets and an initial lack of loan collateral. However, collateral problems have diminished with improving land ownership rights and issuance of Land Use Certificates (LUCs), in theory reducing risk and lowering effective interest rates. Though arguably since in Vietnam's transitional economy, the socialist government from the early 1990s both issued LUCs and provided production loans, farmers en mass obtained such loans whatever the extant property rights regime status happened to be, with LUCs assisting in the increasing formalisation of the loan rationing process. One further shortcoming was the focus on loans rather than savings services, it being generally overlooked that households were joint production-consumption units.

Rural credit markets face two standard hazard problems of *imperfect information* and *imperfect enforcement*, so that their features in developing countries 'can be readily understood as responses to the problems of screening, incentives and enforcement' (Hoff and Stiglitz 1993, p.45). Interest rates are an indirect screening mechanism typically employed in conjunction with rationing and in a typically imperfectly competitive, segmented market with imperfect and costly information, 'may nonetheless allow lenders to charge interest rates far higher than competitive levels' (Hoff and Stiglitz 1993, p.39). The use of collateral, land titles and various local savings schemes in addition to semi-formal and formal linkages with suppliers and buyers, all enable households to obtain production-augmenting finance at lower risk and thence more affordable rates. There has also been a vital paradigm shift worldwide by governments in the supply of rural financial services. That is, from a system of typically poorly managed, concession-based, unsustainable, state-driven agricultural credit (subsidized micro loans being, 'readily treated as political patronage' (Tsai 2004, p.1502)) to one of self-sustaining de-regulated rural financial markets that cover costs, mobilise rural savings and deliver an ever-expanding array of client-driven services. It is now being recognised that even the poor can, and do, save.

THE REFORM AND PERFORMANCE OF VIETNAM'S RURAL FINANCIAL SECTOR

From 1979, when agrarian reforms began, following the evident inability of the existing *social system of production,* to reliably feed the nation and the broader *doi moi* reforms that began in 1986, Vietnam's biomass-based economy has been in transition from a path dependent country-specific variant of classic socialism to market-socialism (Kornai 1992, Chapter 21) underpinned by land reforms, market reforms and price liberalisation. But, whilst rural land has in effect been privatised, the financial sector is still state dominated, with state banks holding over 70 percent of all bank deposits.

After reunification of Vietnam in 1975, the disparate country-wide banking system was consolidated and nationalised and a mono-bank - the State Bank of Vietnam (SBV) - set up to provide central banking policies and commercial banking services. The present two-tier banking system was created over 1988-90 with the separating out of four SBV departments and their upgrading into specialised state-owned commercial banks (SOCBs) (Tam 2000, pp.5-8), the SBV then assuming the role of a supervisory central bank (Dufhues 2003, p.30). From 1989, joint stock banks were permitted. Rural credit cooperatives also flourished in an unregulated banking boom that predictably led to their collapse by the early 1990s besides some private banks, all of which seriously discredited the banking sector, retarding savings mobilisation in Vietnam which remains a cash economy, 'with cash accounting for about 50 percent of the M3 money supply' (Dufhues 2003, p.37). Households, being sensitised by political-economic shocks, still prefer less mobile savings principally comprising dollars, gold stocks and houses, despite their holding costs. The formal banking sector now comprises:

- the State Bank of Vietnam and four commercial banks;
- some 150 joint stock commercial banks, joint venture and foreign banks;
- 950 community savings and credit cooperatives; and
- the two dedicated state-owned rural banks, Vietnam Bank for Agriculture and Rural Development (VBARD) set up in 1988 and the policy bank, Vietnam Bank for the Poor (VBP) established in 1993, and reconstituted in 2003 as the Vietnam Bank for Social Policies (VBSP) (Dufhues et al. 2003; World Bank 2004b).

The pace and success of financial reform in the 1990s was quite modest (Unteroberdoerster 2004), followed by a belated reform thrust in May 2002 as part of the Government's meta-planning instrument, the Comprehensive Poverty Reduction and Growth Strategy (Smith and Le 2003). Consequently, the underperforming, soft-budget constrained dominant state-owned enterprise sector still has priority rights to credit from the SOCBs (36 percent in 2003, reduced from 58 percent in 1998) despite a high level of non-performing loans - about 10-11 percent of total banking credit in 2002 - requiring a sizeable recapitalisation of the state banking sector in 2003 (World Bank 2004b). To be sure, 'a major factor inhibiting private sector investment in agriculture has been the dominant role of state-owned enterprises' (Asian Development Bank 2002, p.3).

Nonetheless, as McCarty (2001, p.5) notes, 'the rapid expansion of the formal banking system to rural Vietnam is the most remarkable achievement of microfinance in Vietnam since 1996. Rural households are more likely to borrow from banks than urban households.' The two government banks – VBARD and the Bank for the Poor (VBP) – dominate rural credit with extensive outreach. By 2001, 38 percent of rural households had credit from VBARD and a further 21 percent with loans from the VBP (Dufhues et al. 2003, p.10). The rural credit market is, however, both repressed and segmented, though real interest rates in the formal sector have tended to rise. During 1997-98, average rural monthly interest rates for farm households were 1.26 percent in the formal sector and 3.95 percent in the informal sector (McCarty 2001, p.10). The informal sector, though crowded out in part by the expanding formal sector, is still important, comprising private moneylenders, relatives and neighbours, and the Ho/Hui – local savings/credit associations. There are also over 80 NGO microfinance schemes, whose expansion is typically limited by their adoption of VBARD's low interest rate spread subsidy policy. This is especially curious as the NGOs could easily have charged full market interest rates while out competing usurious moneylenders and have established in the process, sustainable expanding microfinance operations not dependent thereafter upon donor funds. In 1997-98, some 7 percent of rural households had loans from moneylenders and a further 25 percent reported loans from relatives and neighbours etc. (McCarty 2001, p.5). While in a study of 300 rural households across three provinces, Duong and Izumida (2002, p.322) observed that, 'formal loans accounted for 80 percent of the total and the remainder is from the informal sector.' They also found that (i) the main determinants of borrowing were total farm area and the value of livestock, and (ii) very significantly, that up to 30 percent of households were credit constrained by formal lenders rationing loans. Households were defined as being credit constrained when (i) they demanded more loans than formal/informal markets were willing to lend, or (ii) required loans but couldn't borrow. Consequently, 'the task of the Vietnamese government is to develop the rural financial system to ensure that every household has access to credit and can maximise their production' (Duong and Izumida 2002, p.333). There is also a related task of improving the (demand-side) 'bankability' of poor farmers who fail to access loans due to their low risk-bearing capacity (confidence in their ability to invest, manage and repay small loans), not because of high transaction costs (Buchenrieder and Theesfeld 2000).

Despite extensive reform, capacity building and the influx of government funds, the rural financial sector remains the poor relation. Though the rural sector generates some 27 percent of GDP and employs 70 percent of the labour force, it accounts for only 7 percent of total investment - two-thirds being state-sourced – there being a total failure to mobilise rural savings. For example, VBARD mobilizes 'hot money' funds in urban areas for partial redirection to rural areas (Dufhues et al. 2003, p.11). Accelerating rural financing deepening in Vietnam requires that the inefficiency, insufficiency and feasibility gaps are addressed (Gonzalez-Vega 2003).

An expanding, more efficient, non-subsidised and increasingly privatised rural financial sector is required to underpin a dynamic agricultural strategy that is designed to remedy the sector's main problems of, 'low productivity and profitability, lack of production diversity, low quality and low competitiveness' – the upshot being that, 'Vietnam has not been successful in producing higher quality and higher priced agricultural commodities for export' (Asian Development Bank 2002, p.2). A great deal more local value-adding is necessary, requiring investment in agro-processing facilities, better inter-sector marketing and transport arrangements, as well as enhanced contractual supply arrangements between farmers and processors, in order to better service and manage otherwise fickle markets (IFPRI 2002).

Concluding Comments

Despite impressive economic growth since land reforms commenced in 1979 and the broader *doi moi* reforms in 1986, the large agrarian sector of Vietnam's market-socialist transition economy remains a paradoxical incoherent and unintegrated social system of production. It comprises an amalgam of private land ownership by under-capitalised autonomous household production units subordinated to growth-constraining over-regulation and the supply of key input factors including finances dominated by over-extended state-owned enterprises with a subsidy mentality. The two rural state banks VBARD and the VBP having simply failed to mobilise rural savings – with convenient, positive interest savings products and facilities - in a manner that would help to financially underpin the sustainable growth and value-adding potential of this leading sector, on which 70 percent of the population depend for their livelihood. Rural financial markets are segmented, formal VBARD/VBP loans at administered interest rates are rationed and quarantined for production purposes with LUCs held via 'affirmative asset partitioning' as collateral (see Hansmann and Kraakman 2004). Households are forced to borrow at higher interest rates from the informal market for private consumption on a non-collateralised basis, though typically with adequate reserve equity in their land to obtain lower interest 'second mortgage' loans if their LUCs were otherwise available.

Since then, although over-extended and under-resourced, the Vietnamese Government is ideologically committed to retaining its two rural banks; the growth and mobilisation of rural savings will depend upon the transformation, upgrading and linking together – and inter-sectorally as well - of existing rural savings vehicles: the Ho/Hui, credit associations and local money lenders, as well as the private sector suppliers of key agrarian inputs (eg fertiliser) and purchasers of outputs. The considerable initial inflow of private sector capital required to stimulate the rural financial sector could be intermediated by the establishment of a partly foreign financed private rural bank – with the successful Cambodian microfinance ACLEDA Bank as a possible model (Channy 2003) - perhaps with franchised operations at the local level, or at least socially embedded, upgraded commercial links with the most successful local farmer/credit associations, and both lending at market interest rates and offering an array of market rate savings products. Without establishment of private rural microfinance banking with proven integrity so that it can mobilise foreign and rural savings and compete with the two under-capitalised marginally sustainable state banks, the growth trajectory of Vietnam's agrarian sector – and thereby the entire economy – must remain excessively path-dependent and predestined to achieve considerably less than its potential.

References

Asian Development Bank, (2002) *Report and Recommendation of the President to the Board of Directors on Proposed Loans to the Socialist Republic of Vietnam for the Agriculture Sector Development Program,* viewed 15 September 2003, *http://www.adb.org*

Benjamin, D. and Brandt, L. (2002) *Agriculture and Income Distribution in Rural Vietnam under Economic Reforms: A Tale of Two Regions*, Working Paper 519, William

Davidson Institute, University of Michigan Business School, viewed 14 January 2003, *http://www.wdi.bus.umich.edu*

Binswanger, H. P. and Deininger, K. (1997) *Explaining Agricultural and Agrarian Policies in Developing Countries*, Policy Research Working Paper Series No. 1765, The World Bank, Washington DC, viewed 1 September 2002, http://econ.worldbank.org

Brooks, K. (1990) "Agricultural Reform in the Soviet Union" in C. K. Eicher and J. H. Staatz (eds) *Agricultural Development in the Third World* 2nd edition, John Hopkins University Press, Baltimore, Chapter 29.

Buchenrieder, G. and Theesfeld, I. (2000) *Improving Bankability of Small Farmers in Northern Vietnam*, Discussion Paper No. 8, Centre for Tropical Agriculture, University of Hohenheim, viewed 12 September 2003, *http://www.uni-hohenheim.de/i3v/00068900/26425041.htm*

Channy, I. (2003) *The Case Study of ACLEDA Bank*, paper presented at Paving The Way Forward for Rural Finance: An International Conference, 2-4 June 2003 Washington DC, viewed 16 November 2003, *http://www.basis.wisc.edu/rfc/index.html*

Cleveland, C. (1999) *Biophysical Economics: From Physiocracy to Ecological Economics and Industrial Ecology*, Working Paper No. 9907, Centre for Energy and Environmental Studies, Boston University, viewed 15 September 2003, *http://www.bu.edu/cees/research/workingp.html*

Deininger, K. (2003) *Land Policies for Growth and Poverty Reduction*, World Bank, Oxford University Press, viewed 14 November 2003, *http://econ.worldbank.org*

Deininger, K, and Jin, S. (2002) *The Impact of Property Rights on Households' Investment, Risk Coping, and Policy Preferences: Evidence from China*, Policy Research Working Paper 2930, The World Bank, Washington DC, viewed 15 October 2003, *http://econ.worldbank.org*

Deininger, K. and Jin, S. (2003) *Land Sales and Rental Markets in Transition*, Policy Research Working Paper No. 3013, The World Bank, Washington DC, viewed 14 October 2003, *http://econ.workdbank.org*

Deng, K. G. (2003) "Development and its Deadlock in Imperial China, 221 BC-1840 AD", *Economic Development and Cultural Change*, Vol. 51 No. 2, pp.479-522.

Do, Q-T. and Iyer, L. (2003) *Land Rights and Economic Development: Evidence from Vietnam*, Policy Research Working Paper No. 3120, The World Bank, Washington DC, viewed 15 October 2003, *http://econ.worldbank.org*

Dufhues, T. (2003) "Transformation of the Financial System in Vietnam and its Implications for the Rural Financial Market – an Update", *Journal for Institutional Innovation, Development and Transition*, Vol. 7, viewed 15 December 2004, *http://www.gov.si/zmar/apublic/jiidt/jiidt03/4dufhues.pdf*

Dufhues, T, Buchenrieder, G., Heidhues, F and Dung, P. T. 2003) *Towards demand-driven financial services in Northern Vietnam: A Participatory analysis of customer preferences,* Discussion Paper No. 1, Institute of Agricultural Economics and Social Sciences, University of Hohenheim, viewed 5 September 2003, *http://www.uni-hohenheim.de/i3ve/00068900/28217041.htm*

Duong, P. B. and Izumida, Y. (2002) "Rural Development Finance in Vietnam: A Microeconometric Analysis of Household Surveys", *World Development,* Vol. 30 No. 2, pp.319-335.

Easterly, W. and Levine, R. (2001) "It's Not Factor Accumulation: Stylized Facts and Growth Models", *The World Bank Economic Review*, Vol. 12 No. 2, pp.177-219.

Eggertsson, T. (1996) "A Note on the Economics of Institutions", in L. J. Alston, T. Eggertsson and D. C. North (eds) *Empirical Studies In Institutional Change*, Cambridge University Press, Cambridge, pp.6-24.

Gonzalez-Vega, C. (2003) *Deepening Rural Financial Markets: Macroeconomic, Policy and Political Dimensions*, lead paper for Paving The Way Forward for Rural Finance: An International Conference, 2-4 June 2003 Washington DC, viewed 16 November 2003, *http://www.basis.wisc.edu/rfc/index.html*

Gopal, M. H. (1935) *Mauryan Public Finance*, George Allen and Unwin Ltd, London.

Hansmann, H, and Kraakman, R. (2004) "Agency Problems and Corporate Law" in Hansmann, H, Davies, P. et al., *The Anatomy of Corporate Law*, Oxford University Press, Oxford, Chapter 1.

Hayami, Y. (2001) "Ecology, History, and Development: A Perspective from Rural Southeast Asia", *The World Bank Research Observer*, Vol. 16 No. 2, pp.169-198.

Hayami, Y. and Ruttan, V. W. (1985) *Agricultural Development: An International Perspective*, 2nd edition, The John Hopkins University Press, Baltimore.

Heitger, B. (2003) *Property Rights and their Impact on the Wealth of Nations – A Cross-Country Study*, Working Paper No. 1163, Kiel Institute for World Economics, viewed 15 October 2003, *http://www.uni-kiel.de/ifw/pub/kap/2003/kap1163.pdf*

Hoff, K. and Stiglitz, J. E. (1993) "Imperfect Information and Rural Credit Markets: Puzzles and Policy Perspectives, in K. Hoff, A. Braverman and J.E. Stiglitz (eds) *The Economics of Rural Organization*, Oxford University Press. New York, Chapter 2.

Hollingsworth, J. R. and Boyer, R. (1997) "Coordination of Economic Actors and Social Systems of Production", in J. R. Hollingsworth and R. Boyer (eds) *Contemporary Capitalism: The Embeddedness Of Institutions*, Cambridge University Press, Cambridge, Chapter 1.

Honore, A. M. 1961, "Ownership" in A. G. Guest (ed) *Oxford Essays in Jurisprudence: A Collaborative Work*, Oxford University Press, Oxford, Chapter 5.

International Food Policy Research Institute, (2002) *Fruit and Vegetables in Vietnam: Adding Value from Farmer to Consumer*, viewed 10 October 2003, *http://www.ifpri.org*

International Labour Organization, (2000) *Agrarian Transition in Vietnam*, Working Paper No. 128, viewed 26 September 2003, *http://www.ilo.org*

Klein, B., Meyer, R., Hannig, A., Burnett, J. and Fiebig, M. (1999) *Better Practices in Agricultural Lending*, Food and Agricultural Organisation of the United Nations, Rome, viewed 5 September 2003, *http://www.fao.org*

Kornai, J. (1992) *The Socialist System: The Political Economy of Communism*, Princeton University Press, Princeton.

Kornai, J. (2000) "What the Change of System from Socialism to Capitalism Does and Does Not Mean", *Journal of Economic Perspectives*, Vol. 14 No. 1, pp.27-42.

Kratoska, P. and Batson, B. (1992) "Nationalism and Modernist Reform" in N. Tarling (ed) *The Cambridge History of Southeast Asia, Vol 2, The Nineteenth and Twentieth Centuries*, Cambridge University Press, Chapter 5.

Lal, D. (1988) *The Hindu Equilibrium: Cultural Stability and Economic Stagnation, India c1500 BC – AD 1980*, Clarendon Press, Oxford.

Le, A. (2004) "Counter-Trade and Development: A Case Study of Counter-Trade between Indonesia and Vietnam during the 1990s", in K. C. Roy (ed) *Twentieth Century Development: Some Relevant Issues*, Nova Science Publishers, New York, Chapter 11.

Liebenstein, H. (1989) "Organizational Economics and Institutions as Missing Elements in Economic Development Analysis", *World Development*, Vol. 17 No. 9, pp.1361-1373.

Lin, J. Y. (2002) "Development Strategy, Viability and Economic Convergence", *Economic Development and Cultural Change*, Vol. 51 No. 2, pp.277-308.

McCarty, A. (2001) *Microfinance in Vietnam: A Survey of the Schemes and Issues*, Mekong Economics Ltd, viewed 6 September 2003,
http://econwpa.wustl.edu:8089/eps/fin/papers/0110/0110001.pdf

Malesky, E. et al., (1998) *The Model and the Reality: Assessment of Vietnamese SOE Reform – Implementation at the Firm Level,* Working Paper No. 154, William Davidson Institute, University of Michigan Business School, viewed 14 January 2003, *http://www.wdi.bus.umich.edu*

Martinussen, J. (1997) *Society, State and Market: A Guide to Competing Theories of Development*, Zed Books Ltd, London.

North, D. C. (1981) *Structure and Change in Economic History*, W. W. Norton and Co, New York.

North, D. C. 1996, 'Epilogue: economic performance through time', in L.J. Alston, T. Eggertsson and D. C. North (eds) *Empirical Studies In Institutional Change*, Cambridge University Press, Cambridge, Chapter 10.

Owen, N. G. (1992) "Economic and Social Change" in N. Tarling (ed) *The Cambridge History of Southeast Asia, Vol 2, The Nineteenth and Twentieth Centuries*, Cambridge University Press, Cambridge, Chapter 8.

Polanyi, K. (2001) *The Great Transformation: The Political and Economic Origins of our Time*, Foreword by Joseph E. Stiglitz and a new Introduction by Fred Block, Beacon Press, Boston.

Rajan, R.G and Zingales, L. (2001) "Financial Systems, Industrial Structure and Growth", *Oxford Review of Economic Policy*, Vol. 17 No. 4, pp.467-482.

Ravillion, M. and van den Valle, D. (2003) *Land Allocation in Vietnam's Transition Economy*, World Bank Research Working Paper No. 2951, viewed 4 February 2003, *http://econ.worldbank.org*

Sinath, C. (2001) *Investment in Land and Water in Cambodia*, viewed 4 April 2004, *http://www.fao.org*

Smith, L. and Le, A. (2003) "The Future of Vietnam's Public Sector and State-owned Enterprises in a Developmental Market-Socialist Economy" in L. Montanheiro, F. Kuznik and A. Ochojski (eds) *Public and Private Sector Partnerships: Sustainable Success*, Sheffield Hallam University Press, pp.451-472.

Tam, L. M. (2000) *Reforming Vietnam's Banking System: Learning from Singapore's Model*, Visiting Researchers Series No. 5, Institute of Southeast Asian Studies, viewed 10 September 2003, *http://www.iseas.edu.sg/vr52000.pdf*

Timmer, C. P. (1990) "The Agricultural Transformation", in C. K. Eicher and J. M. Staatz (eds) *Agricutural Development in the Third World*, 2nd edition, The John Hopkins University Press, Baltimore, Chapter 2.

Tsai, K. S. (2004) "Imperfect Substitutes: The Local Political Economy of Informal Finance and Microfinance in Rural China and India", *World Development*, Vol. 32 No. 9, pp.1487-1507.

Unteroberdoerster, O. (2004) *Banking Reform in the Lower Mekong Countries*, IMF Policy Discussion Paper No. 5, International Monetary Fund, viewed 15 December 2004, *http://www.imf.org/external/pubs/ft/pdp/2004/pdp05.pdf*

Wittfogel, K. A. (1957) *Oriental Despotism: A Comparative Study of Total Power*, Yale University Press, New Haven.

World Bank, (2004a) *Vietnam Development Report 2005: Governance*, The World Bank, Washington DC, viewed 15 December 2004, *http://www.worldbank.org*

World Bank, (2004b) *Financial Sector Policy Issues Note: Vietnam Bank For Social Policies*, The World Bank, Financial Sector Group, East Asian and Pacific Region, Washington DC, viewed 15 December 2004, *http://www.worldbank.org*

van Thuyet, P. (1995) *The Emerging Legal Framework for Private Sector Development in Vietnam's Transitional Economy*, Policy Research Working Paper WPS 1486, The World Bank, Washington DC, viewed 28 August 2003, *http://www.worldbank.org*

Zhou, J-M. (1996) *Is Nominal but De Facto Private Land Ownership Appropriate?: A Comparative Study among Cambodia, Laos, Vietnam, Japan, Taiwan Province of China, South Korea, China, Myanmar and North Korea*, EUI Working Paper ECO No. 98/12, Economics Department, European University Institute, Florence.

In: Readings in World Development
Editors: K.C. Roy and S. Chatterjee, pp. 87-102
ISBN 1-59454-947-8

Chapter 9

POVERTY AND ENVIRONMENT: A REVIEW OF ISSUES AND EVIDENCES OF MALAYSIA

Chamhuri Siwar and Norshamliza Chamuri[1]

INTRODUCTION

This paper reviews the state and conditions of the poverty in Malaysia, and discusses the prevailing inter-linkages between poverty and environmental sustainability. The paper is structured as follows: Section 2 provides prevailing poverty conditions in Malaysia and their implications for environmental sustainability. The discussion includes the incidence of poverty and its impact on livelihood, dependence of the poor on natural resources and the sustainability of resource use, constraints faced by the poor in employing environmentally sustainable lifestyle and the inter-linkages between poverty eradication and environmental sustainability. Section 3 provides an overview on the importance of environmental sustainability in national policies and major ongoing national programmes to promote sustainability. Section 4 discusses existing barriers to promoting environmental sustainability, including policy and legal, institutional and infrastructural barriers. Finally, some recommendations are provided for changes in policy and planning mechanism, roles of government, private sector, NGOs, and the need for an integrated approach to promote environmental sustainability and poverty eradication.

POVERTY IN MALAYSIA

Poverty alleviation has been in the pillar of Malaysia's development policy and planning, especially since the inception of the NEP (1971-1990), with its twin objectives of poverty eradication, irrespective of race and restructuring of society to address economic imbalance and job identification by race. The macro-policy of "growth and redistribution" has been

[1] The authors are respectively Senior Fellow, Institute of Environment and Development (LESTARI), and Lecturer, Faculty of Economics and Business, Universiti Kebangsaan Malaysia, 43600 Bangi, Selangor, Malaysia.

carried through in the Outline Perspective Plan 1 (OPP1), which coincided with the NEP, the OPP2, which coincided with the National Development Plan (NDP, 1991-2000), and the OPP3, which coincided with the National Vision Plan (NVP, 2001-2010).

After the NEP, with the significant reduction in the incidence of poverty and the number of poor households, the focus of poverty alleviation was on the hardcore or extreme poor, which consist of the bottom 5 percent of the income distribution. This was to facilitate more direct targeting to the poor and to prevent leakages. However, with the implementation of the OPP3, the targeting of the poor is widened to include those in the bottom 30 percent or those with household income of less than RM1200 per month (Malaysia, 2001a).

INCIDENCE OF POVERTY AND ITS IMPACTS ON LIVELIHOOD

The poverty conditions in Malaysia have improved significantly since the implementation of the NEP. The incidence of poverty has been significantly reduced from 49.3 percent in 1970 to 6.1 percent in 1997, before it increased to 7.5 percent in 1999, as a result of the economic recession (Table 9.1). Poverty is still predominantly a rural phenomenon (Chamuri, 1994a, 1994b) with the incidence and occurrence of poverty relatively higher in the rural compared to the urban sector. However, the phenomenon of urban poverty will be serious in the future with the growing burden of urbanization and industrialization (Chamuri and Tan, 1996, Chamuri, 2000). With the incidence of hardcore poor at 2.5 percent in 1999, the incidence of poverty is targeted to be reduced to 0.5 percent in 2005.

Malaysia's success in poverty eradication could be attributed to its high and sustained economic growth, pro-active and explicit poverty alleviation strategies and programmes, strong institutional and budgetary support and effective delivery mechanism.

Table 9.1: Incidence of Poverty (%) and Number of Poor of Poor Households ('000)

	1970	1990	1995	1997	1999
Total	49.3(1606.0)	16.5(448.9)	8.7 (365.6)	6.1(274.2)	7.5(351.1)
Rural	58.7	21.1(371.4)	14.9(281.8)	10.9(221.8)	12.4(264.3)
Urban	21.3	7.1(77.5)	3.6(83.8)	2.1(52.4)	3.4(86.8)
Hardcore	-	3.6(107.3)	2.1(88.4)	1.4(62.4)	2.5(64.1)

Source: Malaysia Five-Year Plan (Various Plans). Note: Figures in ( ) denote number of poor households. Hardcore or extreme poor is a subset of the poor, determined as those with less than ½ the poverty line income (PLI).

Rapid and sustained economic growth was achieved over the OPP1 (1971-1990) and OPP2 (1991-2000) periods, except for low to negative growth during the recession of the 1980s and the 1997/1998 economic crisis. The Malaysian economy grew at an average rate of 7.8 to 8.6 percent between 1971-80, declined to 5.1 percent due to global recession of the 1980s, climbed to 6.7 percent between 1986-1990 and increased to rapid growth of 8.5 percent between 1991-1995, and declined again to 4.7 percent between 1995-2000, due to the economic crisis of 1997/1998. In 1998, the economy grew at a negative rate of 7.4 percent.

Sustained economic growth has contributed significantly to poverty alleviation and increased quality of life. The Malaysian Quality of Life Indices (MQLI) generally recorded positive trends in terms of income, accessibility to basic needs and services like transportation, health, education and housing, but negative on some aspects of social capital, like public safety and environmental, which declined by 8.0% and 2.8% respectively over the 1980-1998 period (see Table 2).

Table 9.2: Changes in Indices and Malaysian Quality of Life Index, 1980 and 1998

Index	1980	1998	Change (%)
Income and Distribution	77.39	105.82	36.7
Working Life	106.13	118.94	12.1
Transport and Communications	87.36	112.78	29.1
Health	83.24	109.58	31.6
Education	85.97	117.31	36.5
Housing	90.52	107.72	19.0
Environment	103.86 (1985)	100.94	-2.8
Family Life	85.46	113.86	33.2
Social Participation	81.55	97.98	20.1
Public Safety	78.40	72.11	-8.0

Source: Malaysia (1999)

LINKING POVERTY AND ENVIRONMENT

Conceptual Framework

The framework for the analysis links between the concepts of sustainable development, poverty, environmental and natural resources conditions, which brings into focus the interplay between development, poverty, and natural resource degradation (DFID, 2002). The link between poverty and environmental degradation has generally been seen in a causal and effect relationship, in that poverty contributes to environmental degradation which in turn affects poverty (Gow 1992, Reardon and Vosti 1995). However, this relationship may not be that simple. Various studies have dispelled the assertion that poverty causes environmental degradation. In the urban context, a recent study concluded that urban poverty amongst the squatters and low cost flat dwellers do not significantly contribute towards environmental degradation in Kuala Lumpur (Chamuri and Md Wahid Murad, 2002).

Following DFID (2002), the link between poverty and environment may be viewed from a simplified framework, which shows the pathways between environmental conditions and dimensions of poverty, shown in Figure 1 below.

The nature and dynamics of poverty-environment linkages are complex, multi-dimensional and context specific, reflecting geographic locations (rural, urban), economic, social and cultural characteristics of individuals and social groups. Micro and macro policies and institutional arrangements also influenced this linkage.

Environmental conditions such as access to and ownership of natural resources (land, water), ecosystem services (forests, grassland, freshwater, agro and coastal ecosystems), access to safe water and sanitation, pollutants, ecological fragility and the likelihood of natural disasters affect various dimensions of poverty such as livelihoods, health and vulnerability.

Table 9.3: Environmental Dimensions of Poverty (Source: Adapted from DFID, 2002) Examples of Environmental Conditions Dimensions of Poverty

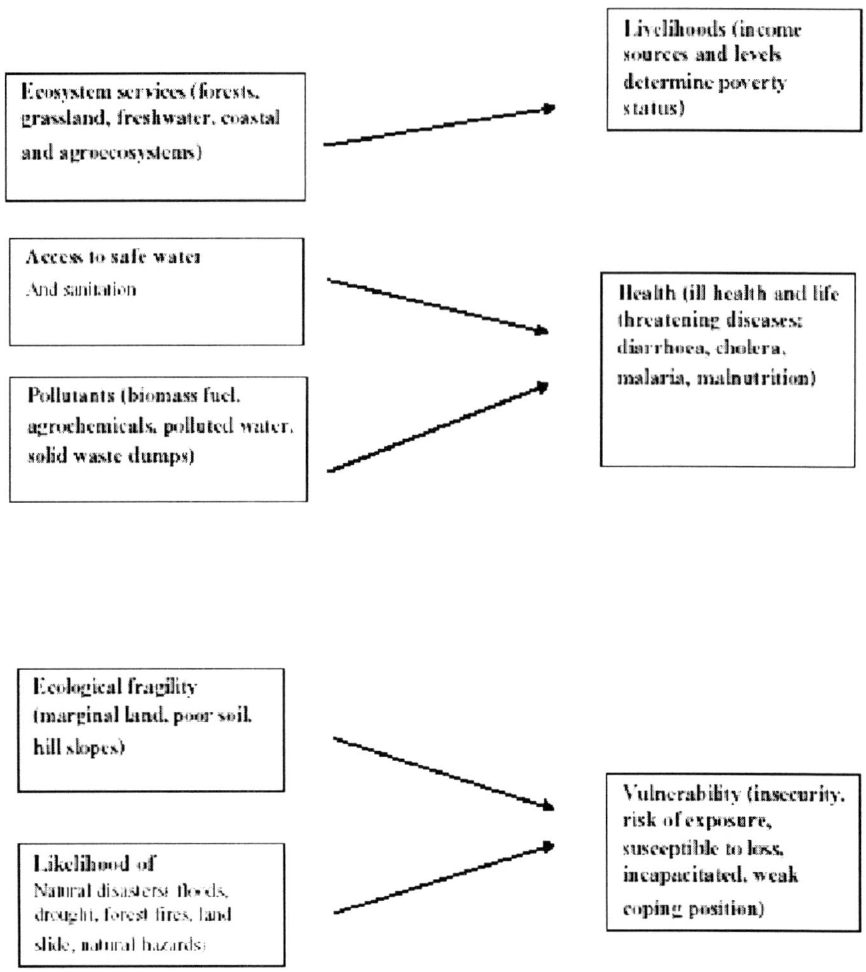

Access to and ownership of natural resources and ecosystem services affect the ability of the poor to sustain their livelihood. In rural areas, limited access to and insecurity of ownership to land and natural resources affect income levels. Landless tenants and farmers with small-sized farms are known to acquire inadequate income and hence to subsist under poverty conditions. Ecosystem services or functions from forests, agriculture, fisheries, etc provide valuable sources of income to rural communities. Ecological vulnerability and low levels of biological and resource productivity also affect livelihood. Hence, sustainable management of these natural resources and ecosystems is important to sustain the livelihood of rural communities.

Environmental health also affects the ability of the poor to move out of poverty. The health status of communities may be affected by environmental conditions such as access to safe water and sanitation and also the presence of pollutants in the air and water. The burden of diseases among the poor may be influenced by environmental factors such as lack of access to clean water, inadequate sanitation and poor hygiene practices. Pollutants from biomass fuels (woods, dung and crop residues), and agrochemicals (pesticides, weedicides) may contribute to the physical burden and ill health of women and children of the poor.

The vulnerability of the poor may be increased due to ecological fragility and exposure to natural disasters like floods, land slides, drought, forest fires, etc. Resource mismanagement or overexploitation may lead to environmental degradation which may contribute to fragility and exposure to natural disasters. Vulnerability leads to insecurity, risks to exposure to environmental hazards, susceptibility to loss, incapacity to recover and weak coping position. The poor are most vulnerable to environmental stresses and shocks, both in the short and long run. In the short run, short term economic difficulty may be prolonged due to incapacity and weak coping ability of the poor.

To summarize, environmental conditions clearly affect the various dimensions of poverty. The livelihood of the poor tends to depend more on natural resources and their environment services. Hence, lack of access, insecurity of ownership of natural resources and degradation of the environment would severely affect the poor. Lack of access to safe water, inadequate sanitation and pollutants from biomass fuels, agrochemicals and waste dumps will severely affect the health status of the poor. The poor will also be more vulnerable to natural disasters and ecologically fragile conditions, causing insecurity, exposure to risks, susceptible to losses, incapacity and weak coping position.

CASE STUDIES

In Malaysia, poverty has traditionally been viewed or analyzed through ethnic, spatial, gender and sectoral dimensions. Ethnically, poverty is relatively still dominant among the Malays, Indians, Orang Asli and various ethnic groups in Sabah and Sarawak. Spatially and sectorally, poverty is still predominantly a rural phenomenon and in the eastern states of Peninsular Malaysia and in East Malaysia. In terms of gender, poverty is predominant among women or women headed households.

In Malaysia, serious attempts to analyse poverty and its link to the environment were only recently made (Nuraain and Mohd. Yaakub 1998, Md Wahid 2002, Md Amzad 2003). The linkages between environment and poverty are numerous and complex. They require locally specific analysis to be understood. Poverty and environment is often viewed in a two-way linkage, as cause and effect. The two-way relationship shows that poverty may cause environmental degradation, which in turn worsens the poverty situation, in a downward spiral. Environmental degradation tends to impact the poor more than the non-poor. It is asserted that the poor tends to settle in environmentally sensitive agricultural or forested areas and also in squatter urban areas. The poor, in trying to meet their short term survival, tend to destroy or exploit unsustainably the natural capital like forest, soil, land, fishery resources, causing severe poverty (World Bank, 1992).

Case studies of the links between poverty and environment could be found among urban squatters, artisanal fisheries, shifting cultivators and Orang Asli.

Urban Poverty: Squatters

Most studies tend to portray squatters as agents of environmental degradation, polluting the urban environment, particularly the areas surrounding their settlements. Since squatter settlements are considered illegal and treated as outside the control of local authorities, they lack proper sewage and waste disposal systems, causing further stress to the environment (Abdul Wahid Murad and Chamuri, 2000). Squatters also faced problems of overcrowding, both in terms of physical and social space. Most squatters have migrated from rural areas, but there is no indication that the migration is related to any breakdown in production base or degradation of the rural environment. Nuraain and Mohd. Yaakub (1998) concluded that the degradation of the environment in the rural areas have not reached a stage where the livelihood of the rural people are threatened so as to force them to migrate to urban areas. Studies have also shown that most of the squatters are not poor measured by the official PLI, but their quality of life is considered low, deprived of various environmental, social, infrastructure and economic services (Chamuri and Mohd. Fauzi, 2000).

Rural Poverty

In the rural areas, case studies linking poverty and environment may be observed among artisan fishermen, shifting cultivators and Orang Asli (indigenous groups).

i) Artisanal Fishermen

Poverty is still predominant among fishermen, especially artisanal fishermen. Some of the environmental issues relate to depletion of fishery resources due to over-fishing by trawlers, fish bombing causing destruction of fish breeding grounds and corals, and also destruction of coastal resources such as mangroves. The activities of trawler boats, especially within the inshore areas, indiscriminately destroy fishing grounds and hence the sustainability of fishery resources. Fish bombing not only kill fish of all sizes, but also cause extensive damage to corals and marine environment. Destruction of coastal resources occurs due to various development projects, such as tourism, logging, industry, construction, earthwork and reclamation development, which destroys mangroves, riverine and estuarine areas which affect the reproductive capacity of fishery resources. Fishery resources may also be destroyed due to industrial pollution, affecting catch, income and the livelihood of poor artisan fishermen (Chamuri and Tan, 1996). From various case studies, Nuraain and Mohd. Yaakub (1998) concluded that poor artisanal fishing communities were victims rather than agents of environmental degradations.

ii) Shifting Cultivators

Shifting cultivators are mostly found in Sabah and Sarawak where between 16 percent and 24 percent of land respectively are under shifting cultivation or rotational agriculture or swiddening. Shifting cultivation is still being practiced among the indigenous communities which are among the poor target groups as a result of unproductive and unremunerative farming system. However, this practice may be decreasing as more shifting cultivators are absorbed into "established swiddening" and resettlement schemes as modern farming as well as tree crops, fruits and a variety of food crops are grown (Nuraain and Mohd. Yaakub, 1998).

The dependence of the poor shifting cultivators on natural resources (eg: forests and land) could lead to unsustainable use of resources. Shifting cultivators contribute to environmental degradation through the slash and burn practice, and also through their direct dependence on land and forests for their livelihood. But the extent of environmental degradation may be as severe compared to frontier development, involving the felling of forest and land clearing.

iii) Orang Asli

The Orang Asli, or indigenous people of Peninsular Malaysia, are among the poorest among the poor target groups. They number about 100,000, populated in about 778 settlements. About 40 percent of them live close to or within forested areas, while the others live as fishermen, waged labourers and permanent agriculturalists of rubber, oil palm and cocoa. The factors contributing to poverty among the Orang Asli are lack of legal ownership to their land, reduction in the resource base of the Orang Asli affecting their simple commodity production system, negative impact on their environment as a result of logging, rapid development involving highways, plantations, land development projects, etc. (Nuraain and Mohd. Yaakub, 1998). The marginalization and lack of integration of the Orang Asli with the mainstream economy also contribute to their poverty.

Although it may seem that Orang Asli contribute to the degradation of the environment, many authors have argued that this is an unfair accusation. Compared to the destruction caused by large scale agriculture, land and highway development projects, the damage done by the Orang Asli traditional rotational production system can be considered minimal, and could be ecologically and scientifically sound and an efficient utilization of forest resources.

Poverty alleviation projects for the Orang Asli have tended to concentrate more on resettling them into resettlement schemes, welfare aid and integrating them with the mainstream and cash economy. The Orang Asli are adapting to changes in their environment, becoming more detached from depending on the forest and traditional rotational system for their livelihood and hence less likely to exploit the natural resources to an extent that will cause serious degradation to the environment (Nuraain and Mohd. Yaakub, 1998).

CONSTRAINTS FACED BY THE POOR IN EMPLOYING ENVIRONMENTALLY SUSTAINABLE LIVELIHOOD

Generally, the poor lack access to basic amenities and ownership to natural resources like land, water and forests. Regarding squatters, their illegal status and non-payment of annual rates and assessment, led to deprivation of proper environmental services like waste disposal, sanitation, clean water and electricity. Furthermore, limitation of built-up, physical and social space put added stress on their environment and livelihood. The quality of life of squatters is generally low, although many may have crossed the official poverty line income (PLI). There may be a need for a higher urban PLI to reflect the higher cost of living in urban areas. Public housing for the poor still could not meet the demand of housing for the low-income groups.

Regarding artisanal fishermen, the open access nature of coastal fisheries deprived them of control and ownership of fishery resources within the coastal areas. The activities of trawler boats indiscriminately robbed them of valuable fishing grounds and fish stocks, causing depletion of fishery resources. Although rules and regulations are available regarding fishing zones limiting trawler boats off the 3 miles boundary, there are limitations of enforcement capacity, in that efforts to step up enforcement of the fishing regulations have not been successful due to resource constraints. In Sabah, efforts to curb fish bombing, mainly done by illegal immigrants, have also met with limited success.

Regarding shifting cultivators and Orang Asli, problem of ownership of land and insecurity of land tenure are the major constraints encountered by them. The process of securing land titles could be tedious, frustrating and time consuming. Whenever their traditional resources are being managed and developed by the State or private sector, they are normally marginalized with only minimal benefit and compensation from such development (Nuraain and Mohd. Yaakub,1998). Efforts to resettle the Orang Asli in resettlement schemes face adaptation problems, with some of them facing difficulty in adapting to sedentary agriculture. Efforts to bring them into mainstream economy and modernization also face difficulty and resistance from those opposing change. Change could be brought about through education, but many Orang Asli children dropped-out of education, which may delay the modernization process.

Importance of Environmental Sustainability in National Policies and Plans

In Malaysia, environmental and natural resource issues continued to be addressed to ensure balanced and sustainable development. During the Seventh Plan period (1996-2000) efforts to integrate environmental considerations into development planning have been intensified, and the relevant institutional, legislative and regulatory mechanisms have been strengthened. In addition, there is the use of cleaner technologies and the introduction of a market-based approach to address environmental and resource issues. Environment education and awareness campaigns have also been launched to foster an environment-friendly society. In the Eight Plan Period (2001-2005), environmental and resource management issues continue to be addressed in a more integrated and holistic manner, including identifying prudent, cost-effective and appropriate management approaches to ensure sustainable and resilient development. Efforts to address air quality, mitigate degradation of rivers, improve marine and groundwater quality, minimization of waste and management of their disposal. Natural resource management will be enhanced by improving land-use planning, sustainable forest management, addressing multiple-use issues in marine areas and extending the Biodiversity Action Plan to various states. Environmental management will be enhanced through the promotion of performance measurement, and market-based instruments, as well as engaging communities in addressing environmental and natural resource issues (Malaysia, 2001).

The Malaysian Government's strategic policy thrusts for environment and sustainable resource management are as follows (Malaysia, 2001):

- Reducing the energy, materials, pollution and waste intensity of urban-industrial activities to address air pollution, mitigate deterioration in water quality and waste disposal;
- Increasing the use of fiscal policy in pursuit of environmental objectives and promoting the use of appropriate market-based instruments and self-regulatory measures among industries;
- Promoting environmental performance measurement and strengthening the database fore environmental decision-making;
- Empowering local authorities and engaging communities in addressing environmental issues; and
- Enhancing land use planning, intensifying biodiversity conservation and the sustainable management of forests as well as improving the management of maritime affairs.

Environmental and natural resource management guided by the National Policy on the Environment, ensures long-term sustainability and improving the quality of life. The policy aims at promoting economic, social and cultural progress through environmentally sound and sustainable development. The objectives of the Policy are:

- To achieve a clean, safe, healthy, and productive environment for both present and future generations
- To conserve the country's unique natural resources and diverse cultural heritage with effective participation by all; and
- To promote lifestyles, patterns of consumption and production, consistent with the principles of sustainable development.

The essence of this Policy is based on seven inter-related and mutually supporting principles which have been identified as:

1. Stewardship of the environment
2. Conservation of nature's vitality and diversity
3. Continuous improvement in health, safety and the quality of the environment for sustained human development
4. Integration of sustainability in all development decisions
5. Commitment and accountability
6. Rational and efficient use of natural resources; and
7. Active participation in the community of nations.

In terms of Natural Resources Management (Malaysia, 1996), Malaysia emphasizes the long-term management of its natural resource base to ensure their sustainable use and development. The Nationals Conservation Strategy (NCS) will be used as the framework for a comprehensive approach to natural resource development. The objectives of the NCS are:

- To conserve natural resources in order to maintain ecological processes, preserve biological diversity, and restore degraded natural resources in a cost-effective manner
- To use natural resources in a sustainable manner as well as to ensure that non-renewable resources are extracted at rates that do not exceed the creation of substitute capital resources; and
- To improve efficiency in resource use and management, give higher priority to renewable resources already exploited, and prevent deterioration of fragile ecosystems with large downstream influences.

National Programmes to Promote Environmental Sustainability

National programmes to promote environmental sustainability fall under strategies, measures, and programmes to improve environmental and natural resource management.

Natural Resources Management

Land Resources

Integrated land use planning and remote sensing technology are used to improve the management of land resources. Balanced and sustainable development in its economic, social, spiritual and environmental aspects form the basis of land use planning and development projects. Physical planning guidelines were established by the Town and Country Planning Department (TCPD), including a National Spatial Plan, Development, Structure and Local Plans. The development of coastal areas, islands, open spaces, housing, retention ponds, solid waste disposal, conservation of trees and environmentally sensitive areas, to ensure sustainable development are covered by these guidelines.

Water Resources

In the past, several states in Malaysia experienced periodic water scarcity, caused by extended dry spells, and compounded by the increasing demand for water, polluted water sources and the encroachment of development into water catchments. In 1998, the Government formed a National Water Resources Council to provide a forum for a holistic approach for the planning and management of water resources. A National Water Resources Study for Peninsular Malaysia was completed to determine the availability of water resources and water demand up to 2050. A river-basin approach to water management and various awareness and *Love Our River* campaigns, were initiated to improve and to promote the wise use of river and river conservation (Malaysia, 2001).

Biodiversity

In 1998, the National Biodiversity Policy, which provides a framework for integrating and consolidating biodiversity programmes and projects, was launched. In line with the Policy, the capacity of several conservation agencies were strengthened and management plans were drawn-up for a number of protected areas. These included the preparation of master plans, a capacity building project, improving management of totally protected areas, and the establishment of nature education and research centres and wildlife reserves.

Forest Resources

In the past few years, efforts to manage forests sustainably were intensified and multiple-use forestry was promoted. The area under permanent forest reserve has been increased. Timber certification in fulfilling Malaysia's commitment towards achieving the International Tropical Timber Organization's Year 2000 objective, when all timber traded in the international market must be produced from forests that are sustainably managed, was initiated. Sustainable forests management includes also non-timber forest, enhancing the protective and recreational role of forests (Malaysia, 2001).

Energy and Mineral

Emphasis is given to the sustainable development of depletable resources in energy production and diversification of energy sources. The potential for the development of renewable energy sources was assessed and encouraged. Several states adopted the Mineral Enactment, which provides for the efficient and sustainable exploration and mining of minerals and the conversion of ex-mining land to other economic use.

Coastal and Marine Resources

Integrated coastal management plans were adopted by several states, to ensure sustainability of coastal resource and to reconcile conflicting use. A National Coastal Zone Policy will be prepared to provide uniform and minimum standards for coastal zone management for all states. A pilot study to develop an integrated shoreline management plan was conducted for north Pahang (Malaysia, 2001).

Other initiatives include programmes to increase the level of environmental awareness and to disseminate environmental information among Malaysians, including the NGOs and the private sector. Several larger corporations have adopted environment-friendly processes with ISO 14001 standards and the emphasis on Corporate Social Responsibility (CRS). At the international front, Malaysia participated in several multilateral environmental negotiations, and also actively implemented its commitments to international initiatives, such as Agenda 21 and sustainable development efforts.

Existing Barriers to Promoting Environmental Sustainability

Developmental Pressure

The main barrier to promoting environmental sustainability is pressure for development arising from rapid growth. Except for the recession years in the early 1980s and the crisis years of 1997/1998, Malaysia has experienced rapid and sustained economic growth, covering the NEP era (1971-1990) and post NEP era (1991-2000). Various development projects were implemented during these eras to fulfill the objectives of poverty eradication, restructuring and transformation of the economy from primary producer to industrialized nation. These development projects which include infrastructural, industrial, agricultural, highway, new township, energy, etc. put pressure on natural resources and the environment, as evidenced from the decline in the quality of environment and also depletion of natural resources. Conflicts may arise between the need to develop and to meet the sustainable development objectives of the country. The need to arrive at a balance between development and conservation is a big challenge for development planning and implementation for sustainability. Rapid development beyond the carrying capacity of resources and the environment will degrade the environment and deplete resources and will be detrimental to the future development and growth of the economy.

Capacity to Implement Regulatory and Market- Based Instruments

Efforts to integrate the environment into development planning has been intensified by strengthening the institutional, legislative and regulatory mechanisms, including the use of cleaner technology, market-based approach and enhancing educational awareness to foster an environmental-friendly society (Malaysia, 2001).

The early response to address the various environmental problems was through legislation. No less than 40 legislations were legislated, many of them sector specific in nature. Among the much legislation, the Environmental Quality Act (EQA, 1974) is probably the most comprehensive in terms of environmental management in Malaysia. It provides the guiding principles for the National Environmental Policy objectives, to integrate environmental dimension in project planning and implementation, provide environmental inputs into resource and regional development planning. A requirement for an Environmental Impact Assessment (EIA) as an integral part of overall project planning was introduced in 1988.

Apart from legislation, market-based instruments, including incentives, pricing, taxes and subsidies, have begun to be used as a means of ensuring the quality of the environment. In Malaysia, the use of market based instruments as a tool for environmental management could be considered at its infancy and seems not to be too popular, compared to its use in many developed countries. However, it has the potential and advantages of a 'win-win' proposition for a more environmental-friendly means of production and gives incentives for producers to cut back on pollution. It also provides revenue for government for financing environment protection measures, thus reducing government budgets for monitoring and enforcement. Market-based instruments also reduce the need for regulation and give more flexibility to producers, giving rise to overall efficiency.

Some of the market-based instruments that could be implemented include externality pricing, pricing of resources, laws on natural reserve conservation, polluter-pay principle, user pays, tax packaging, subsidy and grants, emission trading and control standards. To effectively implement the economic instruments, the objectives must be clear, as well as acceptable to the target groups and to achieve specific community objectives.

While there are efforts to increase compliance through enforcement, there are barriers of enforcements in terms of lack of manpower, finance and institutional capacity of enforcement agencies such as the DOE and local authorities. With the expansion of economic activities, the task of enforcement and monitoring requires greater efforts. The industries are bound to take advantage of lapse in enforcement and loopholes in the law to render legislation ineffective. There may be market barriers arising from the high cost of environmental technologies, purchasing power and the extent of private sector interest in complying with legislations and market-based instruments. There are also infrastructural barriers, related to the level of industrial development for technology absorption, technical skills and capabilities, institutional mechanisms.

CONCLUSION

The paper discusses Malaysia's experience and policies linking the environment and poverty alleviation. A review of the state of the environment in Malaysia, the incidence of poverty, and case studies on the inter-linkages between poverty and environmental sustainability are provided. An overview on the state of environment in Malaysia is provided focusing on critical environmental issues and problems, the importance of environmental sustainability in national policies and major ongoing national programmes to promote sustainability. Existing barriers to promoting environmental sustainability are discussed, including development pressures, policy, legal, institutional and infrastructural barriers in the context of the implementation of various environmental regulations and market-based instruments.

Prevailing poverty incidence and living standards in Malaysia, case studies linking the environment and poverty, and their implications for environmental sustainability, are discussed. The discussion includes the incidence of poverty and its impact on livelihood, dependence of the poor on natural resources and the sustainability of resource use, constraints faced by the poor in employing environmentally sustainable lifestyle and the inter-linkages between poverty eradication and environmental sustainability.

RECOMMENDATIONS

Some recommendations are provided for changes in policy and planning mechanism, roles of government, private sector, and NGOs, especially for an integrated approach to promote environmental sustainability and poverty eradication:

i) Strengthening Mechanisms

Desirable changes in the implementation of policies and planning mechanisms are suggested. These changes include strengthening the capacity for Government agencies related to the implementation of regulatory and market-based instruments for environmental sustainability by providing additional budgetary and manpower support to render effective monitoring and compliance of regulations and implementation of market-based instruments. The increased role for the private sector in the implementation of environmental sustainability, awareness and poverty alleviation projects are suggested, in the context of more concerted and effective CSR.

Public awareness and attitude towards a cleaner environment is still low. Environmental educational and awareness programmes need to be continually enhanced. The private sector and the NGO could increase efforts in enhancing educational and awareness programmes for the general public, such as implementing and encouraging participation in community recycling and social work programmes for the elderly, school children and women groups. The private sector and industries should gradually increase compliance and implement measures towards achieving sustainable industrialization, while preserving the environment increases the welfare of the poor and general population.

ii) Integrated Environmental Sustainability and Poverty Eradication

An integrated approach for promoting environmental sustainability and poverty eradication needs to evolve a win-win policy option for attacking poverty while improving the environment. A partnership with the poor needs to be forged to reduce poverty, improve social equity and enhance environmental quality (UNDP-EC, 1999a, UNDP-EC, 1999b). Among the steps which must be taken include challenging and revising the entrenched myth in the understanding of the interactions between poverty-environment, that: poverty necessarily leads to environmental degradation, poor people are too poor to invest in the environment, and that countries must tackle poverty eradication before dealing with environmental improvement. There is no simple causal link between poverty and the environment and that the linkages between both are complex and require locally specific analysis. However, programmes at alleviating poverty such as by improving welfare and human capital (education, and health), employment and access to resources, basic needs and services will go a long way towards empowering the poor while improving environmental sustainability.

Similarly, the linkages between population growth and environmental degradation are complex. Poverty and population growth does not necessarily lead to environmental degradation. The notion that population growth necessarily leads to environmental degradation may be a myth. While population increase may initially lead to environmental degradation, this linkage may be further influenced by policy and may be context-specific.

Another myth relates to the role of the poor in resource management. Poor people are assumed to lack the technical knowledge for resource management, and that Government can best control resources and that markets always lead to efficient allocation of resources. Further analysis to look at the role of the poor and communities in managing resources and the advantages that could be derived from community-based resource management should be done through case studies on the linkage between poverty and the environment.

Specific policy recommendations touch on i)access to assets, including protecting the current asset base of the poor and expanding the asset base of the poor, ii) asset improvement, involving co-managing resources with the poor and co-investing with the poor, iii) infrastructure and technology development, including supporting infrastructure development for the poor and developing technologies that benefit the poor, iv) employment and compensation for the poor, including employing the poor and compensating the poor, v) market and planning reform, including intervening to overcome the deficiencies of the market, eliminating subsidies for the non-poor, and reforming the planning procedures.

There are also recommendations for sectoral policy options in the areas of agriculture, water resources, forests, urban development, sanitation and waste disposal. In the area of agriculture, there is a need to facilitate access to agricultural assets for the poor, co-invest in on-farm natural resource assets of the poor, employ the poor in efforts to improve the agricultural resource base, develop and promote agricultural technologies with environmental benefits, promote low-risk perennial production in poor and marginal areas, and compensate the poor for conserving or managing resources.

In the area of water resources, specifically involving irrigation and watersheds, there is a need to facilitate access to water for the poor, employ the poor in water resources projects and reform water pricing. In terms of forest resource and management, there is a need to facilitate access to forests for the poor, co-invest and co-manage forests such as in agro-forestry projects, collaborate in protected area management, bring in the private sector, supply forest products through agro-forestry sources and support markets for forest products.

In the area of urban development, there is a need to improve urban transportation, improve housing conditions and housing tenure, reduce the impacts of disasters, improve urban planning and zoning, and strengthen municipal government. There is also a need to improve water supply, waste disposal and sanitation by developing a people-centred approach, develop a community-based ecosystem planning, increase attention to the role of scavenging and recycling (Md Amzad 2003), provide the poor with access to urban services and resources.

There are also recommendations to look on macro and cross-cutting issues such as equity and the distribution of assets, and governance as key elements for integrating poverty alleviation and environmental sustainability. The uses of cross-cutting operational principles are recommended for achieving better integration of poverty alleviation and environmental sustainability. These include prioritizing investments in neglected areas, working across sectors, protecting the asset base of the poor, developing approaches integrating poverty alleviation and environmental sustainability strategies and programmes, decentralizing to the lowest appropriate level, promoting community-based action, understanding gender relationships and foster child development and education, especially among poor households.

REFERENCES

Angelsen, A. and Vainio, M (ed.) *Poverty and Environment,* Bergen: CROP Publications.

Chamuri, S, (1994a), *"Rural Development, Poverty Alleviation and Rural Transformation,"* in INTAN, Malaysian Development Experience: Changes and Challenges, Kuala Lumpur: National Institute of Public Administration (INTAN).

Chamuri, S, (1994b), *"Poverty Profile in Malaysia: Findings from Ten Districts in Peninsular Malaysia,"* in Jamilah Ariffin (ed.), Poverty Amidst Plenty, Petaling Jaya: Pelanduk Publications.

Chamuri, S, (2000), *"Urban Poverty Alleviation and the Financial Crisis: Problems, Prospects and Challenges,"* paper presented at National Conference on Urban Issues and Challenges: Developing Solutions for the 21st Century, Faculty of Human Ecology, Universiti Putra Malaysia, 8-9th May.

Chamuri, S and Siew Hock,T, (1996), *"Perindustrian, Kemiskinan dan Alam Sekitar,"* (Industrialization, Poverty and Environment), in Chamuri Siwar and Nor Aini Idris. (ed.), Kemiskinan dalam Arus Pembangunan Ekonomi Malaysia, Bangi: Penerbit Universiti Kebangsaan Malaysia.

Chamuri, S and Yusof Kasim, M, (1997) *"Urban Development and Urban Poverty in Malaysia",* International Journal of Socioeconomics, 12.

Chamuri, S, Fauzi, M, and Jani, M, (2000) *"Pola Pekerjaan, Pendapatan, Kemiskinan dan Perbelanjaan di kalangan Penghuni Rumah Awam Kos Rendah Dewan Bandaraya Kuala Lumpur,"* (Employment, Income, Poverty and Consumption among Low Cost Flat Dwellers in Kuala Lumpur), Malaysian Journal of Consumer anf Family Economics, 3: 8-21.

DFID, (2002), *" Linking Poverty Eradication and Environmental Management: Policy Challenges and Opportunities,"* Discussion Document prepared for World Summit on Sustainable Development (WSSD), by Department for International Development (DFID), UK, Directorate General for Development, EC, United Nations Development Programme (UNDP), and The World Bank.

DOE, (1997), *Malaysia: Environmental Quality Report 1997,* Kuala Lumpur: Department of Environment.

Gow, D.D, (1992) *"Poverty and Natural Resources: Principles for Environmental Management and Sustainable Development"* Environmental Impact Assessment Review, 12: 49-65.

Malaysia, (1996), *Seventh Malaysia Plan, 1996-2000,* Kuala Lumpur: Percetakan Nasional Malaysia Bhd.

Malaysia, (1999), *Malaysian Quality of Life,* Kuala Lumpur: Economic Planning Unit.

Malaysia, (2001), *Eighth Malaysia Plan, 2001-2005,* Kuala Lumpur: Percetakan Nasional Malaysia Bhd.

Malaysia, (2001a), *Third Outline Perspective Plan, 2001-2010,* Kuala Lumpur: Percetakan Nasional Malaysia Bhd.

Md. Amzad Hossain, (2003), *The Impact of Scavengers' Status on Waste Recycling in Klang Valley, Malaysia*, Ph.D thesis submitted to Faculty of Economics, Universiti Kebangsaan Malaysia, Bangi.

Md. Wahid Murad, (2002), *Poverty and Environment: Case Study of Solid waste Management amongst Squatters and Low-cost Flat Dwellers in Kuala Lumpur City, Malaysia,* Ph.D thesis submitted to Institute for Environment and Development, Universiti Kebangsaan Malaysia, Bangi.

Md. Wahid Murad and Siwar, C, *"The Links between Poverty and the Environment: Solid Waste Management among Squatters in Kuala Lumpur, Malaysia,"* Paper presented at the 16th International Conference on Solid Waste Technology and Management, Widener University, Philadelphia, 10-13 December, 2000

Nuraain Amirah and Mohd. Yaakub Johari, (1998), *"Poverty and Environment: Some Observations from Malaysia,"* in Angelsen A and M.Vainio (ed.) Poverty and Environment, Bergen: CROP Publications.

UNDP-EC, (1999a), *Attacking Poverty While Improving the Environment: Towards Win-Win Policy Options*. Poverty and Environment Initiative (mimeograph).

UNDP-EC (1999b), *Attacking Poverty While Improving the Environment: Practical Recommendations*. Poverty and Environment Initiative (mimeograph).

In: Readings in World Development
Editors: K.C. Roy and S. Chatterjee, pp. 103-114
ISBN 1-59454-947-8

Chapter 10

POLICY FAILURES AND ENVIRONMENTAL EXTERNALITIES: CASE OF OIL PALM IN MALAYSIA AND INDONESIA[1]

Jamal Othman[2]

ABSTRACT

Rising export demand for palm oil may lead to pronounced increases in agricultural land demand for oil palm expansion in Malaysia and Indonesia – two main palm oil producing and exporting countries. However, it is expected that the environmental effects of agricultural land augmentation will depend much on existing governance affecting environmental and forestry management in the two countries. Given the relatively more prevalent policy and institutional failures in Indonesia, it is anticipated that deforestation consequences and open burnings in the country will be stronger, inevitably giving rise to recurring haze externalities in the region. This paper examines environment-trade linkages affecting the oil palm sub-sector in Malaysia and Indonesia. Shifts in export demand for palm oil were simulated and effects on land use in Malaysia and Indonesia were observed under varying assumptions of environmental and forestry policy regimes in the two countries. Inferences on haze effects are provided.

Keywords: Haze externalities, policy failures, palm oil trade, land demand

INTRODUCTION

Unlike acid rains, which characterize the trans-boundary environmental problems in many industrial regions of the world (such as Northeast Asia (Japan, Korea and Taiwan) and

---

[1] Paper presented in the Fourth IIDS International Conference on Development. Organized by IIDS and UI, December 15-19. Bali, Indonesia

[2] * Author is Associate Professor in the Resource and Environmental Economics Program, Faculty of Economics and Business, Universiti Kebangsaan Malaysia, Bangi 43600, MALAYSIA, E-mail: Jortman @pkrisc.cc.ukm.my

Europe), the Southeast Asian region is rather prone to an international environmental pollution of a peculiar kind – the haze. Haze refers to the accumulation of fine particles in the air, which are hardly visible to the naked eye. The particles may result from natural phenomena and/or human activities. The main natural source of haze is forest fires, while haze from deliberate forest burnings, open burnings, emissions from factories and motor vehicles represent conscious human activities. Persistent accumulation of haze particles in the air reduces sun's rays and visibility while imposing health impacts.

For parts of Malaysia and Indonesia, haze is quite an annual phenomenon, which normally occurs in the months of August - October with varying scales. However, the haze of 1997 was unprecedented in terms of intensity, duration and coverage. It started in early August and the sky remained dull until some three months later. The haze caused much inconvenience and disruption to the Malaysian economy. It raised the incidence of respiratory diseases, forced a decline in agricultural crop and fishing yields and caused disruption to transport services, manufacturing output and the tourism industry. A state of emergency was declared for 10 days in Sarawak, a Malaysian state neighbouring the Indonesian Kalimantan. It has been estimated that the value of the 1997 haze damages to Malaysia was some RM800 million or US$320 million (based on exchange rates at the time). This amounted to some US$15 of damage per capita for the country (Shahwahid and Jamal, 1999).

The prime cause of haze has been suspended smoke particulate from large-scale forest and plantation fires, particularly in Southern Sumatra and Central Kalimantan, both in neighbouring Indonesia. Much of these forest fires have been attributed to land clearing practices for extensive ex-situ oil palm expansion.

Palm oil is considered as the "green gold" for the economies of Malaysia and Indonesia. Of 13 major vegetable oils produced by the world, palm oil currently (2001) accounts for 25 per cent of world production. This constitutes an increase of 5 percent from 20 percent in 1995. For the same period, soybean oil (palm oil's main rival) production increased from 27 percent to 29 percent - only a 2 percent change. Given expanding demand and increasing per capita consumption, palm oil looms to be the world's leading vegetable oil in a few years time.

Currently, Malaysia is the world's largest producer of palm oil (a share of 50 percent) followed by Indonesia (23 percent). There are 3.5 million hectares of oil palm plantations in Malaysia and some 3.2 million hectares in Indonesia. In recent years, land supply for oil palm cultivation in Peninsular Malaysia has become more rigid due to the commitments of the country on sustainable resource and forest management. The oil-palm industry has thus expanded to the land rich states of Sabah and Sarawak. Indonesia, with a land area 6 times larger than Malaysia and a more abundant labour resource, will undoubtedly dwarf Malaysia in the near future, in terms of palm oil production and exports. It has been reported that each year about 200,000 hectares of forestland were converted into new oil palm plantations in Indonesia (Aditjondro, 2000). Foreign investments in the Indonesian oil palm subsector, most notably from Malaysian companies, had been particularly active due to the dwindling land supply and rising farm wages in Malaysia. By 1996, a year before the ASIAN Financial Crisis, 45 Malaysian companies along with their Indonesian partners had been able to secure land banks totalling some 1.3 million hectares (Casson, 1999).

Rising demand for palm oil in non-traditional palm oil importing countries and depressed currencies (vis a vis the US dollar) is expected to lead to pronounced expansion in oil palm cultivation in Malaysia and Indonesia, the two main palm oil producing and exporting countries. However, it can be shown that the effects of shifts in export demand on land factor demand and consequently haze impacts will depend much on existing policy regimes affecting forestry and environmental management in the two countries. Of the two countries, Indonesia is more land and labour abundant while its forest and environmental management regime is more susceptible to institutional and policy failures. For instance, while both Malaysia and Indonesia had imposed a regulatory ban on open burnings for land clearance, enforcement capacities of the latter have been relatively weaker. Operationally, plantation firms in Indonesia have been free to use open burnings to clear land with impunity (ASIAN Development Bank, 2001). Thus, it is anticipated that detrimental land clearance practices (forest fires, open burnings) in Indonesia will be more pronounced, inevitably giving rise to recurring haze externalities in the region. For instance, increased export demand for Indonesian timber was not the major factor for deforestation in Indonesia (Barbier et. al., 1995). Distorted market factors such as inefficient prices, subsidies, and institutional failures were found to have played a greater role in the conversion of forest in the country. Tampubolon (1998) had also pointed that given a multitude of factors which essentially constitute policy and institutional failures in Indonesia, the expansion of private sector investments in the oil palm subsector in the country may lead to even more severe forest fires in the next several years ahead. Unless there were quick legal and institutional reforms in Indonesia, it is anticipated that the trans-boundary haze pollution will continue to engulf the Southeast Asian region in the near future.

This study employs output supply exogenous policy models with explicit factor markets to examine land factor demand - trade linkages in the world vegetable oil markets. Specifically, this study simulates shifts in export demand for palm oil and effects on land demand in Malaysia and Indonesia are observed under varying assumptions of environmental policy regimes in the two countries. Inferences on haze externalities and possible strategic solutions for Malaysia and Indonesia are then deliberated.

Linking Trade Expansion and Haze Externalities: Theoretical Framework

The idea of agricultural or industrial production processes giving rise to negative externalities has long been an integral subject in the study of resource and environmental economics. This subsection lays the basic framework in examining the linkages between agricultural output supply, trade and haze externalities. In the subsection that follows, formal treatment of these linkages is provided.

Analysis of agricultural trade-environmental linkages requires knowledge of: i) the underlying agricultural production function which links factor use, type of technology and output supply, ii) how the demand for output is affected by shifts in export demand and related trade policies imposed by producing and competing countries, and iii) how changes in production factors, particularly land, result in externalities, in this case the production of haze. The following equations illustrate these linkages.

Demand for agricultural output

$$q_O^D = f(p_O^D(d_O^D) + p_O^E\ (d_O^E\ )) \tag{i}$$

Demand for land input

$$X_L^D = f(q_O^S\ ) \tag{ii}$$

Supply of land input

$$X_L^S = v_L * r_L \tag{iii}$$

Production of environmental externalities

$$E_h = \gamma * X_L^D \tag{iv}$$

Market clearing condition

$$q_O^S = q_O^D \tag{v}$$

Land market clearing condition

$$X_L^D = X_L^S \tag{vi}$$

The notations *q, d* and *p* in the above equations denote quantity, demand, and prices, respectively. The superscripts *D, E,* and *S* denote domestic demand, export demand and supply, respectively, while subscript *O* refers to the agricultural output which is being modelled.

Equation (i) expresses the demand for agricultural output (q_O^D) which is a function of domestic demand ($p_O^D(d_O^D)$and export demand ($p_O^E(d_O^E)$). Equation (ii) describes the derived demand for land input (X_L^D) that goes into the production of agriculture (q_O^S). Equation (iii) portrays the supply of land factor, where V_L and r_L represent respectively, land supply elasticity and land rents. Equation (iv) depicts the production of environmental externalities, in this study the haze, $E_{k,}$, where its scale and magnitude are determined by the haze coefficient (γ) and the size of new agricultural land (X_L^D) that goes into the production of new outputs. Equation (v) and (vi) describe the market clearing conditions, where no surpluses or deficits in inventory of outputs and inputs were assumed.

From the above-simplified equations, linkages between trade expansion, output and land demand as well as environmental impacts can be traced. It is clear that the direction of impacts on land demand as a result of changes in export demand, output supply, and consequently the resulting haze impacts can be determined, i.e., $\frac{\partial X_L^D}{\partial q_O^S} \succ 0$, $\frac{\partial X_L^D}{\partial d_O^E} \succ 0$, and

$\frac{\partial E_k}{\partial X_L^D} \succ 0$ if $\gamma \succ 0$.

The parameters V_L in Equation (iii) and γ in (iv) are critical in determining the likelihood and magnitude of haze externalities (marginal propensity of haze), i.e., $\frac{\partial E_k}{\partial X_L^D} = \gamma$ and

$\frac{\partial E_h}{\partial V_L} \succ 0$. It is obvious that ∂E_k would not only be contingent on γ, but also on X_L^D which is in turn affected by land supply elasticity (V_L). Thus, V_L and γ may both reflect the relative degree of institutional and environmental policy failures in a country; the higher the parameters, the greater the failures and the resulting haze externalities.

In this study, no attempt was made to establish explicit causality links between deforestation or agricultural land expansion and the production of haze externalities in either Malaysia or Indonesia. Moreover, there were other factors contributing to haze. We rather presume that the likelihood for deliberate open burnings and forest fires for land clearance and consequently the resulting environmental externalities is higher in the case of countries which exhibit greater policy and institutional failures in environmental management.

The Formal Framework – Hertel's Comparative Static Model

There has been virtually no known attempt in the literature to examine theoretically and empirically the association between agricultural expansion and haze externalities. Perhaps the most appropriate framework to date to examine such linkages is the Hertel's model of the farm sector (Hertel, 1989). Hertel's model is single country, comparative static, and partial equilibrium. It relates factor markets, output supply, demand and trade through a system of equations.

The repercussions of domestic and trade policy shocks are examined by the model explicitly via policy-price linkages (interested readers are advised to refer to the paper for the detailed construction of the model). Hertel's model, however, is not capable to examine the impact of shifts in export demand on factor markets. To overcome this weakness, we manipulated Equation 1 of Hertel's model to incorporate shifts in domestic and export demand for farm output. The complete system of equations for the enhanced Hertel's model is presented in Table 10.1. Note that with the exception of Equations 1 and 4, all others are Hertel's original equations. All notations – *p, q, d, D, S, E,* and *O* are as defined earlier while the *hat* notation represents the percentage change in the relevant variable.

Equation 1 was an extension of Hertel's original formulation to incorporate shifts in domestic and export demand. The original Hertel equation for output demand consists of two components – domestic and export demand. By some simple manipulation of this equation, shifts in domestic and export demand can be expressed, respectively, as shifts in the direction of price axis,

$$\hat{p}_O^D = \frac{\hat{q}_O^D - \alpha \in_D^E \hat{p}_O^E}{(1-\alpha)\in_D^D} + \hat{d}_O^D,$$

and

$$\hat{p}_O^E = \frac{\hat{q}_O^D - (1-\alpha)\hat{p}_O^D \in_D^D}{\alpha \in_D^E} + \hat{d}_O^E$$

where $\hat{d}_O^D$ and $\hat{d}_O^E$ represent percentage shifts in domestic output and export demand schedules, respectively. The aggregate farm-level demand elasticity, $\in_D = [(1-\alpha)\varepsilon_D^D + \alpha\varepsilon_O^E]$ is a weighted sum of the farm-level domestic and export demand elasticities, where α is the quantity share of exports in total demand. By solving the two equations above, Equation 1 is generated.

Equation (2) describes the derived demand of a competitive agricultural sector operating under locally constant returns to scale. The variables C_k and σ_{kj} represent cost share of an input and an Allen partial elasticity of substitution (AES), respectively. Equation (3) represents the assumption of zero profits for the aggregate farm sector. Factor mobility including land is addressed in equation (4). The notation V_k denotes supply elasticity for factor *k*. Specifically, it describes the responsiveness of production factors to a change in rents under varying assumptions of factor mobility. By specifying factor supply this way, varying levels of factor supply elasticities can be modelled. Equations 5-7 incorporate exogenous sectoral *ad valorem* output, input, and trade policy variables into the model. The last two equations explain the market clearing conditions for output and inputs.

The above extended version of Hertel's model to incorporate shifts in output demand as well as factor supply schedules has been developed and applied to examine the inter-linkages between factor markets, currency depreciation, and trade for the case of oil palm in Malaysia (Jamal 1997, Jamal 2000). In the current study, the basic exogenous parameters used in the model came from these studies.

We had earlier postulated that the effect of shifts in commodity demand on agricultural land demand would not only be contingent on whether land is in abundance (through deforestation or conversion of other land uses to agriculture), but are also influenced by factors such as the existence of policy or institutional failures. This implies that given the same relative endowment of land, a country that exhibits greater policy and institutional failures will see more pronounced increases in land going into agriculture.

Institutional and policy failures are especially caused by the lack of appropriate environmental regulations and instruments or when these regulations are not adequately enforced – inevitably resulting in unsustainable production practices. This includes perverse public investment incentives, which accelerates the pace of environmental resource degradation. In this study, to what extent these factors affect land mobility is modelled by assuming varying levels of land supply elasticities (V_k – Equation 4). Higher supply elasticities (elastic) would denote greater mobility of land factor from forest conversion due to the existence of the above factors. Although not directly modelled, this study assumes that the value of γ (marginal propensity of haze – see Equation iv) is positive and greater for the case of Indonesia.

All parameters relating to factor substitutions, factor shares and demand elasticities for Malaysia are taken from Jamal (1997, 2000). The same parameters are assumed for Indonesia. This assumption would not, however, alter the course and implications of model results, as this study is more interested to observe the directions and relative extent of changes in land demand and haze externalities (rather than fine-tune numbers of impacts magnitude) as a result of policy and institutional failures - represented by varying levels of land supply elasticities.

In the model simulation, varying values of land supply elasticities in Indonesia, i.e., 0.2 (baseline), 0.7, 1.2 and 2.0 are employed with a 10 percent change in export demand. The model is solved for the endogenous variables of interest using Cramer's Rule.

Simulation Results

A 10 percent shift in export demand was simulated along with varying levels of land supply elasticities to model varying assumptions of policy and institutional failures in a country. The results are presented in Table 10.4.

A range of land supply elasticities were employed, from 0.2 (base line), 0.7, 1.2, and 2.0. Recall that higher land supply elasticities denote greater prevalence of policy and institutional failures, *ceteris paribus*, and hence the less rigid will be land supply to agriculture given the same level of incentives.

Results (Table 10.4) show that the impact of shifts in export demand in a country became more pronounced when a more elastic land supply was assumed, *ceteris paribus*. With increasing land supply elasticity, the model especially shows more significant increases in land demand. For instance, using an elastic land supply of 2.0, land use is expected to increase by a high 8 percent. This compares to 3.0 percent when land supply elasticity was 0.2. Impacts on domestic price are also greater which leads to greater effects on output and export markets.

Higher values of land supply elasticities (1.2 – 2.0) in this study represent a mix of unsustainable agriculture/forest management and less adherents to best practices environmental regulations. The results clearly suggest that if policy failure is more prevalent, shifts in export demand will pose more pronounced impacts on land use and hence the haze consequences (refer to Equation iv). Higher land supply elasticities in this study are thought to represent the case of Indonesia, hence it is expected that given the same magnitude of export shifts, greater oil palm expansion and the resulting haze externalities will be seen in the country.

Summary and Policy Implications

Model results show that the impacts of shifts in export demand on land use are contingent on whether or not there exists related policy or market failures in the country. Malaysia is likely to demonstrate its commitment towards sustainable forest and environmental management; hence demand enlargement is expected to result in smaller deforestation impacts and less detrimental land preparation practices for agricultural expansion. On the other hand, Indonesia will inevitably see larger increases in oil palm land-use due to the greater availability of land from forest conversion, while less stringent environmental policies will lead to recurring haze externalities.

While impacts of demand enlargement on land use in Malaysia may be relatively smaller, land factor has always been crucial in generating oil palm growth in Malaysia. Technical progress is yet to be an important growth factor. This implies that Malaysia may inevitably encroach into environmentally sensitive forest areas should it continue to rely on land expansion to sustain industrial growth. It is therefore clear that more active Rand D activities to improve factor productivity are imperative in the face of dwindling land supply for oil palm expansion.

The implementation of regional autonomy or decentralization of federal powers in Indonesia may or may not lead to greater institutional failures and consequently deforestation/haze impacts. It all depends on to what extent local administrators are resolute in addressing the institutional failures and legal distortions that have been long entrenched in the country. To a large extent, it is also affected by how local policymakers view the relative importance of agriculture and forest resources as an engine of economic development *vis a vis* other sectors in the economy. A move towards reduction of haze externalities will require among others an extended socio-economic evaluation of all land-use options to identify the most socially desirable resource use plan in the affected region.

Negative impacts of large-scale oil palm mono cropping, besides the haze externalities, include biodiversity loss, agrochemical runoffs from fertilizers and insecticides, and land erosion. Some competing vegetable oil producers have also regarded these environmental impacts as sort of “environmental subsidy” for oil palm production. In a trading world charged with green consumerism issues, this regard may have detrimental trade impacts on palm oil, a vital commodity for both Indonesia and Malaysia.

It is commendable that ASEAN formulated a Regional Haze Action Plan (RHAP) in 1997 to prevent and mitigate the damage from recurrent fires and haze (ASIAN Development Bank, 2001). However, from a game theoretic perspective, it will be to the best interest of both Malaysia and Indonesia to address the haze pollution by identifying a comprehensive and sustained “cooperative solution” in oil palm investment. This perspective has been rather understated in the ASEAN RHAP and the subsequent ministerial negotiations. It has been obvious that Malaysia is relatively land and labour scarce while possessing a distinct advantage in capital and related technology. It will be important for Indonesia, through the provincial or regional governments, to espouse more flexible and transparent procedures on matters governing land procurement and to further demonstrate strict adherence to best practices in environmental regulations and enforcements. Successful land-socio development models of Malaysia, for instance the Federal Land Development Authority (FELDA) model, may also be employed and/or adapted in Indonesia to take into consideration the distinctive cultural setting and needs of local communities. Increased Malaysian investments in Indonesia may also help reduce the flow of illegal workers from Indonesia to Malaysia.

Table 10.1: Partial Equilibrium Model of the Farm Sector with Output Demand and Input Supply Shifts (Hertel's Extended Model)

Commodity Demand

$$\hat{q}_O^D = (1-\alpha(\hat{p}_O^D - \hat{d}_O^D)\varepsilon_O^D + \alpha(\hat{p}_O^E - \hat{d}_O^E)\varepsilon_O^E \quad (1)$$ (1)

Derived Factor Demands Under CRS Technology

$$\hat{x}_k^D = \sum_{k=1}^{N} C_k \sigma_{jk} \hat{r}_k^D + \hat{q}_O^S \quad (2)$$ (2)

Zero Profits

$$\hat{p}_O^S = \sum_{k=1}^{N} C_k \hat{r}_k^D \quad (3)$$ (3)

Factor Supplies

$$\hat{x}_k^S = v_k(\hat{r}_k^S) \quad (4)$$ (4)

Ad valorem – Output Subsidy

$$\hat{p}_O^S = \hat{p}_O^D - \hat{O}_O \quad (5)$$ (5)

Ad valorem – Input Subsidy

$$\hat{r}_k^D = \hat{r}_k^S - \hat{i}_k, \quad (k = 1,2,...n) \quad (6)$$ (6)

Ad valorem – Export Subsidy

$$\hat{p}_O^E = \hat{p}_O^D + \hat{t}_O \quad (7)$$ (7)

Commodity Market Clearing

$$\hat{q}_O^S = \hat{q}_O^D \quad (8)$$ (8)

Factor Market Clearing

$$\hat{x}_k^D = \hat{x}_k^S \quad (9) \qquad (9)$$

Table 10.2: Definitions of Variables

Endogenous Variables

$\hat{q}_O^D$	Percentage change in demand for output by country
$\hat{q}_O^S$	Percentage change in supply of output produced by country
$\hat{p}_O^D$	Percentage change in demand (consumer) price of output in country
$\hat{p}_O^S$	Percentage change in supply (producer) price of output in country
$\hat{p}_O^E$	Percentage change in export price of output
$\hat{x}_k^D$	Percentage change in input *k* demand in country
$\hat{x}_k^S$	Percentage change in input *k* supply in country
$\hat{r}_k^S$	Percentage change in input *k* supply price in country
$\hat{r}_k^D$	Percentage change in input *k* demand price in country

Exogenous Variables

E_O^D Consumer demand elasticities in country

C_k Factor share for input *k* in country

σ_{jk} Allen partial elasticity of substitutions between inputs *j,k* in country

V_k Factor supply elasticities for input *k* in country

Ad-Valorem Policies

$\hat{O}_O$	Percentage change in ad valorem subsidy (tax) on output in country
$\hat{t}_O$	Percentage change in ad valorem export subsidy (tax) imposed by country
$\hat{i}_k$	Percentage change in ad valorem input subsidy (tax) imposed by country

Table 10.3: Base Exogenous Parameter Values Used in the Model

Variables	Short-Run
Domestic demand elasticity (Malaysia and Indonesia)	-0.27
Output supply elasticity – baseline (Malaysia and Indonesia)	0.39
Land supply elasticity (V_L) - base line (Malaysia and Indonesia)	0.2
Labour, chemical, durables and other inputs supply elasticities (Malaysia and Indonesia)	0.5 (labour), ∞
Factor shares – land, labour, chemicals, durables, other inputs (Malaysia and Indonesia)	0.5, 0.2, 0.05, 0.1, 0.15
Base exports – Malaysia	80 percent
Base exports - Indonesia	60 percent

SOURCE: Jamal (1997, 2000).

Table 10.4: Impact of 10 Percent Shift in Export Demand under Varying Land Supply Elasticities (V_L)

	$V_L = 0.2$	$V_L = 0.7$	$V_L = 1.2$	$V_L = 2.0$
Land Demand	2.8	5.8	7.0	8.0
Labour Demand	2.3	4.8	5.9	6.7
Domestic Price	7.8	6.0	5.3	4.7
World Price	7.8	6.0	5.3	4.7
Domestic Output	3.1	6.0	7.3	8.2
Export	4.4	7.9	9.4	10.6

REFERENCES

ASIAN Development Bank, (2001), *Fire, Smoke, and Haze. The ASEAN Response Strategy*, Manila: ASIAN Development Bank.

Aditjondro, G.J, (2000), *The Driving Force of Indonesia's Catastrophic Forest Fires.* Online. Http://forests.org/archive/indomalay/drforind.htm

Barlow, C, (2003), *"Palm Oil Policies and Intervention"*, Chapter in E. Pushparajah and Chee K.H. (eds). Glolbalisation and its Impact on the Palm Oil Industry. Proceedings of an International Planters Conference, June 16-18, 2003.

Barbier, E.B, Bockstael, N, Burgess, J.C, and Strand, I, (1995), *"The Linkages Between Timber Trade and Tropical Deforestation – Indonesia".* World Economy, 18(3).

Casson, A, (1999), *The Hesitant Boom: Indonesia's Oil Palm Sector in an Era of Economic Crisis and Political Change.* Program on the Underlying Causes of Deforestation, Bogor Indonesia: Center for International Forestry Research.

Hertel. T.W, (1989), *"Negotiating Reductions in Agricultural Support: Implications of Technology and Factor Mobility"*, Amer. J. Agr. Econ. August: 559-573.

Shawahid H.O, and Othman, J, (1999), Malaysia, chapter in Glover, D., and Jessup T., *Indonesia's Fires and Haze: The Cost of Catatrophe.* ISEAS, Singapore and IDRC, Canada

Tampubolon, S.M.H, (1998), *Land–Use Planning and Management To Reduce the Impacts of Transboundary Pollution from Fires in South East Asia: Key Policy and Resource Management Stakeholders Perceptions.* Center for Development Studies, Institute for Research, Bogor University of Agriculture. Online. Http://www.icsea.or.id/sea-span/scipol2/STUDY123.htm.

Othman, J, (1997), *"Linking Factor Markets, Environment and Trade: The Case of Oil Palm in Malaysia"*, Jurnal Ekonomi Malaysia, 31: 53-69.

Othman, J, Mohd Fauzi Mohd Jani, and Haji Alias, M, (1998), *"World Palm Oil Market Under Freer Trade: Implications for Malaysia.* ASEAN Economic Bulletin**.** Vol. 15. No. 2 :168-183.

Othman, J, (2000), *"Linking Exchange Rates, Market Failures and Agricultural Land Demand"*, Jurnal Ekonomi Malaysia, 34: 21-37.

Othman, J, (2003), *"Linking Agricultural Trade, Land Demand and Environmental Externalities: Case of Oil Palm in South East Asia"*, ASEAN Economic Bulletin. Vol. 20. No.3: 211-22.

Malaysian Palm Oil Board (MPOB) and Ministry of Primary Industries, (2002), *Malaysian Palm Oil Statistics, 2001.* Bangi, Selangor.

Oil World Annual (2002), Hamburg: ISTA Mielke GmbH.

In: Readings in World Development
Editors: K.C. Roy and S. Chatterjee, pp. 115-127
ISBN 1-59454-947-8

Chapter 11

SEARCHING FOR A BETTER CREDIT SYSTEM TO HELP IMPROVE FARMERS' INCOME: A REFLECTION FROM STUDY ON AGRICULTURAL CREDIT USERS IN LOMBOK, INDONESIA

Taslim Sjah, Donald Cameron and Iean Russell

ABSTRACT

There are some indicators that the program for provision of credit to agriculture producers by the Government of Indonesia has failed to achieve its objectives. Agriculture production and farmers' income have not substantially increased and a high proportion of loans have not been repaid. This paper attempts to provide some thoughts on how to not only improve the current system but also to help farmers to obtain a better standard of living.

A survey seeking credit users' perspectives was conducted in Central Lombok, where the current KKP government credit scheme is provided to agriculture producers. Three villages within the regency were sampled, representing various repayment rates of government credit. Data were collected using face-to-face, semi-structured interviews with 65 farmers who had made use of government or other sources of agricultural credit. Additional information was obtained from key informants and secondary sources to supplement data from farmers.

This study found that there was a little evidence of positive impact of credit on agriculture production and farmers' income, although credit has been highly demanded during most of farmers' lifetimes. To have a significant impact on farmers' livelihood, credit should be provided in larger amounts and be extended to wider purposes than farming only. Given the low socio-economic condition of farmers on Lombok, credit interest rate charged should be low, and be provided with simple application procedures. In addition, information on the objectives of credit provision and the lenders' requirements should also be made clearer to borrowers to avoid misunderstanding. This study also revealed that farmers' attitudes toward credit repayment were influenced by examples provided by government officers and other high profile public figures.

Key words: poverty, agricultural credit, lessons learnt, Lombok, Indonesia.

INTRODUCTION

There has been much credit provision through many government schemes to agricultural producers in Indonesia, as the Government believes that the majority of Indonesian farmers experience insufficient capital to practise proper husbandry in their farming activities. The amount of credit has substantially increased from year to year (Table 11.1). The various schemes involved are aimed at increasing agricultural production (particularly rice) as well as farmers' income. Following the achievement of these two goals and in indicating the usefulness of credit application to farm activities, agricultural producers are expected to be able to return the borrowings.

Table 11.1. Nominal value of national farm credit provision by Government of Indonesia, 1995/1996 – 1999/2000

Year	Amount of credit (Rp 000,000,000)
1995/1996	202.5
	229.9
1997/1998	374.0
1998/1999	7,000.0
1999/2000	8,090.0

Source: Kompas (2000; 2000). Note: AUD 1 = Rp 5,000 (during 1999/2000)

Evaluation based upon the purposes of the credit provision indicated that none of the stated program goals has been achieved. Agricultural production apparently failed to increase. As an indication, rice production dropped from 51.1 million tons in 1996/1997 (when farm credit provided was only Rp 200 billion) to 48.7 million tons in 1998/1999 (when farm credit reached Rp 7 trillion) (Kompas 2000). It appears that farmers' income has also not improved (Kompas 2000). Furthermore, some reports suggest that a significant amount of the credit was not repaid, and the amounts in arrears tended to increase as years proceeded. In the 1970s there was about 80% repayment nationally (Kompas 2000; Kompas 2001), whereas in 1998-2000 the repayment rate was only about 30% (Kompas 2000; Kompas 2000). This apparent failure in achieving goals of credit provision induces suspicion that the current credit system has some weaknesses.

This paper attempts to provide some thoughts on how to not only improve the current system but also to help farmers to obtain a better standard of living. The earlier part of this paper explores agricultural producers' needs and perspectives in relation to managing their farms. The later part examines some strategies for improving the credit systems.

METHODS

A survey seeking credit users' perspectives was conducted in Central Lombok, where at the beginning of the survey the KKP (*Kredit Katahanan Pangan*) government credit scheme was provided to agricultural producers. The survey also covered other schemes found in three selected villages (of three districts), including the KUT (*Kredit Usaha Tani*), the PKP (*Program Ketahanan Pangan*), the UPKD (*Unit Pengelola Keuangan Desa*), and private lenders. A face-to-face survey (Babbie 1990; Miller 1991; Fink and Kosecoff 1998) was applied in the recognition of the low level of literacy amongst respondents, language sensitivity, and the lack of telephones. In addition, the face-to-face format afforded opportunities for mixed languages (local dialect and Indonesian) to clarify understanding according to the particular situation. Farmers were selected from three villages of three districts in Central Lombok. The villages were purposively selected to provide a variety of levels of repayment of government credit, on the basis of information gained from the Office of Agriculture and the Bank (*the Bank Rakyat Indonesia, BRI*). The village of Plambik (Praya Barat Daya district) was chosen to represent full repayment of the current government credit (the KKP). The village of Beraim, Praya Tengah was chosen to represent a poor repayment rate, having most unpaid debt from the previous system of government credit (the KUT). The village of Sengkerang, Praya Timur, was selected to represent a population with part completion of repayments. A farmer group using the KKP or KUT schemes was selected within each village with the help of the leaders of farmers or villages meeting the repayment criteria. Other credit users within the three villages were also sampled, and Table 11.2 presents the distribution of sampled respondents. The information on farmers making use of the KUT, private credit, and other credit schemes in those villages was obtained from leaders of the villages and from farmer groups and extension officers, depending on the informants' ability to supply the required information. Data were collected from July 2001 to March 2002, through in-depth, semi-structured interviews with farmers. The overarching philosophy of qualitative research (Patton 1990) was applied. Data were analysed using descriptive statistics, as appropriate. Some results are presented below.

Table 11.2. Respondent distribution by credit schemes and locations of survey

Credit schemes	Locations of survey			Total
	Plambik (Praya Barat Daya)	Beraim (Praya Tengah)	Sengkerang (Praya Timur)	
KKP	10		10	20
KUT	4	11	10	25
PKP	2		2	4
UPKD	3			3
Private	3	3	7	13
Total	22	14	29	65

Current Credit Demand and Actual Borrowing

Agricultural producers who made use of credit, had low socio-economic conditions, including low income, a situation under which they were forced to use outside funds for their farming activities (Sjah et al. 2004). Indeed, farmers had a long experience with credit, particularly from private sources. They perceived credit, either from government or private sources, as debt that must be returned, and it carries risk. Although borrowings carry risk, especially that from private sources, farmers still demand more credit than currently received.

Interviews with farmer respondents revealed that demand for credit by agricultural producers had not been fulfilled. In general, farmers could obtain only about half of the amount they were willing to take. Furthermore, some farmers could not get credit at all. This figure is confirmed for all government credit schemes, except for the PKP credit, which could satisfy 80% of the demand. In contrast, farmers borrowing from private sources could fulfill almost all of desired credit amount (Table 11.3).

Table 11.3. Average desired and actual amount of borrowing of farmer respondents

Credit scheme	Amount (Rp)			Percentage obtained
	Desired	Obtained	Difference	
KKP	1,515,789	822,000	693,789	54
KUT	1,562,632	630,315	932,317	40
PKP	550,000	437,500	112,500	80
UPKD	833,333	450,000	383,333	54
Private	1,069,231	1,060,000	9,231	99
Aggregate	1,329,138	767,729	561,409	58

There were three major reasons for desiring to obtain the credit amount. Of 65 farmer respondents, 30% wanted to meet not only their farm costs, but also to cover costs for running other businesses and for living. This is followed by respondents who calculated the amount of their desired borrowing to be matched with their repayment capabilities (26%). There were 24% of respondents wishing to borrow according to their farm needs at the time. Other reasons for the desired amount were minor (5% or less each), and included: follow the rule of the credit organizers or lenders; participate in the credit scheme; give chance to other people to borrow; and do speculation. Two farmers forgot their reasons for borrowing.

When triangulated with how the farmer respondents decide the desired credit amount, similar factors were dominating but with the first and the second order reversed. The farmers calculated the desired amount to match their farm needs (22 respondents or 33% responses), and to suffice more than farm needs (30%). The third factor calculated was the farmers' repayment capability and also their attitude to risk bearing (16%).

A total of 30 farmers indicated a difference between the amount of credit desired and obtained, and they revealed reasons behind it. The deficit was mainly (80%) due to the rules of credit organizers or lenders, who set out the certain amount below the borrowers' wishes. The allowable amount was determined in such a way that more farmers could borrow. The credit providers think that it is better to serve more people with smaller amounts of credit than to serve fewer people with larger amounts. Implicitly, this indicates that the supply of credit is limited. The second reason for the difference was indeed due to this indication (13% of responses). Two farmer respondents could get more than was set out for each hectare of land because they manipulated their farm sizes when applying for the credit.

The amount of credit obtained by agricultural producers varies amongst the credit schemes. Farmers could get the largest amount from the private money lenders. Among the government schemes, farmers received the biggest amount from the KKP credit, then the KUT, the UPKD, and the PKP credit.

The credit fulfilment was about 50% for all government schemes, except for the PKP credit, which achieved 80% fulfilment. The reason for higher desire fulfilment of the KKP scheme may relate to the fact this scheme was targeted to farmers with smaller farm size (no more than 0.50 hectare). Smaller farm size requires less cost and also generates lower income than that of bigger farms. Accordingly, the farmers wished to take only a small amount of borrowing, and this quite matched with the credit provision.

Private providers are able to supply almost all of the farmers' needs for credit, and attempt to earn profit from lending money. However, given the private providers charge higher costs and are a higher risk source than government credit, farmers generally tended to avoid borrowing from them. If they have to borrow from a private lender, then they calculate very carefully not to exceed the amount urgently needed.

Farmers Did Not Always Allocate Credit to Farming Activities

Agricultural producers seek credit to finance their farming activities. This is particularly true in relation to the government credit scheme, otherwise the farmers would not be allowed to apply. However, funds borrowed may be allocated to other purposes at times.

In practice, the borrowed amount of credit was allocated to the farms by the majority of respondents (74%). The major reason (27 respondents, 56%) for farmers to do this was because the credit amount was just sufficient or even less than the required farm costs. Due to this shortage the farmers had no way to distort the credit allocation. One third of the farmers, who allocated the credit to their farms only, intended to obtain good production so that they can expect to at least repay back their debt. Four farmer respondents had no available reasons to allocate borrowings to their farms.

There were 15 farmer respondents (23%) who admitted distorting the credit allocation. This was due to other immediate needs to be fulfilled at the times (53%) like household consumption and children's school costs, investment in non farming businesses (33%) such as trading, and an indiscipline use of credit (13%). These 15 farmers and others who could not obtain sufficient funds, practice their farming by reducing the use of agricultural inputs (Sjah et al. 2003).

Monitoring by lenders of whether credit was actually allocated for farm needs rarely occurred. Credit officers sometimes visit farmers in the area 1-3 times (Key Informant, KI1-5). The first visit was to ensure that credit was given to the right persons (who are small farmers). Later visits, which are usually made at harvest times, were intended for improving repayment collection.

To What Extent Could Credit Assist Farmers?

Evaluation on what farm credit could do in farming practiced by respondents was based on direct responses obtained from interviewed farmers. Aspects of examination were related to the purposes of farm credit provision.

Firstly, farm credit could help increase agricultural production by 11%. This figure is an average, counted from farmers' own assessment of production improvement due to credit use. Farmers indicated their assessment in percentage or production improvement. If respondents revealed improvement in terms of quantity of production, then this is converted into percentage. Farmers were also asked to provide reasons for their assessments.

The same numbers of farmer respondents indicated 'positive' and 'no' impacts of credit on agricultural production. Of the 30 farmers who indicated a positive impact of credit, 28 thought that the production improvement originated from farm intensification. These farmers suggested that credit availability enabled them to apply more fertilizers, seeds, pesticides, and better maintenance. Two farmers thought the improvement came from timely farm husbandry. They considered that the availability of credit enabled farmers to implement practices without delay, especially in catching up with water availability from rain.

A total of 30 farmer respondents observed that using credit had no impact on increasing agricultural production. These farmers observed no difference in their farm production level with or without credit. The majority of these farmers (16 respondents, 53%) applied the same level of intensification from year to year, such that the production they observed remained the same. There were 10 farmer respondents who experienced production failures due to disease attacks or adverse weather conditions at the time of credit use. Finally, four respondents reported no production differences, explaining this in terms of the small size of their farms and the fact that they were always in debt.

Secondly, farm credit was thought by farmers to improve their income by 5%. Of the 30 farmers who reported a production increase, only 22 (73%) reported income improvement. The income increase was attributed to production increase (21 respondents, 95%), or to both production and price increase together (one respondent, 5%).

Of the eight farmers reporting a production increase, but no income increase, four claimed production costs had increased to the same extent as farm income, three claimed that the production increase was accompanied by a price drop, and one farmer had no record of income and accordingly could not observe any difference.

There were 30 farmer respondents who reported no impact of credit use on income improvement for several reasons. Nearly half of them (14 respondents) reported the same level of intensification either with or without credit, so that the impact of credit could not be determined. Seven of them stated that there was no production increase, and therefore no income increase. Four respondents held the belief that production and income level depended on weather or economic conditions, and that all depended upon luck. The other four respondents stated that there was no difference between use and non-use of credit since they had always been in debt. Another farmer could not determine whether there was any difference, as he had only a small farm, and believed that credit could not have any impact on production or income improvement.

It can be concluded that credit had little impact in terms of substantially increasing agricultural production and farmers' net income. However, the greater role for credit, which was frequently cited by farmers, was in helping poor farmers to sustain their farm production and thus their livelihood.

Finally, there was a mix of repayment levels amongst the credit schemes and borrowing farmers. The farmers using the KKP government credit scheme could be classified into two groups. The first group, from Plambik village in the district of Praya Barat Daya, consisted of 10 farmers who had fully repaid their debt (although these were purposively sampled). The leader of this farmer group reported that other farmers in the group had also met their full responsibility. The second group, also comprised of 10 sampled farmers, was surveyed purposefully to represent late or low repayment levels. These farmers were from the village of Sengkerang, in the district of Praya Timur. The majority of these borrowers had partly repaid their loan (approximately 20-30%) and two had fully met their obligation. The leaders of these farmers indicated the repayment figure was about ten percent.

The repayment rates of the farmers who used the KUT scheme showed very high variation. There was a group of KUT farmers, all from the village of Sengkerang, who had not paid back their borrowing at all. Half of them stated that they had forgotten that they had borrowed the credit in 1998 (the last KUT distribution in the village). Their farmer leader reported the case of zero repayment in his group was caused by production failure at the time credit repayment was due (in 1999). He stated that although the following years had been good for production, farmers have been discouraged in making repayments by the belief that the government would clear the credit.

While the majority of the KUT borrowers sampled in the villages of Plambik and Beraim had met their total obligation, some had only partly repaid and a very small proportion of farmers had made no repayments at all. Some key informants (farmer leaders) reported that the zero repayment had occurred in the case of borrowers who left their villages, at least temporarily (they went to Malaysia or Bali for paid employment). Government officers, including extension officers, were still attempting to collect repayments from all those who had not fully repaid their KUT borrowings.

The PKP scheme, current in 2002, was launched at about the same times as the KKP and distributed to some farmers who could not obtain the KKP credit in the village of Sengkerang. This was due for repayment by December 2001. In 2002, there were 15 of 72 recipients who had only partly repaid or had not repaid at all. Their leader stated that the defaulting farmers had asked for an extension. Two members of the PKP scheme were sampled, but claimed that their time for repayment had not yet fallen due. Farmers who had just finished their repayment were borrowing again under the same scheme. Similarly, the PKP users in the village of Plambik were borrowing for the third time, but repayment on these loans was not due at the time of sampling. Information from the leader indicated that the first credit distribution was successful (100% repayment, with six late in repayment), and so was the second (with eight delayed repayments).

The UPKD credit scheme was utilized only in the village of Plambik. Borrowings under this scheme were due in April 2002, hence the repayment rate could not be assessed at the time of survey. However, one of the sample members had already repaid fully his UPKD borrowing. Informants reported that the previous UPKD distribution had experienced 100% repayment, although some occurred one or two months late.

In addition to government schemes, farmers also had access to private sources of credit. Private credit users surveyed in all three villages comprised of only 13 respondents. Only two of them had their debt due, and they had met their obligation. The remaining respondents could not be rated, given that the time for repayment of their loans had not fallen due. However, the interviews generated a general impression that private credit users had repaid their previous borrowings so that they were allowed to borrow again.

There were many reasons for credit repayment and these have been reported in Sjah *et al.* (2003; 2003). Some points are highlighted here. In order to make credit repayment, three interrelated factors must exist. These are financial capability, positive borrowers' character and positive motivation. The first factor explains that when there is financial capability then repayment is possible to be made. In contrast, borrowers have little chance of repaying their debt when they are in the difficult situation of financial incapability. If financial capability exists, the second factor is required for repayment to occur. Furthermore, financial capability means nothing if borrowers have a 'negative character'. Farmer respondents who were responsible, aware of having debt, committed to keeping a promise, keen to avoid shame, and having respect for credit officers, made repayments. Sometimes the borrower's character was superior to their financial capability. For instance, some farmers were prepared to borrow again (from the same or other lenders) in order to make their repayments on time.

The third factor, borrowers' motivation, could not be underestimated in terms of its importance in influencing repayment of borrowings. In particular, the motivation to obtain future borrowings had led borrowers to repay their debt even before its due date, and this was the case for a majority of farmers using the KKP credit in the village of Plambik, in the district of Praya Barat Daya. Credit officers could motivate borrowers to make the repayment by conducting frequent visits and by being friendly to the borrowers. Another motivation for borrowers to make their repayment as soon as possible was the credit-associated risk. The perceived credit risk that farmers wished to shed included accumulated interest and feeling pressured or burdened for having debt, especially past the due date. As with other small farmers in other areas, such as in Nepal (Hamal and Anderson 1982; Anderson and Hamal 1983), Mexico (Moscardi and de Janvry 1977), and Brazil (Dillon and Scandizzo 1978), credit users in Lombok were risk avoiders.

The case of low repayment of government credit, especially the KUT, was found to be more complex. There were significant numbers of farmers not repaying their debt due to an unrealistic perception that government credit was a gift for the community so that their debt would be cleared. This may have been construed through their experience of credit clearance. This has occurred in the history of government credit distribution in Indonesia, when farmers' debts were cleared, i.e. in 1998 when the government cleared the 1985-1995 farmers' remaining debt (Kompas 2000; Kompas 2000). Farmers may have anticipated credit clearance would also apply to their loans. Kelly (1955) explains this farmers' rationalization as a construction corollary, whereby people anticipate events by construing their replications. This construction may appear in people's attitude, beliefs, opinions, and values (Bock 1976). In addition, the example of prominent borrowers who had not fully repaid their debts may have become excuses for some farmers not to meet their obligation, reasoning for their part that they would be losers if they repaid their loans while others did not.

IMPROVING CREDIT SYSTEMS

The guidelines for improving credit systems can be drawn from four broad implications, relating to credit distribution, monitoring, collection, and education and extension for farmers. Prior to the implementation of these, attention should be given to the amount of credit provided for the individual borrower and the purpose of credit. It was evident that the amount of credit received by farmers was less than the amount desired, and it become apparent that the received amount was too small to have a noticeable impact on agricultural production and farmers' income. The ground for this reasoning is that, with that amount, farmers could just implement a 'minimal' farming practise, instead of an 'optimal' use of agricultural inputs (such as sufficient fertilizer, quality seeds, and proper crop maintenance). Accordingly, farmers generated less than optimal production and income.

Furthermore, given the small size of farm possession and farm families have plenty of spare time during the year, credit provision should not be restricted to only farming purpose but be extended to cover other income generating activities. It was proven that there were 54 farm families out of 65 respondents who could generate substantial extra incomes from engaging in non-farm activities, which mainly include trading and home industries.

As family members are involved in the use of credit (in family's businesses) then family members should also be made responsible in receiving credit. Even, in the case of credit provision to farming purpose only, family members (especially wives) should at least know that their families are using credit. This is to do check and balance in the use of credit as well as in repaying the loan.

Credit Distribution

Credit has to be distributed with the right image and a clear message from the beginning of the provision that receivers have to repay it. One of many reasons for not repaying a loan was that credit clients did not receive the right image and an accurate message. Some recipients perceived the credit as a gift or assistance (free) from government and therefore not needing to be repaid. Of particular importance is the message in the word 'assistance' (*bantuan*) that can convey some different meanings. One is a free gift. Another is that the credit itself is a subsidized loan so that it assists in terms of lowering borrowing costs.

Delivering a clear and accurate message may be done with allocating sufficient time for revealing related information about credit to borrowers, a month or two before its distribution. August or September is an appropriate time to deliver messages about credit that will be distributed at the beginning of the wet planting season, which starts in October or November within the year.

Credit should also be distributed at the right time, allowing farmers to allocate for farm costs. The right time here means that credit is received not too early and not too late. Following the planting season (October or November, depending on locations and yearly variation), credit should be distributed one or two weeks before that. If credit arrives too early, it could be spent on other than farm needs, recognizing that farmers have insufficient income to meet other needs in addition to farm cost needs. In turn, an early credit arrival could result in reduced farming application and predictably lower farm production, which could lead to lower income and then financially lower capability to repay the loan. If credit comes late, farmers tend to seek borrowing from other providers, which in villages are mainly private money lenders. These loan providers usually charge high interest rates, and therefore create difficulties for farmer borrowers. In brief, the right time provision of credit is crucial for farmers to do proper husbandry practices, such as sufficient amount and on-time fertilizing.

Selection processes should ensure the right borrowers. It has been known that some people could borrow without having farm land, or with reporting inaccurate farm size. Selection processes should allow time to check the accuracy of information both by village level government and above that. Without checking, credit could be given to inappropriate borrowers, e.g. those who are not in the farm size range of 0.10 – 2.00 ha. Selection should be done strictly using the requirements of the credit schemes.

Credit Monitoring

Efforts should be made to monitor credit distribution and allocation, and repayment collection. Monitoring of credit distribution and allocation will help prevent leaking or avoid credit being given to people not initially intended. Included in distribution monitoring is to ensure that credit is distributed at the scheduled time or the distribution is not delayed. As mentioned before, delayed distribution can cause farmers to borrow from other lenders (although with higher interest rates) or to sacrifice proper farming practices. Another reason to do monitoring is to avoid people holding the fund from taking benefit by delaying distribution through obtaining daily interest from a bank where the fund is deposited.

It is also important to monitor clients' business activities. As farm credit is provided for farming activity, then monitoring should ensure that the funds are not allocated otherwise. If a non-farming use is detected then monitoring officers should be suspicious that credit could have been given to wrong persons, and action can be taken immediately to prevent a further loss of funds. For clients who did not misuse loans, monitoring is still crucial in knowing the time when their income availability is the best for repayment. The best income available for farmers is just after crop harvest (or more precisely after production sale). Therefore, obviously it is not too hard for monitoring officers to detect this time, when collection effort is best done. Private providers do this monitoring, and collect credit repayments more successfully than government credit officers. Some farmers indicated that they did not repay government loans due to late collection by officers.

Repayment Collection

Knowing the time when the borrowers have income available makes it easier to follow up with repayment collection. Collection at the wrong time, such as before crop production and after income has been spent, is not effective. The farmers' income was very limited and on many occasions was insufficient to cover the costs of living, let alone to manage debt repayments. Collection time is crucial to making good credit repayment.

Furthermore, to encourage repayment, borrowers may require incentives for meeting their obligation on time. An incentive could be in the form of a bonus (taken from the repayment) of a small percentage of interest paid, for those who repay on or before the time.

Another thing to be recognized is the form of repayment, which is not only cash but also in the form of production with suitable price. Many farmers were reluctant to sell their production after harvest for low prices (that is lower than floor price set out by the government itself). If the Government is committed to its policy (of floor price) then it should agree to accept farmers' production at the scheduled prices. It may be a good idea too to do this, so that farmers could not have an excuse for late collection action by the government officers.

Education and Extension for Credit Clients

Finally, attention needs to be paid to education and extension for farmers to make borrowers aware that they have a debt that must be returned. This aspect is an important consideration given that some farmers perceived credit unrealistically. However, it may be a very difficult task, given that some farmers tend not to meet their obligation due to long experiences of observing other people's behaviour of not repaying their debt. Use of examples of good behaviour on the part of big borrowers may be an effective means to change these small farmers' behaviour. Within rural life, farmer leaders play an important role as they are generally heard and followed by farmers (they are elected by the farming community themselves). Thus, education should also be aimed at those leaders and utilise them as agents for changing farmers' behaviour, in addition to education of farmers.

CONCLUSION

Although borrowings, especially that from private sources, are risky, agricultural producers still demand more credit than currently received. The use of credit was found to have little positive impact on agricultural production and farmers' income, but has a significant role in helping farmers to continue farming practices and thus their livelihood. To have a significant impact on farmers' livelihood, credit should be provided in larger amounts and be extended for more than farming purposes only. Given the low socio-economic condition of farmers in Lombok, credit should charge a low interest rate and be provided with simple application procedures. In addition, information on the objectives of credit provision and the lenders' requirements should also be made clearer to borrowers to avoid misunderstanding. This study also revealed that farmers' attitudes toward credit repayment were influenced by examples provided by government officers and other high profile public figures.

REFERENCES

Anderson, J.R, and Hamal, K.B, (1983), *"Risk and Rice Technology in Nepal,"* Indian Journal of Agricultural Economics 38(2): 217-222.

Babbie, E, (1990), *Survey Research Methods,* Belmont, California: Wadworth Publishing Company.

Bock, I.M, (1976), *National Survey of Market Information Requirements of Primary Producers,* Canberra, Agricultural Extension Research Unit, School of Agriculture and Forestry, University of Melbourne.

Dillon, J.L. and Scandizzo, P.L, (1978), *"Risk Attitudes of Subsistence Farmers in Northeast Brazil: a Sampling Approach."* American Journal of Agricultural Economics 60(3): 425-435.

Fink, A. and J. Kosecoff, (1998), *How to conduct a survey: A step-by-step guide,* London: Sage Publications.

Hamal, K.B. and Anderson, J.K, (1982), *"A note on decreasing absolute risk aversion among farmers in Nepal."* American Journal of Agricultural Economics, 26(3): 220-225.

Kelly, G.A, (1955), *The Psychology of Personal Constructs,* New York: Norton.

Kompas, (2000), *Deptan siapkan kredit pengembangan agribisnis* (Department of Agriculture prepares credit for agribusiness development). Kompas: Jakarta.

Kompas, (2000), *Hentikan penyaluran KUT lewat LSM* (Stop distributing farm credit through NGOs). Kompas: Jakarta.

Kompas, (2000), *Kredit usaha tani di persimpangan jalan* (Farm credit is in the cross roads). Kompas: Jakarta.

Kompas, (2000), *Pengembalian KUT hanya 30 persen* (Repayment of farm credit was only 30%). Kompas: Jakarta.

Kompas, (2000), *Petani anggap KUT sama dengan JPS* (Farmers assume farm credit as social food security). Kompas: Jakarta.

Kompas, (2000), *Setelah Bimas, KUT, KKP, lalu...* (After mass supervision credit, farm credit, food sufficiency credit then …). Kompas: Jakarta.

Kompas, (2001), *80 persen dana KUT macet* (80% farm credit fund was congested). Kompas: Jakarta.

Miller, D.C, (1991), *Handbook of Research Design and Social Measurement.* Newbury Park, California: Sage.

Moscardi, E. and de Janvry, A, (1977), *"Attitudes toward risk among peasants: an econometric approach."* American Journal of Agricultural Economics 59(4): 710-716.

Patton, M.Q, (1990), *Qualitative Evaluation and Research Methods.* Newbury Park, California: Sage Publications.

Sjah, T., Cameron, D, and Russell, I, (2003), *"Acceptance and repayment of agricultural credit in Lombok Indonesia: Farmers' perspectives."* Komunitas, Journal of Rural Studies **5**(1-2): 74-91.

Sjah, T., Cameron, D and Russell, I, (2003), *Factors contributing to the performance of agricultural credit in Lombok Indonesia.* 14th International Farm Management Congress: Farming at the edge, Perth, International Farm Management Congress 2003.

Sjah, T., Cameron, D and Russell, I, (2004), "Profile of farmers making use of agricultural credit in Central Lombok, Indonesia." *Agroteksos* 14(1): 59-67.

Sjah, T., Russell, I and Cameron, D, (2003), *Farming under constrained budget: Practices of agricultural credit users in Central Lombok Indonesia.* The 1st Australian Farming Systems Conference, Toowoomba, Queensland, Australian Farming Systems Association (AFSA).

In: Readings in World Development
Editors: K.C. Roy and S. Chatterjee, pp. 129-153
ISBN 1-59454-947-8

Chapter 12

GENDER INEQUALITY AND POVERTY: THE KENYAN CASE

Tabitha W. Kiriti and K. C. Roy

ABSTRACT

Socio-economic conditions in Kenya are deteriorating, and poverty rates are on the rise. This article finds that a significant and rising incidence of absolute poverty exists in Kenya and women suffer from poverty more often than men. This is more pronounced in female-headed households. The high poverty rates among women can be linked to their unequal situation in the labour market, their lack of voice and participation in decision-making in the family/household and other institutions and because gender disparities persist in access and control of human, economic and social reforms.

The female/male ratios in Kenyan decision-making institutions are highly skewed against women and they experience unfavourable enrolment ratios in primary, secondary and tertiary institutions. The share of income earned by women is much lower than men's share. The GDI and GEM, their weaknesses not withstanding, also show that gender inequality exists in Kenya.

INTRODUCTION

Gender inequality involves the denial of opportunities and denial of equal rights on the basis of gender. Enjoyment of opportunities and allocation of resources are based on gender. Gender inequality is generally manifested in unequal rights for women of access to basic social services such as education and health; unequal opportunities for participation in political and economic decision-making, nationally and at the household level; unequal rights for equal work; unequal protection under the law; preference for male children; violence against women and so on. Women face constraints in accessing the basic resources needed to participate fully in productive earning opportunities, thereby increasing their probability of falling into poverty or making it difficult for them to get out of poverty.

This paper examines the link between gender inequality and poverty in Kenya. It first examines the various ways that agricultural resources are unequally allocated based on gender, examines the indicators of gender inequality and then provides a link between these and poverty in Kenya.

Gender Inequality in the Allocation of Agricultural Resources

Access to critical resources provides an alternative way of conceptualising determinants of women's class position, because it is broader and more flexible than the idea of relationship to means of production, and it applies to class and gender struggle both inside and outside the household (Sorensen, 1990). In her work on the Kipsigis society in Kenya, Sorensen (1990) found that besides satisfying the family's need for food, clean clothes and a nice and tidy home, women's activities include participating in cash crop production, tending cattle, and other income generating activities. Men's responsibility for taking care of the family is primarily fulfilled through provision of cash, mainly through wage labour, and production and sale of cash crops such as tea. The pattern of resource control in this society heavily favours men as they control the major means of production, income and surpluses.

Extension of the market system tends to marginalise rural women economically because males take control of cash and often assume responsibility for activities earning cash (Boserup, 1970; Kennedy and Oniang'o, 1990; Sorensen, 1990; Gross and Underwood, 1971). These authors show that cash cropping has reduced the opportunities for rural women to produce subsistence crops and provide food for their families, especially children. It is not uncommon for women's labour in certain tasks, such as weeding, to increase to a greater extent than men's labour when the agricultural chores associated with cash crops become particularly labour intensive (Spring, 1978). Research on time allocation in Africa by Julin (1993) and Henn (1988) support this view.

Where the structure of agriculture is becoming commercialised, women's roles and thus their economic status are changing. In many regions of the Third world, women are still unremunerated for the long hours they contribute to the tending of commercial crops. As revenue-generating cash cropping rises in importance, the proportion of resources controlled by women tends to diminish. This is largely due to the fact that household resources, such as land and inputs, are transferred away from women's crops in order to promote the production of cash crops (Davison, 1988).

Afonja (1986) shows how women's limited access to land has been a critical factor in explaining gender inequality. She demonstrates how the introduction of cocoa and tenancy in Ile-Ife has led to increased economic differentiation among men, while women are unified in a lower stratum of the peasantry with less control over land, crops and income.

Land adjudication and registration has made women's situations worse because land titles belong to men (Saito, 1992). This makes it difficult to access extension services and formal credit. In any case, credit institutions are situated far away in urban areas. Lack of collateral, transaction costs and long distances, limited education and unfamiliarity with banking procedures, increase the opportunity cost of forgone labour because of their multiple obligations in the household and the farm.

Male out-migration has had a number of adverse consequences for women in terms of time and labour and, less directly on the welfare of their families and on the resource base. Women are constantly making adjustments within a changing set of limitations on their time and labour to provide for the family's subsistence and welfare. They are more bound to the homestead, sometimes waiting for remittances that never come or are too little or too late to purchase fertilizer or hire labour for the agricultural season. Agricultural inputs and training are rarely provided to female farmers. Even efforts to reduce poverty through land reform have been found to reduce female income and economic status because they distribute land titles only to male heads of households (Todaro, 1997). Cultural and social barriers to women's integration into agricultural programs remain strong because in many countries, women's income is perceived as a threat to men's authority. While men are taught new agricultural techniques to increase their productivity, women, if involved at all, are trained to perform low-productivity tasks that are considered compatible with their traditional roles, such as sewing, cooking, or basic hygiene. Women's components of development projects are frequently little more than welfare programs that fail to improve economic well being. Furthermore, these projects tend to depend on the unpaid work of women, while men are remunerated for their efforts (Todaro, 1997).

Households with a male present are 14 times more likely than those headed by a female to have received detailed data on credit and new improved farming practices of all kinds (Spring, 1978; Staudt, 1985). When new agricultural technologies are introduced, women are by-passed in training, credit extension and land reform programs. Extension agents tend to be men who deal with male clients. An increase in family income arising from cash crop production results in a new loss to women as in some societies males take possession of any cash income earned by females, or most of it, and use it for their own ends. Just as Sen (1981) demonstrated that famine could occur in the midst of an increase in aggregate food availability, poverty amongst women and children can increase with rising aggregate family income (Tisdell, 1999).

There is widespread discrimination against women in that few agricultural extension services are directed to them, few women are contacted, female-headed households are less visited and supported by advisers and also members from female-headed households join farmers training centres at a lower rate than members from male-headed households. Most of the males who visit training centres are old retired men who attend because of their high status in society (World Bank, 1989; Bay, 1982). Female-headed households in general have less access to agricultural advice than male-headed ones (Staudt, 1985). Whether the women have large farms, are rich, poor or innovative, the pattern of gender discrimination remains. This may have negative implications for the food production, since women provide most of the food. Women's access to new agricultural technology is limited. Technologies appropriate for household activities, farming objectives, and production conditions for women are lacking. They overlook the requirements of women. The inadequate supply of suitable labour and energy saving farm and household technologies for women's activities impairs women's productivity. This is because technology is mainly male oriented such as heavy machinery, tractors, ploughs and so on. Women use crude implements such as hoes, machetes, cutlasses and so on, which are very slow and labour intensive. Lack of title or secure tenure and access to small dispersed and remote plots are strong disincentives to adopting new agricultural techniques. Diseconomies of scale not only reduce women's yields but cause extension agents to dismiss women as non-adopters of new technologies (Roy and Tisdell, 1993; Saito, 1992; Staudt, 1985).

Culture and Allocation of Resources

Men's control over labour as a factor of production can translate into claims on women's labour for cultivation of the husband's compound or fields. In effect, the culturally determined rules of access to and control over resources may constrain women as much as external biases in providing access to farm support services (Palmer, 1991). The cultural norms actually may predetermine unequal access to agricultural inputs, marketing services, and farmers' organisations because of the link between farm support services and land title, for which women are rarely eligible (Jiggins, 1989).

In households where women and men have separate accounting unit resources (labour and working capital), household resource use is most efficient when they enjoy equal access to land and other factor markets and in product markets (Palmer, 1991). Unequal access means unequal barter or bargaining capabilities and sub-optimal resource allocations.

The intra-household allocation of resources cannot be disassociated from relations of power within the household and within the community with overlapping livelihoods. The access to and control over productive resources are also a function of social status, which can be ascribed or achieved. The norms and set of values embedded in a particular culture bring with them entitlements or rights ascribed to certain categories of persons to particular shares, often related to basic subsistence needs, such as food and clothing. The way in which domestic groups confer power to some members based on age and gender differences, reflects the norms of distributional justice of the group or society. An individual is, therefore, subject to socially determined valuation that becomes internalised through a socialisation process. The inequality of those valuations is evident between men and women. Male domination, perceived as embedded in cultural norms and institutions, characterises intra-household power relations and resource allocation patterns (Kiriti, et al, 2003b).

Most formal and legal rights to land have been given to men, while women only have user rights to some of the land. This may affect their productivity because of lack of security. Women in Kenya do not inherit land, which means that they depend on their male relatives both when it comes to land distribution and decisions about farming. If a woman chooses to remain unmarried, is divorced or widowed, she does not have any rights to land and will be in a very exposed situation. This lack of security and access to land means that women cannot undertake large investments. An increase in legal rights to land and support could increase overall productivity.

Ethical practices also make it difficult for women to access extension services since most extension officers are men. Information is usually passed on to men who do not pass it on to women. Saito et al. (1994) found that in Kenya, extension positively affected the gross value of output of male farmers but not of female farmers, all other variables being held constant. Male extension agents are generally unaware of the need to communicate differently with women and view women as farmer's wives and not farmers by their own right. Rural women tend to be shy and reluctant to speak up in the presence of male agents from the same village. They lack confidence because they are less educated and have less contact with the outside world. They see men as authority figures whose decisions they are to follow (Roy and Tisdell, 1993; Saito 1992; Kennedy and Peters, 1992).

Where wives head households due to the continued absence of husbands (*de facto*), output may be low because women are not decision-makers. Men, though absent, want to make all the decisions concerning the household and the allocation of resources (Kiriti, et al, 2003a). They control the output, which they sell but do not buy the inputs. Women rely on remittances which come from their husbands and when it comes it is either too little or too late that it can't be used to buy inputs.

ALLOCATION OF RESOURCES AND BARGAINING POWER

The diversity of needs and interests among family members, and the allocation of the scarce resources, are determined by the degree of decision-making power possessed by each negotiating party (Bennett, 1983). Furthermore, not all household members have equal bargaining power to enforce their own definition of utility and therefore not all members benefit equally from the way resources are actually allocated. This view interprets observed inequalities in the distribution of household resources, not as the most efficient reaction to the prevailing wage/price situation or as evidence of the household's maximising behaviour, but as evidence of structural asymmetries in the economic, social, and legal position of men and women, which give the two unequal bargaining power (Bennett, 1983).

Bargaining power or a household member's ability to realise personal allocational priorities, can be influenced by the individual's contribution to the household income and some studies have shown that increases in women's income have given women more decision-making power and control over the distribution of resources within the household. Acharya and Bennett (1983) found that women's involvement in market activities gives them much greater power within the household in terms of their input in all aspects of household and resource allocation decisions. At the same time, confining women's work to the domestic and subsistence sectors reduces their power vis-à-vis men in the household.

Bargaining models often define an individual's "threat points" in terms of his or her market earnings or individual assets. Increasing one's economic valuation improves that individual's bargaining power. The greater a woman's net control of income, the greater her leverage in other household economic and domestic decisions, and the greater her overall "voice and vote" (leadership) in the relationship. Tisdell (1999) identifies five factors that may increase the threat power of a married woman in relation to her husband or partner; (1) her capability of finding independent employment and the level of income earned by her; (2) her ownership of property and ability to transfer, inherit and bequest property; (3) her rights to collective family assets in the event of dissolution of marriage; (4) her ability to institute divorce proceedings, especially if the legal hurdles to divorce are minimal; and (5) contacts with influential networks in a community.

However, legal, institutional, and social factors also affect bargaining power. For example, property rights could easily have a much bigger impact than changes in relative earnings of men and women (Folbre, 1992). The World Bank (1996) says that women and children are more vulnerable because tradition gives them less decision making power and less control over assets than men, while at the same time, their opportunities to engage in remunerative activities, and therefore to acquire their own assets, are more limited.

Compared with men, women are disadvantaged in their access to and control of a wide range of assets. With fewer assets and more precarious claims to assets, women are more risk-averse, more vulnerable, have a weaker bargaining position within the household, and consequently are less in a position to respond to economic opportunities. Access to land is not an end in itself. Access to land and other productive resources are critical in creating wealth and generating growth.

The next section examines the indicators of gender inequality. Some of the indicators, especially the human development index (HDI), gender-related development index (GDI) and the gender empowerment measure (GEM), were introduced by the UNDP in its 1995 and 1997 Human Development Reports.

Human Development Index

The UNDP (1998) defines human development as a process of enlarging people's choices. It tries to measure it by the Human Development Index (HDI). HDI measures the overall achievements in a country in three basic dimensions of human development: longevity, knowledge and a decent standard of living. It is measured by life expectancy, educational attainment (adult literacy and combined primary, secondary and tertiary enrolment) and adjusted per capita income in US$ purchasing power parity (PPP). Longevity and knowledge refer to the formation of human capabilities. Income is a proxy measure for the choices people have in putting their capabilities to use. HDI is the equally weighted sum of deprivation of a country with respect to each of the three components: life expectancy at birth, literacy, and real income per head (UNDP, 1995).

The HDI sets a minimum for each of these components and then shows where each country stands in relation to these scales expressed as a value between 0 and 1. For example, since the minimum adult literacy rate is 0 percent and the maximum is 100 percent, the literacy component of knowledge for a country where the literacy rate is 75 percent would be 0.75. Similarly, the minimum for life expectancy is 25 years and the maximum 85 years, so the longevity component for a country where life expectancy is 55 years would be 0.5. For income, the minimum is $100(Purchasing Power Parity)(PPP) and the maximum is $40000(PPP). Income above the average world income is adjusted using a progressively higher discount rate. The scores for the three dimensions are then averaged in an overall index. The HDI facilitates the determination of priorities for policy intervention and the evaluation of progress over time. It also permits instructive comparisons of the experiences within and between different countries (UNDP, 1995).

The HDI offers an alternative to GNP and GDP for measuring the relative socio-economic progress at national and local levels. Comparing HDI and per capita income ranks of countries, regions or ethnic groups within countries highlights the relationship between their material wealth and income on the one hand and their human development on the other. A negative gap implies the potential of redirecting resources to human development.

Table 12.1 shows the Human Development Indices for Kenya and Kenya's HDI rank compared to other UN member countries. Compared to other nations, Kenya failed to improve its human development ranking – it was 134th position in 1975 and remained there in 2000.

Table 12.1: Human Development Indices for Kenya: 1994 – 2000

Year	HDI Rank (among UN member countries)	HDI Value
1975	134	0.443
1980	134	0.489
1985	134	0.512
1990	113	0.533
1994	134	0.463
1995	137	0.523
1997	136	0.519*
1998	138	0.506*
1999	134	0.513*
2000	134	0.513*

Source: UNDP: Human Development Reports (various issues)
* Not comparable with other figures

The table shows that Kenya has not been faring well even when compared with other countries. The lower the HDI value, the worse the state of human development is in a country.

It should be noted that the treatment of the income variable used to calculate HDI from 1997 onwards is different to its treatment in 1994 and 1995. In the two years mentioned, income above the cut-off point of world average per capita income was discounted using a drastic discounting formula. In 1997, the discounting was made more gradual by taking the logarithm of income throughout, as recommended by Kelley (1991). The improvement in methodology and data affect the HDI ranks of almost all countries. Thus, although the HDI of Kenya in 2000 is higher than in 1994, this does not mean that its state of human development has improved. In fact, when individual variables are taken into account, it can be seen that there was a fall in life expectancy and a fall in the real GDP per capita.

Criticism of the Human Development Index

The HDI has been criticised for some of its choices of components, weights, implicit trade-offs, and aggregation rules (Ravallion, 1997; Kelley, 1991; Srinivasan, 1994; Tisdell, 1999; Tisdell, et al, 2001; Bardhan and Klasen, 1999). These authors argue that the fixed weights used in the calculation of HDI involve value judgements. The variables used may not be independent of each other and the linearity of HDI implies a constant rate of substitution between these variables. They also argue that the HDI is too restrictive in the attributes it takes into account in assessing welfare. For example, it does not take into account such factors as security of income, employment and psychological well-being. It also fails to consider the distributional aspect of its variables. The process of averaging ignores the differences between men and women, rural and urban poor, different ethnic and racial groups and so on.

A country's overall HDI can conceal the fact that different groups within the country have very different levels of human development. This can be improved through disaggregation. Using the data for the HDI components pertaining to each of the groups into which the HDI is disaggregated, treating each group as if it were a separate country arrives at disaggregated Human Development Indices. Such groups may be defined relative to geographical or administrative regions, urban-rural residence, gender and ethnicity.

Using disaggregated Human Development Indices at the national and local levels helps highlight the significant disparities and gaps: among regions, between the sexes, between urban and rural areas and among ethnic groups. This can help guide policy and action to address gaps and inequalities. It can also enable community groups to press for more resources, making the HDI a tool for participatory development.

Gender Related Development Index (GDI)

The GDI involves a variation on HDI. It uses the same variables as the HDI but the GDI adjusts the average achievement of each country in life expectancy, educational attainment and income in accordance with the disparity in achievement between women and men. It incorporates a measure of gender equity into a measure of absolute levels of human development. The GDI methodology imposes a penalty for inequality in that GDI falls when the disparity between achievements of men and women increase. Thus, GDI is simply HDI adjusted for gender inequality. It reflects disparities between gender in health, education and income. For this gender-sensitive adjustment, the UNDP uses a weighting formula that expresses a moderate aversion to inequality, setting the weighting parameter, ϵ, equal to 2. This is the harmonic mean of the male and female values.

In the life expectancy component, it is assumed that, given equal treatment, women would outlive men by an average of five years (UNDP, 1995). If female life expectancy exceeds male life expectancy by less (or more) than five years, a gender gap is held to exist. For example, if female life expectancy is 42 and male life expectancy 40, then a gender gap of two years against females is assumed to exist. The range of possible life expectancies assumed in the HDR is 60 years. The GDI adjusts the maximum and minimum values for life expectancy, to account for the fact that women tend to live longer than men. For women, the maximum value is 87.5 years and the minimum value 27.5 years; for men the corresponding values are 82.5 and 22.5 years.

In the literacy and school enrolment (education) component of the index, women and men are assumed to have the same potential achievement (100 percent literacy and school enrolment) so that any gender differences in literacy rates or school enrolment rates constitute a gap with a maximum possible gap of 100 percent.

To calculate the index for income, the values of real per capita GDP (PPP$) for women and men are calculated from the female share and male share of earned income. These shares, in turn are estimated from the ratio of the female wage to the male wage and the percentage shares of women and men in the economically active population. The estimates of female and male per capita income (PPP$) are treated in the same way as income is treated in the HDI and then used to compute the equally distributed income index. The equally distributed income index is defined as the level of achievement that, if attained equally by women and men, would be judged to be exactly as valuable socially as the actually observed achievement (Anand and Sen, 1995). The equally distributed income index is given by: {[Female population share x (adjusted female per capita PPP$ GDP)$^{-1}$] + [Male population share x (adjusted male per capita PPP$ GDP)$^{-1}$]}$^{-1}$. The indices for life expectancy, educational attainment and income are added together with equal weight to derive the final GDI value.

However, the GDI has been criticised by Tisdell, et al. (2001); Bardhan, and Klasen (1999) for: (1) pre-assigning of a notional value to the sensitive indicator; (2) it is not clear why the same weighting parameter, ϵ, should be applied to the three gaps, particularly since the nature, size, and significance of the gaps differ greatly; (3) allowing the weighting parameter, ϵ, to vary among countries allows for an elastic ruler, which makes the GDI ineffective in international comparisons; (4) GDI may conceal significant gender inequalities since its components are aggregate measures. Thus, for Kenya, female inequality regionally between its tribes, between urban and rural areas, between races and so on may rise considerably without this being reflected in any change in the GDI. Furthermore, (5) GDI ignores the impact of past (and present) pre-natal discrimination in mortality; (6) by concentrating on the life expectancy measure, the overall assessment ends up neglecting the life expectancy measure completely and the education measure largely by giving too small penalties for gaps in these achievements; (7) use of gender disaggregated per capita GDP is a weak indicator of gender inequality because most countries do not report their per capita GDP in terms of men and women. Hence, using GDP per capita disaggregated by gender is unsatisfactory and renders GDI internationally incomparable; (8) because gender-specific attributions of income per head cannot be readily linked to the aggregate GDP per capita in the calculation of GDI, inequalities within the household are difficult to characterise and assess (Anand and Sen, 1995, pp. 12); and (9) using female income shares to calculate GDI does not take into consideration the increased burden of work that women face as their work for paid employment is added onto their other responsibilities of looking after the family and subsistence farming. Also, Kiriti, et al. (2003a) found that access to paid employment is not a sufficient condition for the improvement of the status of women especially at the household level.

Table 12.2 seems to demonstrate an improvement in the status of women in Kenya in the period 1995-2000 as the GDI rose from 0.459 to 0.512 between 1995 and 2000. However, it fell slightly to 0.512 in 2000 compared with 1997 indicating a small deterioration in the status of women. There has been virtually no change in GDI in Kenya since 1997. However, the methodology used in 1995 is different from the 1997 and therefore the two GDI coefficients may not be comparable.

Table 12.2: Kenya's Gender Related Development Index: 1995-2000

Year	GDI
1995	0.459*
1997	0.517
1998	0.508
1999	0.511
2000	0.512

Source: UNDP: Human Development Reports (various issues)

* Not comparable with other GDI values

It is possible for gross inequality between females and males to increase and for GDI to remain constant other things being equal. GDI may conceal significant gender inequalities since its components are aggregate measures (Tisdell, et al, 2001). This is because gender inequality only relates to the average situation of males compared to the average for females.

Gender Empowerment Measure (GEM)

The Gender Empowerment Measure (GEM) measures the extent of gender equity in economic and political power. The GEM uses variables constructed explicitly to measure the relative empowerment of women and men in political and economic spheres of activity. It thus attempts to measure gender equity in participation in governmental and managerial decision-making, professional roles, and economic activities generally.

This is important for several reasons: First, gender equity in access to economic and political opportunities is of intrinsic importance as it determines the status of women in society. Second, it may be that women (and men) are more effective promoters of their own cause. If this is the case, then gender equity in economic and political power may be an effective way to reduce other gender inequalities in society. Third, a society that neglects the economic and political potential of half of its population is likely to perform worse than a society using its talent regardless of gender (Bardhan and Klasen, 1999).

The GEM is calculated in four steps. First, indices for administrative, managerial, professional and technical positions are calculated. This involves calculating male and female shares of administrative, professional, technical and managerial positions. These are broad, loosely defined occupational categories. Because the relevant population for each category is different, a separate index for each is calculated and then added together. Secondly, women and men's percentage shares of parliamentary seats are calculated which reflects political participation and decision-making power. Third, an index for gender relation shares of earned income is calculated. This involves calculation of the male and female shares of earned income similar to that used for the GDI. For all three variables the methodology of population weighted ($1-\epsilon$) averaging to derive an "equally distributed equivalent percentage" (EDEP) for both sexes together is used. Each variable is indexed by dividing the EDEP by 50 percent. Fourth, an income variable is used to reflect power over economic resources. It is calculated in the same way as for the GDI except that unadjusted rather than adjusted real GDP per capita is used. Fifth, the gender empowerment measure is computed which involves adding together the three indices for economic participation and decision making, political participation and decision making, and power over economic resources (UNDP, 1999).

The UNDP does not have a GEM value for Kenya due to non-availability of data and therefore Kenya is not ranked. However, as mentioned earlier, women held only six (3.6 percent) seats out of 202 seats in parliament in 1997, and 17 seats (8.1 percent) in 2002. This was a huge improvement since before the first multi-party elections of 1992 there were no elected women in parliament. There are also an insignificant number of women professionals and technical workers, and very few female administrators and managers.

Criticism of the Gender Empowerment Measure

However the GEM has been criticised (Tisdell, et al, 2001) for: (1) its focus on the sources of income but not the users of income since a female may earn cash income but it may be mainly controlled and utilised by her husband. In most African societies, Kenya included, women may earn income but the man controls it or it may be used for the sustenance of the whole family, not solely for the well being of the woman (Kiriti, et al, 2003a); (2) it is questionable how well GEM fully captures economic and political power held by women and their roles in the development process; (3) GEM does not reliably allow for inter-country comparison due to the flexibility of the earnings gap indicator and the weighting and averaging procedures; (4) the choice of representation in parliament ignores the fact that there are some parliaments that do not have any power thereby making it difficult to interpret the share of female political representation. A country may have very high female participation in parliament and hence a high GEM ranking but this does not reflect the actual political power of women; (5) the GEM focuses too much on representation at the national level and in the formal sectors of the economy; (6) the GEM neglects many important aspects of women's economic and political roles that exist outside of national politics and the formal economy, as is the case in many developing countries; and (7) in most developing countries, for example Kenya, where poverty levels are high, most women may not be interested in being members of parliament or even local authorities, let alone being managers. Their interest is, in basic, survival.

Education and Literacy Levels

In the developing world's 900 million illiterate people, women outnumber men two to one. And girls constitute the majority of the 130 million children without access to primary school. In sub-Saharan Africa (SSA), the average number of years of schooling for the female adult population in 1960 was only 1.1 years, which was barely half of the schooling achievement by men. Females in SSA experienced the lowest average annual growth of total years of schooling between 1960 and 1990 of all regions (an annual increase of 0.04 years, raising the average years of schooling of the adult female population by only 1.2 years between 1960 and 1990). The female-male ratio in the growth of total years of schooling was only 0.89 meaning that females experienced a slower expansion in educational achievement than males (Blackden and Bhanu, 1998).

Beginning in the early 1990s in Kenya, government expenditure on education, health and other social services decreased due to rising pressure from the World Bank and the IMF to reduce government expenditure. The need to undergo fiscal adjustment because of unsustainable fiscal deficits and mounting payment obligations on its external debt constrained the government's ability to increase the education budget. Attempts to solve the resource shortage by shifting costs to families and communities ran into difficulties. Extremely low per capita incomes limited the ability of many communities and households to contribute more private funds to the education of their children. The additional burden on low-income households had a negative effect on school enrolment, especially enrolment of girls, as the demand for education is price sensitive in low-income households (Kabubo and Kiriti, 2001).

As can be seen from Table 12.3, gross enrolment ratios in primary education fell in comparison to 1990. They reached a low of 84.9 per cent in 1995. While the downward trend was reversed as indicated by the 1998 figure, primary school enrolment ratios were still lower in 1998 than in 1991. It is also probable that the quality of education of those in school declined while secondary school ratios also show a decline. This decline halted in the mid-1990s and in fact, in 1998 the secondary education enrolment ratio was higher than in 1991.

However, there is no doubt that an increasing number of the poor are missing out on education in Kenya or receiving little education. The distribution of educational opportunity cannot be deciphered from these aggregate statistics. But, they influence UNDP's indices of development such as its Human Development Index (HDI) and its Gender Development Index (GDI). The fact that the secondary enrolment ratio was higher in 1998 than in 1991, but the primary school enrolment ratio was lower in Kenya, suggests that in the 1990s, inequality of income has exerted a rising influence on access to education.

The gender gap in primary school enrolments is measured as the ratio of female to male enrolment at this level times 100. The gender gap in secondary school enrolment is measured as the ratio of female to male enrolment at this level times 100. These two are measures of women's status as far as education in early years is concerned.

Where places in school are limited and resources are scarce, girls are at a particular disadvantage. Parents may prefer to educate sons, both because expected benefits are higher due to better job prospects for sons and dependence on sons in old life (Kiriti and Tisdell, 2003a), and costs are lower because of the low opportunity cost of their time in terms of help in the household (Mincer and Polachek, 1974).

Table 12.3: Gross Enrolment Ratios for Primary and Secondary Levels of Education for Kenya by Gender: 1991-1998

Year	Primary enrolment				Secondary enrolment			
	Total	Male	Female	Gap	Total	Male	Female	Gap
1991	93.0	94.5	91.5	3.0	27.9	31.5	24.4	7.1
1992	91.7	92.9	90.5	2.4	27.3	30.7	23.9	6.8
1993	90.5	91.1	89.8	1.3	25.7	28.5	22.8	5.7
1994	86.9	87.1	86.6	0.5	24.8	27.0	22.6	4.4
1995	84.9	84.9	83.2	1.7	24.8	26.4	22.4	4.0
1998	90.7	91.4	90.0	1.4	29.9	31.5	28.2	3.3

Source: UNESCO Datasets

Table 12.3 shows that the enrolment ratios of females in both primary and secondary schools are lower than that of males. However, the gender gap, though exhibiting a declining trend in both primary and secondary school levels, is much wider in secondary schools. The data indicates that while enrolment levels are high for both girls and boys in primary schools (although enrolment ratios for females are lower than those of males), there is a higher drop-out of female students than of male students and enrolment ratios are much higher for males than for females in secondary school.

The gender gap in adult illiteracy is measured as the percentage of illiterate females in the 25 years and above age group minus the percentage of illiterate males in the same age group.

Adult illiteracy rates are largely a reflection of historical trends in primary school enrolment. A higher gender gap is a reflection of women's lower status since literacy is the forerunner to a host of expanded opportunities for women including earning power, control over health and child-bearing, political and legal rights and so on.

Table 12.4: Adult Illiteracy Rates for Kenya by Gender

Year	Adult Illiteracy			
	Total	Male	Female	Gap
1970	na	44.0	74.0	30.0
1980	na	30.0	57.3	27.3
1990	29.2	19.1	39.2	20.1
1995	23.0	14.7	31.1	16.4
1999	17.6	11.1	24.0	12.9

Source: UNESCO Datasets

As seen from Table 12.4, in 1970, 74 percent of the adult female population was illiterate compared to 44 percent of adult males. By 1999, 24 percent of the adult female population remained illiterate compared to 11.1 percent of the adult male population. Table 12.4 demonstrates that there exists a gender gap in adult illiteracy in Kenya although it seems to be declining but at a slow pace between 1990 and 1999. Low enrolment ratios for females in institutions of higher learning and high illiteracy rates means that women cannot participate effectively in decision-making institutions.

Although the data indicate increased access to education for women and a decrease in the gender differences between men and women, it does not take into account the availability of facilities, the quality of education, for example, size of classes and so on. Furthermore, the fact that women in Kenya have access to education does not necessarily lead to their empowerment. Kiriti, et al. (2003a) found that in patriarchal societies, customary conventions play a major role in determining the socio-economic status for women.

Female/Male Ratios in Decision-Making Institutions

The effectiveness of Kenya's development efforts and the ability to sustain them are dependent on the full utilisation of all human resources (both men and women). But, socio-economic indicators show that Kenyan women are disadvantaged compared to men in respect of their participation in decision-making. The vast majority of Africa's women find their total livelihood within agriculture and the informal sector. For example, women constitute 95 percent of the agricultural labour force in Lesotho and 54 percent in Tanzania. The UN Economic Commission for Africa (1998) estimates that over 70 percent of Africa's food is produced by women. Women account for 53 percent of all informal sector workers. In Botswana, between 55 percent and 75 percent of all informal sector's businesses are owned and operated by women. In the formal sectors of Africa's economies, women continue to play marginal roles. Their participation rate is less than 30 percent. For example, out of the total in wage employment, women account for 19.9 percent in Angola, 30.7 percent in Botswana,

21.3 percent in Kenya, 14.69 percent in Malawi, 28.8 percent in Swaziland and 16.59 percent in Zimbabwe (Sivard, 1995).

Most women in formal sector employment are concentrated in low-paying semi-skilled and non-skilled jobs. Women's representation in technical and professional fields is still limited. Their representation in major decision-making positions is also extremely limited. There are various reasons accounting for this. First, early socialisation practices emphasise the primary role of women as mothers and wives and influence girls' total expectations for future participation in the labour force and the choice of career paths. Second, women's overall limited educational attainments, as well as the types of curricula used in schools, emphasising stereotypical roles for women, create further barriers. Career guidance and counselling likewise tends to channel girls into traditional female fields such as nursing and home economics. Third, women's multiple responsibilities as mothers, wives, employees and employers create role conflicts that at times could result in compromises in careers. Women's careers tend to be interrupted during their childbearing years, resulting in loss of seniority. In addition, as women are usually expected to move with their husbands, the interrupted career syndrome further compromises their career progression. Fourth, organisational policies and procedures are often influenced by cultural perceptions of women's roles and capabilities. This leads to women being discriminated against in recruitment, and in promotion to senior positions as it is assumed that women lack the qualities essential for successful managerial careers (Mincer and Polachek, 1974).

African culture is a barrier to development because it perpetuates culturally sanctioned biases against women and provides excuses for men. Cultural biases operate at all levels ranging from national institutional level, government policy, community level, household and individual levels (Kiriti, et al, 2003b). In Africa, women's participation at all levels of decision-making is low. In Parliament, the highest level of decision-making, women are under represented. In 1995, at the time of the Beijing Platform for Action, only 10 percent of the members of legislative bodies were women. In 1998, this had increased to 12 percent, still a very low percentage. The UNDP in its Human Development Report of 1995 states that there should be a target of 30 percent of women in all spheres of political and social life for an impact to be felt.

The Beijing Platform for Action (1995) states that women's equal participation in political life plays a pivotal role in the general process of the advancement of women. Without the active participation of women and the incorporation of women's perspectives at all levels of decision-making, the goals of equality, development and peace cannot be achieved. Incorporation would ensure women's equal access to and full participation in power structures and decision-making. It would also increase women's capacity to participate in decision-making and leadership. However, eight years later many of the injunctions in the Beijing Platform for Action still remain agendas for the future and there are even some issues that some governments, for example Kenya, have refused outright to take into account saying that they go against their cultures.

According to the United Nations Division for the Advancement of Women (UNDAW, 1996) the percentage of women in both ministerial and sub-ministerial levels ranges from zero percent (in about 15 countries), to 30 percent in 2 countries. Only 3.5 percent of the world's cabinet ministers are women, and women hold no ministerial positions in 93 countries of the world. In Kenya, most women in high government positions are in such ministries as education, culture, social welfare, women's affairs and so on. Women in Kenya rarely achieve elective office, and are severely under-represented at top positions in political parties. Out of a total of 202 seats in parliament, women occupied only 6 seats after the 1992 first multi-party elections. These increased to 17 in the 2002 elections out of 210 seats. In Kenya, women are under represented in the judiciary, in local authorities and even in government administration. Female lecturers in universities and institutions of higher learning represent only 10 percent of the total teaching staff.

The above statistics show that despite the fact that many governments have adopted and adapted affirmative action measures and the rhetoric of gender equality, women constitute nowhere near half of the personnel in decision-making structures although they are around half of the global population. The threshold of 30 percent advocated by the UNDP Human Development Report (1995), as a prelude to the 50 percent is still a dream for most women.

LIFE EXPECTANCY

Life expectancy is an important human development indicator. Pierre-Yves, et al. (1999) found a strong relationship between national health-care spending and life expectancy. Considering that most African governments have reduced their expenditures on almost all the sectors, due to structural adjustment pressure from the World Bank and the IMF, this suggests that life expectancy in most African countries is going to decline.

Sala-I-Martin and Barro (1995) found a strong and positive relationship between life expectancy and economic growth; a 13-year increase in life expectancy is estimated to raise the annual growth by 1.4 percentage points. Croix and Licandro (1999) argue that there are several channels through which life expectancy affects economic growth directly, for instance, when the probability of dying young is high, the shortened time horizon makes it optimal for people to start working early in their life and not to stay at school for too long. Moreover, when life expectancy is short, the depreciation rate of human capital is high, making its accumulation more difficult. Since the human capital accumulated in school is an important engine of growth, we should thus expect a country's growth rate to depend upon life expectancy.

Development economics literature shows that an increase in economic growth leads to a higher life expectancy due to better nutrition, reduced infant mortality rates and improved medical care. Life expectancy for both men and women in the world's richest countries is about 80 years, which is almost twice that in the world's poorest countries - 45 years (UNDP, 1998). The problem here however, is of deciding what the causal is and what is the dependent factor; a kind of mutual causation problem or "chicken and egg problem" exists.

The average life expectancy for sub-Saharan Africa is 51.1 years, the lowest for all regions in the world. Table 12.5 shows life expectancy in Kenya for selected years.

It can be seen that when Kenya attained independence in 1963, life expectancy was only 44.7 years. It rose to 50.5 years in 1970, increasing life expectancy coinciding with a growth in GDP of 6.5 percent between 1963-1974 (Republic of Kenya, 1991), and subsequently to 58.3 years in 1990. However, this fell to 47 years in 2001. Kenya started implementing structural adjustment programs in 1994. These reduced government expenditure in such sectors as health, education, transport, social services and so on. This has meant shifting the cost of consultation and drugs to households. Considering their already low per capita incomes, most sick people avoid medical facilities thereby raising morbidity rates and the mortality rate. This has contributed to the decline in the life expectancy for both male and females to less than 50 years. The female life expectancy in 1980 was 57 years compared to 53 years for males. In 2000, it was 47 years for both females and males.

Table 12.5: Life Expectancy in Kenya in Years: 1963-2001

Year	**Life expectancy at birth**	**Female**	**Male**	**Female less male**
1963	44.7	na	na	Na
1970	50.5	52	48	6
1980	54.9	57	53	4
1990	58.3	59	55	4
1994	53.6	na	na	na
1995	53.8	53	52	1
1996	49	na	na	na
1997	52	53.0	51.1	1.9
1998	51.3	52.2	50.5	1.7
1999	50.8	48	47	1
2000	47	47	47	0
2001	47	47	46	1

Source: UNDP: Human Development Reports (various issues)

A further reason for declining life expectancy is that Kenya had been relying on donor aid to fund various programs in its health sector. For the last eight years, Kenya has been cut off as a donor aid recipient due to its non-compliance with conditions given by the World Bank, IMF and various bilateral aid agencies. This has resulted in some doctors moving to Southern Africa and to other more developed countries worsening the situation in Kenya.

As mentioned earlier, life expectancy for both men and women in the world's richest countries is almost twice that in the worlds poorest. Much of this differential is due to very high infant mortality rates in low-income countries, which is in turn due to the gap in living standards, particularly nutritional status and medical care. In most of the world, women have a longer life expectancy than men, but differentials are narrower in developing than in developed countries, and in some cases reversed from the norm. In the developed countries, women's life expectancy is on average six to seven years longer than men's. But in most developing countries the gap narrows to three years or less (UNDP, 1995). For example, in Kenya the differential was only four years in 1980 and it fell to one year in 2001. On the whole, the trend in the differential has been downward since 1970 reflecting retrogression in socio-economic conditions in Kenya. The life expectancy gap reflects patterns of discrimination, which give preference to male over female infants and children early in life in nutrition, in medical care, in the mother's scarce time, and so on; discrimination that often continues into adulthood.

Table 12.6 shows that the child mortality rates for Kenya have been rising since the country started implementing structural adjustment programmes in 1995. In addition, it is found that the child mortality rates for female children rose by 15.2 percent between 1997 and 2000 compared to 9.1 percent for male children. Consequently, in 2000 female mortality rates of children under 5 years exceeded that of males.

Furthermore, AIDS-related illnesses in Kenya have taken their toll and contributed to a reduction in life expectancy and an increase in infant and child mortality. The HIV prevalence rate in Kenya for adults aged between 15 and 49 years in 2001 was 15 percent (World Bank, 2002). According to UNAIDS (2002), the majority of those suffering the impact of the epidemic live in the rural areas and are mainly the poor. In 2000, only 20 percent of the HIV-positive population in Kenya lived in the urban areas.

Table 12.6: Child Mortality rates per 1000 live births for Kenya: 1970-2000

Year	Infants 0-1 years	Children under 5 years	Mortality rate (children under 5 years)	
			Male	Female
1970	102	156	na	na
1990	63	97	na	na
1991	62	96	na	na
1995	73	111	na	na
1997	74	112	33	33
1998	76	124	na	na
1999	76	118	na	na
2000	77	120	36	38

Source: World Bank: World Development Indicators, (various issues)

Table 12.7 provides estimates of people living with HIV/AIDS in Kenya and sub-Saharan Africa between 1999 and 2001. By the end of 2001, about 2.5 million people in Kenya were estimated to be living with HIV/AIDS.

Table 12.7: People Living with HIV/AIDS in Kenya and sub-Saharan Africa: 1999-2001

Region	Year	Total Adults and Children	Adults (15-49 years)	Women (15-49 years)	Men (15-49 years)	Children (0-14 years)
Sub-Saharan Africa (Millions)	End 1999	24.4	23.4	12.0	11.4	1.0
	End 2001	28.5	25.9	na	na	2.6
Kenya (Millions)	End 1999	2.1	2.0	1.1	0.9	0.078
	End 2001	2.5	2.3	1.4	0.9	0.22

Source: Reports of the Global HIV/AIDS Epidemic and UNAIDS Assessment of the Epidemiological Situation in Kenya, 2002

In Kenya 1.4 million women in the age bracket 15-49 years were HIV-positive compared to 0.9 million men in the same category by the end of 2001.Women and girls are more vulnerable to HIV because of their limited access to economic and educational opportunities, and the multiple household and community roles they are responsible for. Also, women and girls are subject to social norms that deny them sexual health knowledge and practices that prevent them from controlling their bodies. The gender division of labour and male urban migration keeps men away from their wives for long periods leading to promiscuity and the spread of HIV. Women in the rural areas may also find themselves discriminated against when trying to access care and support when they are HIV-positive. UNAIDS (2002) reports that in Kenya, women who are HIV-infected are divorced even when their husbands have infected them. Family resources are more likely to be devoted to buying medication and arranging care for ill males than females. Because of lack of hospital facilities in rural areas and lack of income, those in rural areas affected by AIDS may find it difficult if not impossible, to obtain hospital care. Therefore, they mostly have to be cared for at home. Generally this is the burden of females.

As the country loses young productive people to AIDS, the effects have an influence on all sectors of the economy. The loss of income of the breadwinner, increased medical expenses and increased time taking care of the sick persons may lead to reduced agricultural output. Households fall into deeper poverty and women are left bearing even larger burdens as workers, educators, mothers and, ultimately, as caregivers, as the burden of caring for the ill family members rests mostly with women and girls. Of HIV-positive pregnant women in Kenya, 30 percent give birth to HIV-positive babies who are likely to die before 5 years of age, increasing the child mortality rate. UNAIDS (2002) predicts that between 2000 and 2020, 55 million Africans will die earlier than they would have in the absence of AIDS.

The decrease in adult life expectancy, increase in child mortality rates, the narrowing of the difference between female and male life expectancy and the increase in the child mortality rates for female children presents a worrying trend for Kenya.

GDP Per Capita Levels

GDP is a measure of the value of all the final goods and services newly produced in a country during some period of time. GDP per capita based on purchasing power parity (PPP US$) accounts for price differences between countries and therefore better reflects people's standard of living. In theory, at the PPP rate, 1 PPP dollar has the same purchasing power in the domestic economy as 1 US dollar in the US economy.

Table 12.8 lists the real GDP per capita for Kenya for a selected number of years, but the data are not disaggregated between men and women. However, taking the share of income earned for females in 1995 (the only available data), women earned only 41.79 percent of total earnings compared to men's 58.22 percent. Yet, this was only in formal paid employment and it does not reflect availability of income to the females in the family.

From Table 12.8, it is seen that Kenya's GDP per capita peaked in 1995 and thereafter started declining during the implementation of structural adjustments programmes and the withdrawal of donor aid to Kenya. This pattern of decline mirrors the increase in the incidence of poverty and a decline in life expectancy in Kenya during this period. According to the World Bank (1999), Kenya recorded negative real GDP growth rates in 1999. During this time the percentage of the population living on less than a dollar a day was 50.2, implying that they were living in absolute poverty. The World Bank stresses the importance of increased income as a major determinant of wellbeing and poverty reduction. To help raise incomes, the World Bank and other donor agencies have recommended commercialisation of agriculture. However, Kiriti and Tisdell (2003b) found that commercialisation of agriculture has led to gender inequality in families in Kenya. Even when household income goes up, food availability goes down due to male control of household income.

Table 12.8: Kenya's GDP per Capita: 1985-2000

Year	GDP per capita (USPPP$)
1985-88	1010
1990	1058
1991	1350
1992	1400
1993	1400
1994	1404
1995	1438
1996	na
1997	1190
1998	980
1999	1022
2000	1000

Source: UNDP: Human Development Reports (various issues)

However, GDP per capita only reflects average national income. It does not reveal income distribution. GDP per capita is an aggregate at the national level and so it does not uncover inequalities of access to income within households, for example, the availability of that income to wives. Per capita GDP may show an increasing trend but only benefit the male population who are the main beneficiaries of income-earning assets in Kenya.

Poverty Rates

Income poverty means the lack of material well-being; lack of income to meet basic needs like food, shelter and clothing. Food poverty is measured by the per capita consumption of the required daily intake of the basic recommended calories per adult equivalent (2250 calories). Several international bodies consider persons to live in absolute poverty when their income is less than a dollar a day to meet food, shelter and other basic needs (FAO, 1984, UNDP, 1995). Fifty four per cent of the people in sub-Saharan Africa live in absolute income poverty on this basis.

Poverty rates in Kenya are substantially lower in urban areas than in rural areas (Republic of Kenya, 1998). In 1992, the absolute urban poverty rate in Kenya was 29.3 percent compared with 46.4 percent in rural areas. In 2000, national incidence of absolute income poverty in Kenya rose to 50 percent but the data are not disaggregated between urban and rural areas. Nevertheless, the incidence remains highest in rural areas.

Of 1.3 billion people in absolute poverty globally, the majority are women who are mainly found in rural areas. Poverty among women has been linked to their unequal situation in the labour market, their poor treatment under social welfare systems and their inferior status and power in the family (UNDP, 1995).

Women bear a significant responsibility for the family's subsistence. In virtually all societies, women are the main carers in a family and they are often willing to sacrifice their own welfare for the benefit of other family members, especially their children (Tisdell, 1999).

In many countries, women are also important economic providers for the family giving considerable economic support to their children. But their capacity in some developing countries to fulfil this responsibility has been significantly affected by such factors as unequal sharing of household resources, unequal access to earning opportunities, to agricultural land and by the decline in common property resources and forests (Roy and Tisdell, 1993).

Women and men experience poverty differently, and different aspects of poverty (deprivation, powerlessness, vulnerability, its seasonality) have gender dimensions (World Bank, 1996). Vulnerability reflects the dynamic nature of poverty such as defencelessness, insecurity and exposure to risk. Vulnerability is a function of assets. The more assets people have, the less vulnerable they are. Assets include stores, concrete productive investments, human investments, collective assets and claims on others for assistance. Both absolute and food poverty are associated with lack of physical and human assets (World Bank, 1997). Women and children are more vulnerable because tradition usually gives them less decision-making power over assets than men, while at the same time their opportunities to engage in remunerated activities, and therefore to acquire their own assets, are more limited (World Bank, 1995, 1996; Blackden and Bhanu, 1998). Greer and Thorbecke (1986a, 1986b), Collier and Lal (1980), and Republic of Kenya (1991, 1998), show that food poverty and absolute poverty occur mainly among female-headed households.

Tisdell (2000) found that there is gender imbalance in the formation of Human Resource Capital (HRC) in India and other less developed countries. In many developing countries, females are deprived of HRC compared to men. They have less access to education, and often have less availability of food and medical services. This often results in higher fertility rates and higher population growth reinforcing higher poverty rates.

However, Lipton (1995), Ravallion and Lanjouw (1995) argue that women are not generally over-represented in poor households. Their findings and those of Appleton's (1996) are at odds with the findings by other authors, for example, World Bank (1993) and Quisumbing, Haddad and Pena (2001), who found that women are disproportionately represented among the poor. The World Bank's Participatory Poverty Assessment (1995) for Kenya shows that while 25 percent of the study population was categorised as very poor, there were nearly twice as many female-headed households (44 percent) as male-headed households (21 percent) in that category. The remaining 35 percent represented male-headed with no wife present. Greer and Thorbecke (1986a, 1986b), Collier and Lal (1980), and Republic of Kenya (1991, 1998) also find that female-headed households account for the high proportion of the poor in Kenya. Mwabu, et al. (2000) using the cost of basic needs (CBN) and food energy intake (FEI) approaches in computing poverty rates for Kenya, found that poverty rates were marginally higher in female-headed households (41 percent) than in male-headed households (38 percent) where husband and wife live together.

The World Bank's Participatory Poverty Assessment (1995) for Kenya found that to cope with increased levels of poverty, female heads of households in Kenya consistently limit the number of meals eaten. They found that one third of the female-headed households had only one meal per day while the rest had two meals. Some women resort to begging for food, others rely on brewing alcohol despite being harassed by police.

Apart from lack of physical and human assets, women are generally immobile because of greater responsibilities for childcare, household provisioning, doing household chores and home-based agricultural activities. The cultural norms are such that women find it hard to venture out to look for work or in certain traditions, to mix with men. This prevents them from gathering information on job opportunities. They are cut off from channels of communication, or the information they receive is filtered through the (male) head of household or community leaders.

Poverty rates generally decline as the level of education increases (Mwabu, et al, 2000; Schultz, 1960). Education and training reduce the chances of falling back into poverty. Females in Kenya generally have lower levels of education compared to males. A long-term remedy to alleviate poverty would be to invest in poor people, especially women, particularly in their education and training, and to bring them into the mainstream of development

Women not only suffer from income poverty but also human poverty. Human poverty means that opportunities and choices most basic to human development are denied. Human poverty is more than income poverty. It involves the denial of choices and opportunities most basic to human development to lead a long, healthy, creative life, acquire knowledge, and enjoy a decent standard of living, freedom, dignity, self-esteem and the respect of others (UNDP, 1998a; 1998b).

One way of measuring human poverty, although it is far from adequate, is by using the human poverty index (HPI) introduced by UNDP in the Human Development Report of 1997. The HPI is a composite index of different features of deprivation in the quality of life that helps to judge the extent of poverty in a community. HPI-1 measures human poverty in developing countries. The variables used are: (1) The percentage of people expected to die before age 40; (2) the percentage of adults who are illiterate; and (3) deprivation in overall economic provisioning measured by: (a) the percentage of people without access to health services and safe water and (b) the percentage of underweight children under five. The HPI is constructed by taking a simple average of the three variables.

The trend in the HPI for Kenya between 1997 and 2000 is evident from Table 12.9. This table shows that the value of the HPI for Kenya has been rising and the poverty ranking of Kenya increased compared to other developing nations.

Table 12.9 also shows that the percentage of people living below the poverty line rose from 42 percent in 1992 to 50 percent in 2000 implying that half the population in Kenya was living below the poverty line in 2000.

Table 12.9: Human Poverty Index for Kenya: 1997-2000

Year	Human poverty index		Population below absolute national poverty line
	Rank among developing countries	Value (%)	
1992	Na	Na	42.0
1997	35	27.1	Na
1998	49	28.2	47.0
1999	51	29.5	Na
2000	49	31.9	50.0

Source: UNDP: Human Development Reports (various issues)

However, it is difficult to reflect all dimensions of human poverty in a single quantifiable composite indicator. Lack of political freedom, lack of personal security, inability to participate in the life of a community and threats to sustainability cannot be measured and quantified in a simple aggregate. Also, the HPI does not reflect gender inequality. It also does not show how the increased poverty burden is shared between men and women. It does not reveal who among those who suffer from human poverty are females. It also does not show the disparities in poverty between rural and urban areas or among different ethnic communities.

CONCLUSION

This paper finds that absolute poverty exists and is rising rapidly in Kenya and that poverty is more pronounced in female-headed households. This can be linked to discrimination in the labour market, in access to education, in decision-making and in access and control of human, economic and social resources.

General indicators have shown declining GDP per capita, increased poverty rates especially for women, reduced life expectancy, a narrowing of the difference in female/male life expectancy rates, increased child mortality rates and an increase in the female child mortality rates. This deterioration results in an increased burden on women who are carers of the family and indicates a deterioration of the status of women. Consequently, there is a need to learn how women and families are coping with growing poverty and the high incidence of AIDS and whether this has led to an increase in gender inequality. This paper advocates the use of household level gender disaggregated data because gender inequality manifests itself not just at the national level but has its roots at the household level where culture plays a very important role in allocation of resources and decision-making.

REFERENCES

Acharya, M. and Bennet, L, (1983), *"Women and the Subsistence Sector: Economic Participation and Household Decision-Making in Nepal"*, World Bank Staff Working Paper No 526. Washington. D. C.: World Bank.

Afonja, S, (1986), *"Changing Modes of Production and the Sexual Division of Labour Among the Yoruba"*, In Eleanor Leacock and Hellen I. Safa (eds), Women's Work, South Hadley, MA: Bergin and Garvey Publishers, pp. 122-135.

Anand, S. and Sen, A, (1995), *"Gender Inequality in Human Development: Theories and Measurement"*, HDR Office Occasional Paper No. 19, New York: UNDP.

Appleton, S, (1996), *"Women-headed Households and Poverty: An Empirical Decomposition for Uganda"*, Centre for the Study of African Economies Working Paper No. WPS/95-14: Oxford University.

Bay, E. G, (1982), *Women in Africa: Studies in Social and Economic Change*, Stanford, Calif: Stanford University Press.

Bennet, L, (1983), *Dangerous Wives and Sacred Sisters: Social and Symbolic Roles of High Caste Women in Nepal*, New York: Columbia University Press.

Blackden, C. and Bhanu, C, (1998), *Gender, Growth and Poverty Reduction: Special Program of Assistance for Africa, 1998 Status Report on Poverty in sub-Saharan Africa*, World Bank Technical Paper No. 428, Washington, D.C.: World Bank.

Boserup, E, (1970), *Woman's Role in Economic Development*, New York: St. Martin's Press.

Collier, P. and Lal, D, (1980), *Poverty and Growth in Kenya*, Washington D. C.: World Bank Staff Working Paper.

Croix, D. and Licandro, O, (1999), *"Life Expectancy and Endogenous Growth"*, Economics Letters, Vol. 65, No. 2, pp. 255-263.

Davison, J, (1988b), *Agriculture, Women, and Land: The African Experience*, Boulder and London: Westview Press.

FAO, (1984), *"Integrating Nutrition into Agricultural and Rural Development Projects: Six Case Studies"*, Nutrition in Agriculture, No. 2, Rome: FAO.

Folbre, N, (1992), *"Introduction: The Feminist Sphinx", In Nancy Folbre, Barbara Bergmann, Bina Agarwal and Maria, Floro (eds)*, Issues in Contemporary Economics, Vol. 4: Women's Work in the World Economy, Hong Kong: Macmillan Academic and Professional Ltd, pp. 23-30.

Greer, J. and Thorbecke, E, (1986a), *"Food Poverty Profile Applied to Kenyan Smallholders"*, Economic Development and Cultural Change, Vol. 35, No. 1, pp. 115-141.

Greer, J. and Thorbecke, E, (1986b), *"A Methodology for Measuring Food Poverty Applied to Kenya"*, Journal of Development Economics, Vol. 24, pp. 59-74.

Gross, D. and Underwood, B, (1971), *"Technological Change and Calorie Costs: Sisal Agriculture in Northern Brazil"*, American Anthropologist, Vol. 73, pp. 725-740.

Henn, J. H, (1978), *Peasants, Workers and Capital in Cameroon,* Unpublished PhD Thesis, Harvard University.

Jiggins, J, (1989), *"How Poor Women earn Income in sub-Saharan Africa and What Works against Them"*, World Development, Vol. 17, No. 7, pp. 953-963.

Julin, E, (1993), *Structural Change in Rural Kenya*, Unpublished PhD Thesis, University of Gotenborg, Sweden.

Kabubo, J. and Kiriti, T, (2001), *"Macroeconomic Adjustment, Poverty and Economic Growth: An Analysis for Kenya"*, African Journal of Economic Policy, Vol. 8, No. 1, pp. 42-58.

Kelley, A, (1991), *"The Human Development Index: Handle with Care"*, Population and Development Review, Vol. 17, No. 2, pp. 315-324.

Kennedy, E. and Oniang'o, R, (1990), *"Health and Nutrition Effects of Sugarcane Production in Southwestern Kenya"*, Food and Nutrition Bulletin, Vol. 12, pp. 261-167.

Kennedy, E. and Peters, P, (1992), *"Household Food Security and Child Nutrition: The Interaction of Income and Gender of Household Head"*, World Development, Vol. 20, No. 8, pp. 1087-1099.

Kiriti, T. and Tisdell, C, (2003a), *"Family Size, Economics and Child Gender Preference: A Case Study in the Nyeri District of Kenya"*, International Journal of Social Economics [Forthcoming].

Kiriti, T. and Tisdell, C, (2003b), *"Commercialization of Agriculture in Kenya: Case Study of Policy Bias and Food Purchases by Farm Households"*, Quarterly Journal of International Agriculture, Vol. 42, No. 4, pp. 435-453.

Kiriti, T. Tisdell, C. and Roy, K, (2003a), *"Female Participation in Decision-making in Agricultural Households in Kenya: Empirical Findings"*, International Journal of Agricultural Resources, Governance and Ecology, Vol. 2, No. 2, pp. 103-124.

Kiriti, T. Tisdell, C. and Roy, K, (2003b), *"Institutional Deterrents to the Empowerment of Women: Kenya's Experience",* In K. C. Roy (ed), Twentieth Century Development: Some Relevant Issues, New York: Nova Science [Forthcoming].

Lipton, M, (1995), *"Market, Redistributive and Proto-reform: Can Liberalisation Help the Poor?"* Asian Development Review, Vol. 13, No. 1, pp. 1-35.

Mincer, J. and Polachek, S, (1974), *"Family Investment in Human Capital: Earnings of Women",* Journal of Political Economy, Vol. 82, No. 2, pp. S76-S108.

Mwabu, G. et al. (2000), *Poverty in Kenya: Profiles and Determinants*, A Joint Research Project by the Department of Economics, University of Nairobi and the Ministry of Planning and National Development, Nairobi: African Economic Research Consortium (AERC).

Palmer, I, (1991), *Gender and Population in the Adjustment of African Economies: Planning for Change*, Geneva: International Labour Office.

Pierre-Yves, C. Pierre, Q. and Caroline, P, (1999), *"Health Care Spending as Determinants of Health Outcomes*", Health Economics, Vol. 8, No. 7, pp. 627-639.

Quisumbing, A. Haddad, L. and Pena, C, (2001), *"Are Women Over represented among the Poor? Analysis of Poverty in 10 Developing Countries"*, Journal of Development Economics, Vol. 66, No.1, pp. 225-269.

Ravallion, M. and Lanjouw, P, (1995), *"Poverty and Household Size",* Economic Journal, Vol. 105, No. 433, pp. 1415-1434.

Republic of Kenya, (1991), *Economic Survey*, Nairobi: Government Printer.

Republic of Kenya, (1998), *National Poverty Eradication Plan; 1999-2015*, Nairobi: Government Printer.

Republic of Kenya, (2002), *Mainstreaming Gender into the Kenya National HIV/AIDS Strategic Plan: 2000-2005*. Nairobi: The Gender and HIV/AIDS Technical sub-Committee of the National AIDS Control Council, November 2002.

Roy, K. C. and Tisdell, C. A, (1993), *"Technological Change, Environment and Poor Women, Especially Tribal Women in India"*, Savings and Development, Quarterly Review, Vol. 17, No. 4, pp. 423-439.

Saito, K, (1992), *Raising the Productivity of Women Farmers in sub-Saharan Africa: Overview Report*, World Bank, Women in Development Division, Population and Human Resources Department.

Saito, K, Mekonnen, S, Spurling, D, (1994), *"Raising the Productivity of Women Farmers in sub-Saharan Africa",* Discussion Paper 230 Washington, D.C.: World Bank.

Sala-i-Martin, X and Barro, R. J, (1995), *Economic Growth*, New York: McGraw Hill.

Schultz, T. W, (1960), *"Human Capital Formation by Education"*, Journal of Political Economy, Vol. 68, No. 6, pp. 571-583.

Sivard, R. L, (1995), *Women: a World Survey* (2nd Ed.). Washington D.C.: World Priorities.

Sorensen, A, (1990), *"The Differential Effects on Women of Cash Crop Production: The Case of Smallholder Tea Production in Kenya*", CDR Project Paper 90.3.

Spring, A, (1978), *Women in Ritual Symbolic Roles*, New York: Plenum Press.

Srinivasan, T, (1994), *"Human Development: A New Paradigm or Reinvention of the Wheel?"* The American Economic Review, Vol. 84, No. 2, pp. 238-243.

Staudt, K. A, (1985), *Agricultural Policy Implementation: A Case Study from Western Kenya*, West Hartford Conn. Kumarian Press.

Tisdell, C. A, (1999), *"Sen's Theory of Entitlement and Deprivation of Females: An Assessment with Indian Illustrations"*, Social Economics, Policy and Development, Working Paper No. 2, University of Queensland.

Tisdell, C. A, (1999), *"Sen's Theory of Entitlement and Deprivation of Females: An Assessment with Indian Illustrations"*, Social Economics, Policy and Development, Working Paper No. 2, University of Queensland.

Tisdell, C. A, (2000), *"Asset-Poor Women in India and the Relevance of Amartya Sen's Analysis"*, Artha Beekshan: Journal of the Bengal Economic Association, Vol. 9, No. 2, pp. 9-19.

Tisdell, C. A. Roy, K. and Ghose, A, (2001), *"A Critical Note on UNDP's Gender Inequality Indices"*, Journal of Contemporary Asia, Vol. 31, No. 3, pp. 385-399.

Todaro, M. P, (1997), *Economic Development*, Sixth Edition, London and New York: Addison Wesley Longman Limited.

United Nations, (1995), *Beijing Declaration and Platform for Action: Fourth World Conference on Women*, 15th September 1995.

United Nations Development Programme, (1995, 1996, 1997, 1998, 2000), *Human Development Report*, New York: Oxford University Press.

United Nations Development Programme, (1998b), *Overcoming Human Poverty*, New York: Oxford University Press.

United Nations Division for the Advancement of Women, (1996), *Women and Decision-making: Percentage of Women in Government 1996*, Bethesda: United Nations Secretariat.

United Nations Economic Commission for Africa, (1998), *African Women and Economic Development*, Addis Ababa: African Centre for Women.

United Nations Program on AIDS, (2002), *Report on the Global HIV/AIDS Epidemic and UNAIDS Assessment of the Epidemiological Situation in Kenya, 2002.* United Nations Secretariat.

Women Fighting AIDS in Kenya, The Communication Initiative Website, 2001.

World Bank, (1989), *Kenya: The Role of Women in Economic Development. A World Bank Study*, Washington, D.C.: Oxford University Press.

World Bank, (1993), *Kenya: Country Gender Profile*, World Bank, Gender Unit.

World Bank, (1995), *Participatory Poverty Assessment in Kenya*, The World Bank Participation Sourcebook, Washington, D. C.: The World Bank Group.

World Bank, (1996), *The World Bank Annual Report*. Washington, D. C.: The World Bank.

World Bank, (2002), *World Development Indicators*. Washington, D.C.: The World Bank.

In: Readings in World Development
Editors: K.C. Roy and S. Chatterjee, pp. 155-172 ISBN 1-59454-947-8

Chapter 13

INDONESIA, ASEAN AND THE ASEAN REGIONAL FORUM: CONVERGENT TRENDS IN REGIONAL AND NATIONAL DEVELOPMENT

R. James Ferguson

INTRODUCTION: INDONESIAN 'CENTRALITY'

Indonesia, conceptualized as a cultural grouping and region as well as a modern nation, has for centuries had a pivotal geo-political and international role in Southeast Asia and the wider corridor of Indo-Pacific interactions stretching from East Africa to Japan and the western Pacific. As early as the 7th to 8th centuries, major civilisations were linked by these routes, e.g. contact between China and the *mandala* system of Srivijaya, which flourished in the 7th-13th centuries, focusing on south-east Sumatra, but with influence spread through the splendour of its court and its trading networks, as well as its control of the Malacca and Sunda straits (Simkin 1968, pp112-117; Mackerras 1992, pp94-95; Highham 1989, p342; Watson 1992, pp78-79; SarDesai 1994, pp41-43; see also, Kautilya *Arthasastra* 261). Likewise, Majapahit through the 14th to early 16th centuries[1] was part of an extended island domain, with trading networks focused on east Java, linking cultures and commodities in Southeast Asia and China. Kenneth Hall has suggested that: "Collective recognition of the fourteenth and fifteenth century east Java-centered Majapahit polity are the basis of contemporary self-definitions of 'nation' and 'region' among the Javanese, Balinese, Malays, and other island peoples" (Hall 2001, p89). In this sense, Indonesian islands and cultures have had a deep regional engagement that precedes the territorial unity framed by Dutch colonialism.[2] Likewise, it is possible to conceptualise the cultural and regional foundations of ASEAN as

---

[1] The traditional date for extinction of the Majapahit polity, but not its influence, is 1527 (Hall 2001, p99).

[2] It is unwise, of course, to conceive of Indonesia as a 'New Srvijaya', in part because none of these earlier formations exactly coincide with the modern borders of Indonesia, e.g. western Sunda was probably not included in Majapahit domains (SarDesai 1994, p53). The parallel here is of regional engagement rather than strict national and territorial delimitation (for the diverse conceptual usages of Majapahit by early Indonesian nationalists including Sukarno, see SarDesai 1994, p53; Hall 2001, pp104-105; Hoey 2003).

going back indirectly to the trading networks and shared political structures of the 15th century (Hall 2001, p108; Ferguson 2001).

This deep regional interaction remains a crucial component for the development of modern Indonesia in the 20th and 21st centuries. In the last forty years Indonesia has had a central role in the Non-Aligned Movement (NAM), in the creation of the Association of Southeast Asian Nations (ASEAN), and in wider dialogue processes such as the ASEAN Regional Forum (ARF) and the ASEAN-Plus-Three group (ASEAN plus China, Japan and South Korea). Indonesia has positioned itself as a developing, multi-religious state with a strong claim to supporting cooperation and dialogue in the wider region.

ASEAN as a whole, and to a lesser degree Australia, Japan and the U.S., for the 1980s and the early 1990s had viewed Indonesia as a known, stabilising factor in the wider region (regardless of human rights problems and self-determination crises in East Timor, Papua and Aceh). The potential and centrality of Indonesia has long been noted:

> . . . Indonesia is a tremendous potential market for the region and globally and, as by far the largest country in Southeast Asia, it is a regional power of importance. Moreover, the archipelago sits astride the Indian and Pacific Oceans, and the Straits if Malacca that flow between the Indonesian island of Sumatra and Malaysia carries more than 40 percent of the world's ship-borne commerce, making a stable Indonesia desirable for global commercial activity. Moreover, the outcome of how Indonesia deals with the future will almost certainly have a ripple effect in other, smaller countries in the region facing similar economic and political situations. (Snow 2003, p157)

At the same time, from late 2003, Indonesia has helped push forward pro-active new policies for ASEAN, both in enhancing regional integration, and deepening 'strategic partnerships' with India and China. As a whole, though tensions continue over the South China Sea, over low Chinese labour costs affecting ASEAN's competitiveness (Suryodipuro 2002, p208; see further Tham 2003, p34), and Chinese military modernisation, there has been a distinct opening up of relations between ASEAN and China. China has gradually turned towards a dialogue approach with Southeast Asia, e.g. via the Indonesia hosted South-China dialogue process and then via convergence on a Code of Conduct for the South China Sea. Furthermore, once Vietnam withdrew from Cambodia, and once US-China relations improved, Indonesia moved to normalise and improve relations with PRC, as had all ASEAN members by 1991 (see further Ba 2003). This process was aided by some improvement in Sino-Vietnam relations, by the formation of the ASEAN-Plus-Three, by the acceptance of the Declaration on the Conduct of Parties in the South China Sea, and the 2002 agreement for an ASEAN-China free trade agreement to begin by 2010 (Chin 2003, pp19-20). This reduced recent historical impediments in the centuries old relationship between Indonesia and China. Here, Indonesia has continued to play a moderating role among ASEAN, China and the USA in terms of regional influence (Odgaard 2003).

In spite of successes at the diplomatic and regional level, Indonesia in recent years has had to face severe problems that have challenged its goals of national resilience, development and democratic transition. These include rapid if uneven economic reform, a new political openness that accelerates local and national political competition, coming to terms with the difficult path of independence for East Timor, renewed military crises in Aceh and political tensions in Papua (see McGibbon 2003), and sustained ethno-religious and inter-communal violence in Maluku and Central Sulawesi, including problems in Ambon and Poso, (Crouch 2003, p27).[3] Likewise, Indonesia was perceived internationally as one leg of a failed 'Asian' capitalism. Through 2002, domestic Indonesian growth (GDP) has returned to approx. 3.5-3.6%, but this was from a 'low baseline' with uncertain sustainability both at the economic and social levels (Chin 2003, p3; ADB figures via www.aric.adb.org). Real GDP growth for 2003 was 4.1% with projections of growth in GDP for 2004 being around 4.6% (DFAT 2004; Ikhsan 2003, p49). This will probably not be enough by itself to seriously reduce unemployment and poverty levels (though the government had hoped that poverty might decline by 4-7% through 2004, Perdana 2002).[4] The issue to be confronted is not just reform, but the sustainability of the reform process (Ikhsan 2003, pp54-55).

Although Indonesia has begun to stabilise, there are still major concerns about low growth in merchandise exports, continued unemployment (probably higher than the reported 8.1% figures for 2002, Tham 2003, pp27-29, with many engaged in informal sectors or underemployed), and some slowing of the restructuring on non-performing loans and assets through the Indonesian Bank Restructuring Agency (Tham 2003, p31; Smith 2003, pp111-112). Concerns have also been expressed about the Social Safety Net (SSN) program, and the National Movement for Poverty Alleviation. Although a number of communities have been aided by these programs, up to 10-14% of the early SNN loans may have been 'corrupted' and gone to the 'non-poor' (Ananta 2003, p20; see further Hatmadji and Mursitama 2003).[5]

At the regional level, there has also been a number of intensifying transnational problems, including international terrorism, undocumented migration flows, deportation of illegal workers (as has recently soured Malaysia-Indonesia relations and deepened problems along the Thai-Myanmar border), money laundering, people smuggling, and piracy across international borders (Suryodipuro 2002, pp211-212; Singh and Chin 2003, pix; see below). Transboundary environmental damage, especially the 'haze' from major fires in Sumatra and Borneo,[6] plus ongoing concerns about resource extraction from EEZ (exclusive economic zones) have also engaged ASEAN nations in disputes and new areas of cooperation (see Tan and Boutin 2001; Glover and Jessup 1999). These factors have placed a number of new pressures on Indonesia that give it a problematic prominence in the 21st century structuring of

---

[3] These were partly stabilised from late 2001 onwards, in part due to peace efforts by respective religious communities (Smith 2003, p107).

[4] Though calculations vary, most show some reduction in poverty through 2001 (BPS and LPEM figures),[4] with World Bank figures revealing a longer and slower decline through 2001-2002 (see Ikhsan 2003, figure 3.8, p41; for poverty mapping from the village level up in selected provinces, see Suryahadi et al. 2003). Poverty in the developmental context, of course, needs to look at not just a 'poverty line' based on income, but also include issues such as transient verses chronic poverty, and those vulnerable to dropping below the poverty line due to 'capability deprivation' (Perdana 2002). Poverty in a developmental sense should include measures of opportunity, empowerment, security, and capability (UNFPA 2001), thereby incorporating measures sensitive to social vulnerabilities and a wider notion of privation (Ogata and Sen 2003; Kumar 1999; Ferguson 2003).

[5] For efforts in the directions of a long-term National Poverty Reduction Strategy Paper, see SMERU 2003.

[6] The 1997-1998 fires destroyed some 8 million hectares of forest, with regional damage estimates of at least US$4.5 billion and some 70 million people affected regionally (Schweithelm and Glover 1999). Fires in following years were of a lesser order but still created strong regional concerns. By 2003, some estimates suggested that a total of 10 million hectares had been effected, with a regional economic loss of up to US$9.3 billion (*Jakarta Post* 2003b). This led to efforts to monitor regional air pollution, with problems being seriously operationalised within ASEAN in 1998, using some ADB funding, utilising the 1995 ASEAN Co-operation Plan on Transboundary Pollution and the 1997 Regional Haze Action Plan. By late 2003 this led to the ASEAN signing of the Agreement on Transboundary Haze Pollution, with strong monitoring, regulation, and cooperative mechanisms that were praised by the UNEP (*Jakarta Post* 2003b).

non-traditional 'global threat perceptions'. These problems have emerged as parallel problems for ASEAN, which has only begun to tackle them with mixed results (Chin 2003, p10).

Likewise, regional free trade agendas, services and investment agreements have yet to be fully developed. Regional integration via the AFTA and AIA (ASEAN Investment Area) remained limited, and few foreign investors perceive the region as a 'single market', in spite of efforts to push forward these goals over the last four years, including recent work (2000-2003) on the Initiative for ASEAN Integration (IAI) and proposals for an ASEAN Economic Community by 2020 (Chin 2003, p20; Suryodipuro 2002, p207). Via ASEAN Concord II, it is hoped that there will be a strong liberalisation of services by 2012, and shared trade regulations by 2020 (*Credit Control* 2003). The aim here would be not so much to increase inter-regional trade as to 'enhance the region's global competitiveness' (Tham 2003, p35). However, ASEAN may need to return to a developmental agenda that aids stability in newer members, and especially in one of its core creators, Indonesia.

National and Regional Diversity

Within this context, there are strong linkages and parallels between the wider ASEAN and the Indonesian experience. The diversity of the 'ASEAN-plus' and ASEAN Regional Forum (ARF) region, stretching across the entire Indo-Pacific area, is paralleled by the great diversities of Indonesian culture and society.

Within Indonesia, in spite of the relative dominance of Javanese populations, the archipelago has a diverse ethnic and religious mix that has only been partially explored in recent censuses (see Suryadinata *et al.* 2003). The problem of ethnicity, identity, custom and religion among diverse socio-economic groups has received renewed attention during the difficult years of transition. Survey data suggests that ethnic diversity remains the norm for most across Indonesia, with strong regional variations. Collations of data from the 2000 census show that Javanese comprise almost 42% of the population, followed by Sundanese (approximately 15%), then by another 7 major groups with over 2% of the total population (Suryadinata *et al.* 2003, Figure 1.2.1, p13). One sensitive issue has been the under-reporting of Chinese ethnic identity, and though there was a slight increase in the 'absolute' number of Chinese reported between 1930-2000, this has been masked by sensitivity to inter-ethnic tensions (Suryadinata *et al.* 2003, p11, pp73-75). Indonesia has 88% Muslims, and smaller numbers of Christians (8.92%) and Hindu's (1.81%), who nonetheless are concentrated in key regions, e.g. Christian communities in North Sumatra, East Nusa Tenggara (86%), North Sulawesi (52%), West Kalimantan (30%) and Papua (83%), and Hindus in Bali, East Java, and Central Kalimantan (Suryadinata *et al.* 2003, pp104-105, p114, p120; Rabasa 2003, p14, Table 1).

ASEAN, too, has had to lift itself above conflicting national and ethnic interests to promote active cooperation between very different groups. To a limited degree, ethnic diversity across and between states has recently come to be viewed as an asset, e.g. recognition of the cultural and sub-group linkages between Thailand and China, or India and Singapore.[7] Within the great diversity of Indonesia, likewise there has been some limited

[7] As noted by the Indian Deputy Prime Minister in a lecture given in Singapore during 2002, (Advani 2003, p6). However, past historical and religious ties do not necessarily translate into current affinities, and Southeast

ability to make real the dictum of 'unity in diversity'. However, when combined with economic crises, military engagement at the territorial level,[8] police-military rivalries, and community violence, there have been real limits to ethnic justice and balance within specific Indonesian localities (Smith 2003, p108). Here, a sense of communal and inter-communal justice is needed to reduce violence and fear, and allow national development. Likewise, developing states have to cope with the realities of ethnic identity and mobility. In the case of Indonesia, there is a complex legacy from the earlier, government sponsored transmigration scheme, aimed at reducing pressure on high population islands such as Java, and used as an integrative assimilation strategy (Tirtosudarmo 2003, p218). In some cases the scheme caused changes in local ethnic and religious ratios, heightening conflict between migrants and local populations, e.g. in Ambon (Maluku) and Poso (Sulawesi), and resulted in some return flow of migrant families (Crouch 2003, p31; Tirtosudarmo 2003, p213; Rabasa 2003, pp28-31). In the case of eastern Indonesian cities, alongside Javanese, groups such as the Bugis, Butonese and Makassarese were often viewed as comparatively successful economically, leading to ongoing local tensions (Tirtosudarmo 2003, p230).

Thus, it has been recognised by Indonesian commentators that separatist movements, e.g. in Aceh and Papua, in part flourished because 'the social discontent in the region' was 'a product of a long conflict in the region which is basically related to justice, honour and prosperity of the people' (Yudhoyono 2002, p5). Likewise, serious tensions have been experienced among Dyak and Madurese villages in West Kalimantan through early 1997 and again in 1999-2000 (Tirtosudarmo 2003, pp231-234). On this basis, administrative decentralisation and fairer access to resource revenues will not by themselves be enough to ensure the social harmony needed for development. The Indonesian government has gone part of the way in this direction by trying to develop a 'comprehensive approach' drawing on social, political, and economic factors, as supported by Susilo Bambang Yudhoyono (Coordinating Minister for Political and Security Affairs), in contrast to more hardline military approaches (Crouch 2003, p20). However, the comprehensive approach has been difficult to engage in Aceh due to continued military conflict, and is hampered by a number of factors in Papua, including perceptions of impunity in a locally unreformed military sector (McGibbon 2003, p195).

Though problematic in several areas, the democratic transition in Indonesia is remarkable in other aspects. After the elections of 2004, it will create an MPR (People's Consultative Assembly) entirely based on freely elected officials in the DPR (House of Representatives, or Parliament) and the DPD (House of Regional Representatives), including the removal of

---

Asians rightly resist the idea that their cultures are overly derivative of Indic civilisations (Limaye 2003, pp40-41). The tendency to view Southeast Asian cultures as mere extensions of either India or China was 'largely a by-product of the colonial period' (Hall 2001, p88), when European's set up a hierarchical of civilisational development.

[8] Still present at the territorial level of involvement by the TNI from village level upwards, see Darwin 2003, p228; Mietzner 2003, p250, and in areas viewed as a security zone, e.g. the extension of the military state of emergency in Aceh through November 2003 for another six months, *Tempo Interactive* 2003b.This territorial engagement has been debated closely in the last three years, with two reform options failing to change the status quo (Mietzner 2003, pp245-251). Part of the issue here is the need of the army to secure up to two thirds of its funding from outside of the central government budget, in part through running some 250 or more business enterprises (Crouch 2003, p31). Likewise, local government has sometimes been billed via 'stability funds', or funds allocated for TNI operations 'ranging from security interventions to disaster relief and developmental programs' (Mietzner 2003, p255).

military and police non-elected seats in the DPR (Smith 2003, p101; Crouch 2003, p18).[9] Press censorship has been lifted, and a wide range of NGOs, civil society groups, peasant federations, labour unions, citizens' forums (*forum warga*) and village democracy processes, via the Village Representative Board (BPD), have begun in earnest (Anlöv 2003, pp78-84). Through 2000-2001 local elections were held in most of Indonesian's 52,000 villages (Anlöv 2003, p80). Organisations aiming at public accountability and improved governance have also sprung up around the country, e.g. numerous 'Watch' organisations monitoring the government, parliament and judiciary, as well as groups such as Indonesia Corruption Watch, the Presidium of the Papuan Council (PDP) and the Forum for NGO Cooperation in Papua (Rasyie 2003, p70; Malley 2003, p110; McGibbon 2003, pp196-197).

The other great initiative that Indonesia has undertaken is its decentralisation program. Decentralisation has been viewed over the last decade as a major strategy to aid democratisation and development, and by 1997 had been adopted in varying degrees by 75 developing countries (Colongon 2003, p88; see also Malley 2003, p103). Under the Indonesian initiative (via laws 22/1999 and 25/1999), there has been a serious devolution of economic and administrative power to district level, resulting in higher autonomy and local responsibilities that were implemented from early 2001 onwards (Smith 2003, p105; Malley 2003, p109). Governance areas devolved include 'public works, health, education and culture, agriculture, transportation, trade and industry, investment, the environment, land affairs, cooperatives and labour' (Colongon 2003, pp91-92). Jakarta has seriously reduced the power of the centre through some devolution of decision-making, through the relatively untied General Allocation Fund (DAU), and through the more targeted Special Allocation Fund (DAK) designed to help 'poorer regions maintain and improve services such as public education, health, environment, transportation and water supply' (Rasyid 2003, p68). Local funding has in many cases increased, with developmental expenses being the second largest area of local government expenditure, after salaries,[10] in 2002 (25% and 57% respectively, Colongon 2003, p94). It has been difficult, however, to meet some official developmental targets for these local budgets, i.e. 30% of the budget to go to education, and 15% to health (Colongon 2003, p94). Thus, in 2002 developmental expenditure for education was 26.8% and 9.1% on health (Rohdewohld 2003, p272).

In most cases power was devolved not to the provincial level, but to the district level below this (*kabupaten/kota*), thereby reducing the likelihood of political fragmentation and separatism (Aspinall and Fealy 2003, pp3-4). Though a serious benefit for local interests and democratisation, there have been serious problems in the framing of these laws, including administrative confusion, problematic local taxation laws, power capture by old elites, some political 'bossism' at the local level, and possible entrenchment of local corruption during transition (see Bell 2003; Aspinall and Fealy 2003, p5; Rasyid 2003, p66; Malley 2003, pp102-103). There have also been claims of local vote buying, corruption, and collusion by some leaders to enrich themselves (Malley 2003, p110), and concerns about uneven gains for women at the local level (Satriyo 2003). The national government now has to oversee

[9] Free and fair elections could prove problematic in Aceh if it is still under a military state of emergency, an issue of direct concern to the Indonesian government (*Tempo Interactive* 2003b). Local elections have also reduced the numbers of the *bupati* and mayors drawn from the military and police, with career-path civil servants being the major new source (Malley 2003, p113).

[10] More than 2.3 million civil servants have been moved from central to district government administration (Rohdewohld 2003, p260).

approximately 360 local governments to ensure that their laws comply with national statutes, a slow and difficult task, with the Indonesian Chamber of Commerce suggesting that up to one thousand 'local regulations' have been inappropriately passed (Rasyid 2003, p67; Aspinall and Fealy 2003, p6). Likewise, there has been a concern that decentralisation might increase the gap between poor and rich regions within the country (Aspinall and Fealy 2003, p5).

Beyond this, Aceh and Papua have been singled out under special laws (Special Autonomy Laws of August 2001 and November 2001) framing high levels of provincial resource control and autonomy (as Special Autonomous Provinces), approximately 70% for Aceh and 80% for Papua (Smith 2003, p105, p106; Crouch 2003, p28). Under this legislation Papua, in particular, would benefit from recognition of indigenous verses non-indigenous Papuans, affirmative action in relation to representation in the bureaucracy, and the ability of the provincial government to control migration into the territory (McGibbon 2003, pp200-201). Unfortunately, both provinces have been subject to ongoing conflict, military engagement, and political uncertainty (Smith 2003, p106). These factors have meant that the two regions that might have benefited most, and towards which autonomy laws were strongly directed, have not yet gained strong advantages 'on the ground' from these daring reforms. In turn, the fate of these two areas remains a major challenge for the legitimacy of a democratic Indonesia.

Bearing in mind these factors, the Indonesian polity has made a relatively successful democratic transition, in spite of serious conflicts in some regions and uneven progress (see Suhardi 2003) towards decentralisation.[11] However, a secure developmental path for all Indonesians remains problematic, in part because of the nexus among national, security and transnational problems.

Transnational and Transboundary Effects

Nation-building and development have been problematic throughout Southeast Asia during the second half of the 20th century because (with the partial exceptions of Thailand and Singapore) these processes had not been fully established before globalisation processes began to open international borders and deregulate key aspects of national economies. Countries in ASEAN have sought to shift from developing to more developed countries at the same time as competitive pressures, opening of markets and globalisation trends have accelerated. Though Singapore might be viewed as a relative success in this dual challenge, other states are still struggling with this simultaneous agenda. In such a setting, key transnational problems can overwhelm national capacity, undermine national governance, and require more coordinated regional and multilateral responses. For Indonesia, the regional setting has posed ongoing challenges during the transition period. This can be seen in several cases where transnational contexts undermine national goals. These issues have not always been adequately moderated by regional cooperation, as can be seen in several examples.

The problem of legal and illegal labour flows has been both a resource and a problem for Indonesia. Thus, hundreds of thousands of Indonesians have worked, both legally and illegal

[11] It should be noted, of course, that the decentralisation program is only through the initiation and installation stages, and has yet to be consolidated and stabilised, as viewed in the 2000-2007 timeline suggested by the Ministry of Home Affairs (Colongon 2003, p101, footnote 8).

in nearby countries, especially Malaysia. These trends became problematic during the Asian financial crisis, and again in 2002 when Malaysia cracked down again on illegal workers, leading to the outward movement of tens of thousands of Indonesians who could not always make it home (Smith 2003, p111). The perceived poor treatment of these workers caused tensions between Malaysian and Indonesian officials, e.g. between the Malaysian Foreign Minister, Datuk Seri Syed Hamid Albar and Amien Rais (Smith 2003, p11). In the end, however, Malaysia remains dependent on Indonesian labour in key areas, e.g. in the construction industry (Aziz and Hashim 2002). This provides both benefits and risks for Malaysia, which has up to one fifth of its labour force based on foreign labour, forming part of its industrialisation path towards the goals of 2020 (Aziz and Hashim 2002, p175).

In this area ASEAN cooperation needs to go beyond existing trade and investment agreements. Just as in the large numbers of Burmese workers in Thailand,[12] and the almost global reach of Filipino labourers, Southeast Asia is both the source and destination for sustained labour flows. In 1997, Malaysia alone hosted some 1.2 million registered workers, mostly from Indonesia, Bangladesh, and the Philippines (see Azizah 2000; Liow 2003).

Although ASEAN has conducted recent dialogues for integration of labour rules at the regional level, and some regional use of foreign labour through the 'growth circles' and 'sub-regional economic cooperation' strategy,[13] much more needs to be done to avoid key bilateral tensions. Thus, the securitisation of these undocumented workers, as seems to be the trend in Malaysia, will not solve the problem (see further Liow 2003). Likewise, there have been strong calls from Indonesians for this issue to be more effectively handled at the ASEAN level: -

'ASEAN countries urgently need a commitment to formulate and implement the minimum standard for safe migrant worker placement policies, pressure for the conclusion of a bilateral agreement among ASEAN member countries on migrant workers with agreed minimum standards, and preparation for an ASEAN regional convention regarding migrant workers' protection and prevention of the trafficking of women and children'. (Jakarta Post 2003a).

Likewise, regional piracy has remained a serious problem for both Indonesia and ASEAN, with increasing incidents reported through the 1990s (a global total of 469 in 2000, with 119 of these being in Indonesian waters), and has come to the attention of Japan, India and the United States (see Liss 2003, p55; Young and Valencia 2003, p271). Generally, it is likely that piracy cases are under-reported, in part due to repercussions for large cargo carriers, while local attacks on small boats and fishermen may not technically be viewed as 'piracy on the high seas'. Piracy in Southeast increased 37% through the first half of 2003, and there have been recent fears that terrorists could use oil or LPG tankers to create a major disaster in a port or in narrow regions such as the Malacca Strait (*Australian* 2003a). Although the nexus between piracy and terrorism has yet to be established (possibly operational planning by the Abu Sayyaf group provides one example, *Australian* 2003a),[14] it

[12] Almost 4,000 illegal workers were returned to Myanmar in 2002, while there may be as many as 140,000 illegal migrants from Myanmar still within Thailand (Xinhua 2002b).

[13] From 1992. this included the Brunei-Indonesia-Malaysai-Philippines East ASEAN Growth ASEA (BIMP-EAGA), the Indonesia-Malaysia-Thailand Growth Triangle (IMT-GT), and the Indonesia-Malaysia-Singapore Growth Triangle (IMS-GT), while the Mekong Basin acts as it own natural economic territory (see Suryodipuro 2002).

[14] This is a nexus explored by the commercial operation, Aegis Defence Services (a London based consultancy). However, in terms of attacked targets for 1999-2003, maritime assets comprise less than 1%, as noted in an

indicates another layer of regional instability that has a link to poverty and gaps in regional governance. Increases in regional piracy have been noted since 1997, and the focus of activity has shifted from the Malacca Strait, then into Indonesian and Philippines waters and the South China Sea. This is a warning that piracy should not be viewed just as robbery on the high seas or across state jurisdictions (for modern definitions, see Djalal 2002, pp106-107), but as reliant on distinct political and economic conditions.

Wider regional cooperation and training initiatives, with some recent Japanese financial support for the creation of a new anti-piracy centre to be established in Southeast Asia (*Agence France Presse* 2003), has already begun through regular workshops and technical working groups, as well as the establishment of a Maritime Transport Working Group (MTWG), often hosted by Indonesia and other ASEAN states (Djalal 2002, p108-112; Suryodipuro 2002, p214). Likewise, the U.S. has welcomed the idea that Indian naval escorts might play a role in monitoring shipping on routes up to the eastern routes into the Malacca Strait, and there has been increased maritime coordination among India, the U.S. and Japan (Limaye 2003, p49; Suryodipuro 2002, p212). Recent search and rescue operations (November 2003) between Indian and Chinese navies have signalled increasing bilateral cooperation (Wu 2003). Here, the problem of improved documentation, international communication and tracking, and new registry procedures may be needed to cope with the issue of 'phantom' ships, seizure of entire cargoes, and re-registration of stolen vessels (Liss 2003, p63). Strengthened regional cooperation, based on existing agreements among Indonesia, Malaysia, and Singapore from 1992 onwards, and joint naval patrols by Malaysia and Thailand, and Malaysia and the Philippines (via Border Patrol Coordinating Groups), are needed to reduce these problems (Djalal 2002, pp109-110). Further coordination with the International Maritime Bureau Regional Piracy Center (IMBRPC) in Kuala Lumpur and the International Maritime Organization (IMO) has also been suggested (Djalal 2002, p113), while through to late 2003, an IMO regional office was established in the Philippines (*AFX News* 2003). In the wider region, Japan has been keen to develop a comprehensive regional approach to piracy, and has supported ASEAN in its ASEAN Maritime Policy and Development Framework Plan 2002-2007 (Suryodipuro 2002, pp214-217).

The last example we can briefly mention is the much highlighted problem of transnational terrorism. Part of the problem is the mobility of small groups that can pick targets at will on almost a global scale. Recently calls have been made for new methods to make key infrastructures (service points, transportation systems, communications, computer networks, and energy infrastructure) less vulnerable to terrorist attack (Advani 2003, p19; see further Lukasik et al 2003). This approach, though well meaning, has been found to be problematic even in countries such as the U.S. and Australia, and can only be fully applied to particular cases with a known logistic structure and limited territorial extensions, e.g. the Port of Singapore. Rather than approach this from a defensive or technological perspective alone, it can also be tackled by addressing the social capital and human security sides of the equation. In this setting, although security cooperation and local policing remain important, it is also important that the local culture remain critical of radical groups that may directly or indirectly host such activities.

overview of the Aegis "October 2003 Terrorism Report", located at http://www.aegisdef.com/sep2003terrorist report.htm.

In the case of Indonesia, 'a more immediate and strong counterbalance will come from mainstream Muslim groups, including Muhammadiyah and Nahdatul Ulama' (Soesastro 2002, p15; Rabasa 2003, p37). Indonesia should not be viewed as a haven of terrorism, but rather as a transitional, developing country in which terrorists have been able to use existing tensions in order to find a temporary niche from which to link regional and global networks (see further Singh and Chin 2003, pix). Thus, Jemaah Islamiyah (JI) had links in Malaysia, Singapore, Indonesia and Thailand, plus a probable wider linkage to Al-Qaeda funding and training (Chin 2003, p2003; Abuza 2003; Smith 2003, p104). Likewise, it has been suggested that Al-Qaeda had contact with the Moro Islamic Liberation Front (MILF) and Abu Sayyaf in the Philippines (Chin 2003, p10), though the political credentials of the latter organisation remain very weak. In the long run, it will be 'cooperation with mainstream and moderate Muslims' that will be crucial in disempowering such radicals (Wanandi 2003, p105). Hence, these and related problems need to be situated as a regional process drawing on cooperative and multilateral solutions (see below).

Furthermore, human insecurity within Indonesia does not in the main derive from high profile acts of horror such as the Bali bombing, though Indonesian deaths do need to be noted in these events. Day to day economic insecurity, communal violence, sporadic riots and violence, the role of organised crime through *preman* (gangers) (Ananta 2003, p14), an ongoing role for 'political thugs' and bosses (*preman politik*) (Antlöv 2003, p73), unresolved conflicts in Aceh and Papua, the impact of Military Operations Areas and 'civil militias' (Darwin 2003, pp110-112), plus unfinished democratic and decentralisation transitions are in fact of greater impact on national and regional development.

HUMAN SECURITY AT THE REGIONAL LEVEL

The question remains open as to what roles ASEAN, the ARF via its ongoing security dialogue,[15] can play in buffering and moderating these national and transnational problems. A more secure regional environment should allow Indonesia to proceed with its most pressing national goal: the eradication of poverty and human vulnerability within a state undergoing transition to a more just and open society.

ASEAN was originally established as a means to promote economic development and regional resilience: peace was needed to meet these national goals, as was the disengagement of great-power conflicts regionally (Palmer and Reckford 1987, p5). Even after the 1997-1998 crisis, ASEAN remained committed to accelerated regional development. Through the Hanoi Declaration of 1998, ASEAN hoped to build rapid recovery through deepening regional cooperation. Specific plans to counter the social impact of the financial and economic crisis included action plans on 'Rural Development', "Poverty Eradication' and 'Social Safety Nets' (*Hanoi Plan of Action,* 4.1-4.3) The Hanoi Action Plan included efforts for the core ASEAN nations to accelerate the AFTA and to push ahead with the proposed ASEAN Investment Area (AIA) (*Hanoi Declaration*, 12; *Hanoi Plan of Action* 2.2). Although the process on AFTA has been somewhat delayed, the general tenor of recent

[15] The ASEAN Concord II re-iterated in declaration 6 that 'The ASEAN Regional Forum (ARF) shall remain the primary forum in enhancing political and security cooperation in the Asia Pacific region, as well as the pivot in building peace and stability in the region.' (see BBC 2003c).

ASEAN meetings has been to increase regional economic cooperation and integration, in part in order to prepare for deeper engagement with China and global trade flows.

There is a three-way linkage among democratic, developmental and security agendas, both at the national and regional levels. Though in the short term a transition to democratic institutions can lead to deepened political instability and reduce economic governance, in the long term more open, accountable and citizen-oriented governments are likely to provide the legal framework in which local business and international investment can flourish. In Indonesia, there has been marked progress in the holding of open elections, in reform of the Constitution, and in the increased activity of the annual MPR (People's Consultative Assembly) meetings (Soesastro 2002, p11), as well as increased activity in local government and civil society organisations. Through 2002-2003, the gradual strengthening of civil society in Indonesia has laid the basis of providing a vigorous partner in local and grass roots development (Yudhoyono 2002, p8). Active civil society groups, especially in Indonesia, Thailand, and the Philippines, combined with their engagement with INGOs and 'epistemic or knowledge communities', will open another avenue for a more vigorous regional cooperation among civil societies across Southeast Asia. In the long run, such cooperation may be able to envisage a multilateral, 'participatory regionalism' that is built as much on progressive democratisation as on national sovereignty in Southeast Asia. (modifying Acharya 2003).

These few examples indicate the deep relation between security and development. In the words of the Indian Deputy Prime Minister (Advani 2003, p7): 'The two are inseparably inter-related. One cannot think of development without security, or security without development.' This was developed into six 'lessons' linking national and regional development. These can be somewhat summarised as (based on Advani 2003, pp9-10): -

1. 'A just cooperative order, with the willing participation of all members of society, provides a stable basis for addressing the security concerns of the world'. (Advani 2003, p9)
2. Due to interdependence, no single nation 'can enjoy security and development at the cost of others'. (Advani 2003, p9)
3. National security 'is enhanced through collective security - subregional, regional as well as global security; (Advani 2003, p10)
4. Development is 'best achieved through collective development - through subregional, regional and global cooperation.' (Advani 2003, p10)
5. Exclusive and extremist ideologies undermine such cooperation and development. "The intolerance, extremism, hegemonism and proneness to violence that such ideologies breed pose a great threat to development and security - both within nations and to the world as a whole.' (Advani 2003, p10)
6. 'Pockets of extreme poverty in various parts of the world endanger the social fabric, undermine economic development and the environment, and threaten political stability in many countries.' (Advani 2003, p10).

Several key agencies allow Indonesia to expand its zone of regional cooperation. These international, multilateral organisations include ASEAN, AFTA, the ARF, the ASEAN-plus-three, APEC, and the West Pacific Regional Cooperation forum[16] (Yudhoyono 2002, p7;

[16] Includes Australia, East Timor, Indonesia, New Zealand, Papua New Guinea and the Philippines.

Smith 2003, p111), though the latter has yet to have had a strong impact on developmental conditions in East Indonesia.

It is important to link transnational pressures back to the developmental and security nexus. From this perspective, 'human emancipation, far from standing apart from international security, is in fact co-extensive with it: ensuring the protection and prosperity of the individual, through truncating the inequities and social tensions which might later erupt through the types of conflicts at the heart of more traditional security concerns' (Lizée 2002, p510). More recently, the International Commission on Human Security,[17] ASEAN academics, and Thailand in particular have become more interested in the human security debate, with Thai initiatives resulting in the ASEAN-PMC Caucus on Social Safety Nets (Lizée 2002, pp510-511; Capie and Evans 2002, p144). On this basis, states are only one layer in the human security equation, with non-state, regional and international actors having important roles (Lizée 2002, p512).

Trends reiterated through late 2003 suggest that ASEAN is still actively seeking regional stability in Asia as a precondition to economic growth. Among the most recent developments has been the signing of the ASEAN Concord II (Bali Concord II), designed to prepare the ground for the 'proposed' ASEAN Community based on the three 'pillars' of an ASEAN Security Community, an ASEAN Economic Community, and an ASEAN Socio-Cultural Community (*Borneo Bulletin* 2003; BBC 2003c). The plans for the future ASEAN Security Community made special note of the need to strengthen national and regional capacities to deal with terrorism and 'other transnational crimes', as well as recognising that 'maritime issues and concerns were transboundary in nature' (BBC 2003b). The ASEAN Security Community concepts were predicated on, and subscribed to 'the principle of comprehensive security', therein 'recognising the strong interconnections among political, economic and social realities' (BBC 2003c).

CONCLUSION

Indonesia has experienced a rapid transition since the crisis years of 1997-1998. Indonesians rightly hope that current democratic and constitution reforms will lay the basis for a just, stable and diverse nation-state (Yudhoyono 2002, p6). However, these expectations have been modified and somewhat reduced (Soesastro 2002, p11) by uneven economic growth, and by a wide range of security problems that have placed international and local pressures on Indonesian governance. These problems, reconceptualised as human security in the wider sense, have undermined some areas of development over the last two years. They will not be solved, however, at the point of a gun, nor even by heightened surveillance and intelligence-sharing. Well-known national and regional resources of 'cooperative security' and 'human security' can be further mobilised to improve conditions more effectively. Here, ASEAN, and to a lesser degree the ASEAN-plus-three and the ARF, remain important organisations for deepening cooperation on the two key issues of human security and human development. Indonesia, in turn, is a lynch pin in regional cooperation and future stability.

REFERENCES

Abuza, Z, (2003), *"Funding terrorism in Southeast Asia: the financial network of Al Qaeda and Jemaah Islamiya"*, Contemporary Southeast Asia, 25 no. 2, August 2003, pp169-199.

Acharya, A, (1999), *"Realism, Institutionalism, and the Asian Economic Crisis"*, Contemporary Southeast Asia, 21 no.1, April 1999, pp.1-29.

Advani, Shri L.K, (2003), *New Approaches to Security and Development*, Singapore: SEAS.

Aegis, (2003), *"October 2003 Terrorism Report"* [Overview], London, Aegis Defence Services, 2003 [Internet access at www.*aegisdef.com/sep2003terroristreport.htm*]

AFX News, (2003), *"Maritime group plans Asia offices to help combat attack threats"*, November 20, 2003 [Access via LexisNexis Database]

Agence France Presse, (2003), *"Malaysia bids for Japan sponsored anti-piracy centre"*, November 11, 2003 Tuesday [Access via LexisNexis Database]

Aldrich, R. J, (2002), *"Dangerous liaisons: post-September 11 intelligence alliances"*, Harvard International Review, 24 no. 3, Fall 2002, pp50-54

Ananta, A (ed.), (2003), *The Indonesian Crisis: A Human Development Perspective*, Singapore: ISEAS.

Ananta, A, (2003), *"What Do We Learn from the Crisis? Insights on Human Development in Indonesia During 1997-99"*, in Ananta, A (ed.), *The Indonesian Crisis: A Human Development Perspective*, Singapore: ISEAS, pp3-28.

Antara, (2003), *"NKRI's Existence to be Defended at All Cost, Says Min.Yudhoyono"*, Antara - The Indonesian National News Agency, June 24, 2003 [Access via LexNexis Database].

Antlöv, H, (2003), "Not Enough Politics! Power, Participation and the New Democratic Polity in Indonesia", in Aspinall, E and Fealy, G (eds), *Local Power and Politics in Indonesia: Decentralisation and Democratisation*, Singapore: ISEAS, pp72-86.

Aspinall, Edward and Fealy, Greg (eds), (2003), *Local Power and Politics in Indonesia: Decentralisation and Democratisation*, Singapore: ISEAS.

Aspinall, Edward and Fealy, Edward (2003), *"Introduction: Decentralisation, Democratisation and the Rise of the Local"*, in Aspinall, E and Fealy, G (eds), *Local Power and Politics in Indonesia: Decentralisation and Democratisation*, Singapore: ISEAS, pp1-14.

Australian *"Terror Fears for High Seas Piracy"*, 8 October 2003a, p37

Australian *"Marine Bill on a Slow Boat"*, 8 October 2003b, p37

Aziz, A. R. A, and Hashim, H, (2002), *"Immigrant Entrepreneurs in Malaysia: The Case of Indonesian Construction Subcontractors"*, The Indonesian Quarterly, 30 no. 2, 2002, pp175-194

Azizah, K, (2000), *"Indonesian Immigrant Settlements in Peninsular Malaysia"*, Sojourn: Journal of Social Issues in Southeast Asia, 15 no. 1, April 2000, pp100-122

BA, A. D, (2003), *"China and ASEAN"*, Asian Survey, 43 no. 4, July/August 2003, pp622-687.

BBC *"Text of India-ASEAN 'Comprehensive Economic Cooperation' Agreement"*, BBC Monitoring Asia Pacific, 8 October 2003a [Access via LexisNexis Database].

[17] Their home page is located at http://www.humansecurity-chs.org/

BBC *"Indonesian President Issues Statement on ASEAN Summit"*, BBC Monitoring Asia Pacific, 8 October 2003b [Access via LexisNexis Database].

BBC *"Indonesia: Full Text of ASEAN Leaders' 'Bali Concord II' Declaration"*, BBC Monitoring Asia Pacific, 7 October 2003c [Access via LexisNexis Database].

Bell, G. F, (2003), *"Indonesia: The Regional Autonomy Laws, Two Years Later"*, in Singh, D and Chin, K. W (eds) Southeast Asian Affairs 2003, Singapore: ISEAS, pp117-134.

Borneo Bulletin *"Brunei Sultan Urges ASEAN to Tackle Terrorism, Deepen Economic Integration"*, 8 October 2003 [Access via LexisNexis Database].

Capie, D, and Evans, P, (2002), The Asia-Pacific Security Lexicon, Singapore: ISEAS.

Chandrasekaran, R, (2003), "Is Indonesia Unravelling", in Mansbach, R.W. and Rhodes, E (eds) *Global Politics in a Changing World Order*, Boston, Houghton Mifflin Company, pp151-155.

Chon, K.W. (2003), *"Southeast Asia in 2002: From Bali to Iraq - Co-operating for Security"*, in Singh, D and Chin, K.W (eds), Southeast Asian Affairs 2003, Singapore: ISEAS, pp3-23.

Colongon, A. A, (Jr) (2003), "What is Happening on the Ground? The Progress of Decentralisation", in Aspinall, E and Fealy, G (eds) *Local Power and Politics in Indonesia: Decentralisation and Democratisation*, Singapore: ISEAS, pp87-102.

Credit Control (2003), *"China and Southeast Asia"*, Country Risk Analysis, 24 no. 5, pp25-26

Crouch, H, (2003), "Political Update 2002: Struggling to Maintain Momentum", in Aspinall, E and Fealy, G (eds), *Local Power and Politics in Indonesia: Decentralisation and Democratisation*, Singapore: ISEAS, pp15-34.

Darwin, M, (2003), "Freedom from Fear: Social Disruption and System of Violence in Indonesia", in Ananta, A (ed.), *The Indonesian Crisis: A Human Development Perspective*, Singapore: ISEAS, pp105-158.

Di Meglio, R. R, (1970), "Arab Trade with Indonesia and the Malay Peninsula from the 8th to the 16th Century", in Richards, D.S. (ed.), *Islam and the Trade of Asia: A Colloquium*, Oxford: Bruno Cassirer, pp105-135.

DFAT, (2004), "Indonesia: Fact Sheet", Canberra, Department of Foreign Affairs and Trade, [Internet Access via http://*www.dfat.gov.au/geo/indonesia/index.html*]

Djalal, H, (2002), *"Piracy and the Challenges of Cooperative Security and Enforcement Policy"*, Indonesian Quarterly, 30 no. 2, pp106-116.

Eng, P, (1999), *"Transforming ASEAN"*, The Washington Quarterly, 22 no.1, Winter 1999, pp49ff [Internet Access via Infotrac SearchBank]

Ferguson, R. J, (1999), *"East Asian Regionalism: The Challenge of Political Reform and Systemic Crisis in the Late 1990s"*, Paper Presented at the Centre for the Study of Globalisation and Regionalisation Conference, After the Global Crisis: What Next for Regionalism? University of Warwick, 16-17th September 1999

Ferguson, R. J, (2001), "Trading Cultures: Regional and Global Interactions in the Indo-Pacific Region", in Sen, R. (ed.), *Economic Development in the 21st Century*, Bombay: Deep and Deep, pp289-337

Ferguson, R. J, (2003), "Environmental Sustainability in India and China: Prospects and Risks", in K. C. Roy and R. N. Gosh (eds), Twentieth *Century Development: Some Relevant Issues*, N.Y: Nova Science.

Garofano, J, (1999), *"Flexibility or Irrelevance: Ways Forward for the ARF"*, Contemporary Southeast Asia, 21 no. 1, April 1999, pp74-94.

Garofano, J, (2002), " *Power, Institutions, and the ASEAN Regional Forum: A Security community for Asia?* ", Asian Survey, 42 no 3, May-June 2002, pp502-521.

Glover, D, and Jessup, T, (eds) (1999), *Indonesia's Fires and Haze: The Cost of Catastrophe,* Singapore: ISEAS.

Hall, K. R, (2001), *"The Roots of ASEAN: Regional Identities in the Strait of Melaka Region Circa 1500 C.E.* ", Asian Journal of Social Science, 29 no. 1, pp87-119.

"Hanoi Declaration of 1998", Strategic Digest, 29 no. 3, March 1999, pp352-355.

"Hanoi Plan of Action", Strategic Digest, 29 no. 3, March 1999, pp356-368.

Hatnadji, S. H and Mursitama, T N, (2003), "Social Safety Net Programmes in Indonesia: Some Efforts to Survive", in Ananta, A (ed.), *The Indonesian Crisis: A Human Development Perspective*, Singapore: ISEAS, pp266-295.

Higham, C, (1989), *The Archaeology of Mainland Southeast Asia: From 10 000 B.C. to the Fall of Angkor*, Cambridge: Cambridge University Press.

Henderson, J, (1999), *Reassessing ASEAN*, Adelphi Paper 328, London: IISS, May 1999.

Hoey, B. A, (2003), *"Nationalism in Indonesia: building imagined and intentional communities through transmigration"*, Ethnology, 42 no. 2, Spring 2003, pp109-126.

Ikhsan, M, (2003), "Economic Update 2002: Struggling to Maintain Momentum", in Aspinall, E and Fealy, G (eds), *Local Power and Politics in Indonesia: Decentralisation and Democratisation*, Singapore: ISEAS, pp35-62.

Jakarta Post *"ASEAN must find the best way to solve issues of migrant workers"*, October 9, 2003a [Access via LexisNexis Database].

Jakarta Post *"UNEP Hails ASEAN Haze Pollution Agreement"*, 1 December 2003b [Access via LexisNexis Database].

Jones, D. M, and Smith, M. L, (2002), *"From Konfrontasi to Disintegrasi: ASEAN and the Rise of Islamism in Southeast Asia."*, Studies in Conflict and Terrorism, 25 no. 6, Nov/Dec 2002, pp343-356.

Kautilya, (1967), *Arthasastra, trans. by R. Shamasastry*, Mysore, Mysore Printing and Publishing House.

Kumar, A.K, (1999), *Shiva Poverty and Human Development in India: Getting Priorities Right, UNDP, Occasional Paper no. 30*, [Internet Access http://*www.undp.org.in/report/PHDI.htm*].

Limaye, S. P, (2003), *"India's Relations with Southeast Asia Take a Wing"*, in Singh, D, and Chin, K. W, (eds) Southeast Asian Affairs 2003, Singapore: ISEAS, pp39-51.

Liss, C, (2003), *"Maritime Piracy in Southeast Asia"*, in Singh, D and Chin, K. W (eds), Southeast Asian Affairs 2003, Singapore: ISEAS, pp52-70.

Liow, J, (2003), *"Malaysia's illegal Indonesian migrant labour problem: in search of solutions"*, Contemporary Southeast Asia, 25 no. 1, April 2003, pp44-64.

Lizee, P. P, (2002), *"Human Security in Vietnam, Laos, and Cambodia"*, Contemporary Southeast Asia, 24 no. 3, December 2002, pp509-527.

Lukasik, S. J, Goodman, S. E, and Longhurst, D. W, (2003), *Protecting Critical Infrastructure Against Cyber-Attack*, Adelphi Paper 359, London: IISS.

Mackerras, C, (1992), *Eastern Asia: An Introductory History*, Melbourne: Longman Cheshire.

Malik, J. M, (2002), *"Dragon on terrorism: assessing China's tactical gains and strategic losses after 11 September"*, Contemporary Southeast Asia, 24 no. 2, August 2002, pp252-291.

Malley, M. S, (2003), *"New Rules, Old Structures and the Limits of Democratic Centralisation"*, in Aspinall, E and Fealy, G (eds), Local Power and Politics in Indonesia: Decentralisation and Democratisation, Singapore: ISEAS, pp102-118.

Mansbach, R. W and Rhodes, E (eds), (2003), *Global Politics in a Changing World Order*, Boston: Houghton Mifflin Company.

McGibbon, R, (2003), "Between Rights and Repression: The Politics of Special Autonomy in Papua", in Aspinall, E and Fealy, G (eds), *Local Power and Politics in Indonesia: Decentralisation and Democratisation*, Singapore: ISEAS, pp194-213

Meilink-Roelofsz, M.A.P, (1963), Asian Trade and European Influence In the Indonesian Archipelago Between 1500 and About 1630, The Hague: Martinus Nijhoff.

Mietzner, M, (2003), "Business as Usual? The Indonesian Armed Forces and Local Politics in the Post-Soeharto Era", in Aspinall, E and Fealy, G (eds), *Local Power and Politics in Indonesia:* Decentralisation and Democratisation, Singapore: ISEAS, pp245-258.

Nye, J. S, Jr (2003), *"The velvet hegemon: how soft power can help defeat terrorism"*, Foreign Policy, May-June 2003, pp74-75 [Access via Infotrac Database].

Odgaard, L, (2003), *"ASEAN's Security Concerns About China"*, Security Dialogue, 34 no. 1, March 2003, pp11-24.

Ogata, S and Sen, A, (2003), *Final Report of the Commission on Human Security, N.Y: Commission on Human Security* [Internet Access at http://*www.humansecurity-chs.org/finalreport/index.html*].

Palmer, R. D, and Reckford, T. J, (1987), *Building ASEAN: 20 Years of Southeast Asian Cooperation*, N.Y: Praeger.

Perdana, A. A, (2002), *"Transient Poor, Chronic Poor, and the Vulnerability to Poverty"*, Indonesian Quarterly, 30 no. 1, pp4-7.

Rabasa, A. M, (2003), Political *Islam in Southeast Asia: Moderates, Radicals and Terrorists*, Adelphi Paper 358, London: IISS.

Ramcharan, R, (2000), *"ASEAN and Non-interference: A Principle Maintained"*, Contemporary Southeast Asia, 22 no. 1, April 2000, pp.60-88.

Rasyid, M. R, (2003), "Regional Autonomy and Local Politics in Indonesia", in Aspinall, E and Fealy, G (eds), *Local Power and Politics in Indonesia: Decentralisation and Democratisation*, Singapore: ISEAS, pp63-71.

Richards, D.S. (ed.), (1970), *Islam and the Trade of Asia: A Colloquium*, Oxford: Bruno Cassirer.

Rohdewohld, R, (2003), "Decentralisation and the Indonesian Bureaucracy", in Aspinall, E and Fealy, G (eds), *Local Power and Politics in Indonesia: Decentralisation and Democratisation*, Singapore: ISEAS, pp259-274.

Sardesal, D.R, (1994), *Southeast Asia: Past and Present, 3rd edition*, Boulder: Westview Press.

Satriyo, H. A, (2003), "Decentralisation and Women in Indonesia: One Step Back, Two Steps Forward", in Aspinall, E and Fealy, G (eds), Local Power and Politics in Indonesia: Decentralisation and Democratisation, Singapore: ISEAS, pp217-229.

Schweitheim, J and Glover, D, (1999), "Causes and Impacts of the Fires", in Glover, D and Jessup, T (eds*), Indonesia's Fires and Haze: The Cost of Catastrophe*, Singapore: ISEAS, pp1-13.

Simkin, C.G.F, (1968), The Traditional Trade of Asia, London: Oxford University Press.

Singh, D and Chin, K. W (eds), (2003), *Southeast Asian Affairs 2003*, Singapore: ISEAS.

Smeru, (2003), *Consolidation of Existing Participatory Poverty Assessments (PPA) in Indonesia: An Inception Report*, Jakarta: SMERU Research Institute and Pradipta Paramitha, November 2003.

Smith, A. L, (2003) *"Indonesia in 2002: Megawati's Way", in Singh, D and Chin, K. W (eds), Southeast Asian Affairs 2003*, Singapore: ISEAS, pp97-116.

Snow, D. M, (2003), *Cases in International Relations: Portraits of the Future, N.Y: Longman.*

Soesastro, H, (2002), *"Indonesia Under Megawati"*, Trends in Southeast Asia, No. 2, January 2002, pp9-20.

Straits Times *"ASEAN, China Sign Non-Aggression Pact"*, Straits Times Interactive, 8 October 2003 [Internet Access].

Suhardi, E, (2003), *"Rediscovery of local governance in the decentralized Indonesia"*, Jakarta Post, 12 November 2003 [Access via LexisNexis Database].

Suryadinata, L, Arifin, E. N and Ananta, A, (2003), *Indonesia's Population: Ethnicity and Religion in a Changing Political Landscape*, Singapore: ISEAS.

Suryahadi, A et al., (2003), *Developing a Poverty Map for Indonesia: An Initiatory Work in Three Provinces*, SMERU Research Report, Jakarta: SMERU Research Institute, May 2003.

Suryodipuro, S, (2002), *"ASEAN: The Challenge of Integration, Cohesion, and Maritime Cooperation"*, The Indonesian Quarterly, 30 no. 2, pp207-219.

Tan, A. T. H. and Boutin, J. D. K (eds.), (2001), *Non-traditional Security Issues in Southeast Asia*, Singapore: Select Publishers for the Institute of Defence and Strategic Studies.

Tempo Interactive *"Government Refuses Further Dialog with Gam"*, 17 November 2003a [Internet Access via http://www.tempointeractive.com/].

Tempo Interactive *"DPR Accepts Extension of Military State of Emergency in Aceh"*, 14 November 2003b [Internet Access via http:*//www.tempointeractive.com/*].

Tham, S. Y, (2003), "Economic Overview of Southeast Asia in 2002", in Singh, D and Chin, K. W (eds), *Southeast Asian Affairs 2003*, Singapore: ISEAS, pp24-38.

Tirtosudarmo, R, (2003), "Population Mobility and Social Conflict: The Aftermath of the Economic Crisis in Indonesia", in Ananta, A (ed.), *The Indonesian Crisis: A Human Development Perspective*, Singapore: ISEAS, pp213-244.

Tow, W. T, (2003), *"Apocalypse Forever? International Relations Implications of 11 September"*, Australian Journal of Politics and History, 49 no. 3, September 2003, pp314-325.

UNFPA, (2001), *The State of World Population 2001, United Nations Population Fund*, [Internet Access at *http://www.unfpa.org/swp/swpmain.htm*].

Wanandi, J, (2003), *"Regional Perspective on Asia Pacific Security: A Southeast Asia View"*, The Indonesian Quarterly, 31 no. 2, pp101-110.

Warren, J. F, (2002), *Iranun and Balangingi: Globalization, Maritime Raiding and the Birth of Ethnicity,* Singapore: Singapore University Press.

Watson, A, (1992), *The Evolution of International Society: A Comparative Historical Analysis,* London: Routledge.

Wu, D, (2003), *"China agency says search-and-rescue naval exercise with India 'complete success'"*, BBC Monitoring Asia Pacific - Political, November 14, 2003 [Access via LexisNexis Database].

Xinhua, *"Thailand to Join System of Sharing Intelligence Against Terrorism"*, Xinhua News Agency, Feb 26, 2002a [Access via Infotrac Database].

Xinhua *"Nearly 4,000 illegal Myanmar workers return from Thailand"*, Xinhua News Agency, July 17, 2002b].

Xinhua *"Roundup: Jakarta postpones plan to split Papua"*, Xinhua News Agency, August 28, 2003, Thursday [Access via LexisNexis Database].

Young, A. J. and Valencia, M. J, (2003), *"Conflation of Piracy and Terrorism in Southeast Asia: Rectitude and Utility"*, Contemporary Southeast Asia, 35 no. 2, August 2003, pp269-283.

Yudhoyono, S. B, (2002), *"Indonesia's Political and Security Challenges"*, Trends in Southeast Asia, No. 2, January 2002, pp1-8.

In: Readings in World Development
Editors: K.C. Roy and S. Chatterjee, pp. 173-181
ISBN 1-59454-947-8

Chapter 14

Experiences Gained in Poverty Alleviation and Lessons Learnt

K. C. Roy and S. Chatterjee

Introduction

Throughout the developing world, almost every country has been implementing its economic development programmes under some form of economic planning. In the large and populous poor countries of Asia and Africa, poverty is heavily concentrated in rural areas where the vast majority of population live. Hence, an important objective of the development planning in these countries has been to achieve a reduction in the level of absolute poverty in the shortest possible time.

However, since poverty is an outcome of economic, social and political processes that interact with and re-enforce each other in ways that worsen or ease the deprivation that these poor people face every day, attacking poverty requires promoting security with actions at local, national and global levels. The lessons that we learn from the successful poverty reduction strategies adopted in East Asian and South East Asian countries suggest that rapid and politically sustainable progress on poverty has been achieved by pursuing a strategy that has promoted the productive use of the poors' most abundant asset, labour, and provided to the poor the basic social services such as primary health care, family planning, nutrition and education. In China, communes have played the leading role in making provisions for social services for the rural poor, and the states adoption of free market economic policies generated high growth and transformed China into the world's manufacturing hub, creating opportunities for the utilisation of its abundant labour.

Policy Requirements for Poverty Reduction

In discussing the main issues in poverty alleviation and development in Chapter One, Kartik Roy and Srikanta Chatterjee have argued for the need for achieving economic growth first by developing countries before they undertake measures to redistribute income to the poor to alleviate their poverty. But the adoption of a pro-growth and pro-market economic strategy requires a strong activist pro-growth state (political institution), society and a robust law enforcement institution. Furthermore, they have also called for the implementation of a population growth reduction strategy which by slowing down the rate of population growth will facilitate the rapid reduction in poverty level in a country. A successful implementation of a poor population growth reduction strategy, in the final analysis, also depends on the capability of the political and social institutions to implement such a policy. Hence, they have adopted an institutionalist approach to analyse the problem of poverty alleviation and development.

Since the institutional capabilities of East Asian and South Asian countries to implement growth promoting and poverty reduction strategies are greater than those of South Asian countries, poverty has fallen dramatically to a very low level in all East Asian and in a number of South East Asian countries, relative to the decline in poverty level in South Asian countries. However, as already discussed in Chapter One, poverty has many dimensions which include economic and cultural poverty, both of which increase poor peoples' vulnerability and exposure to risk, which, in turn, makes them voiceless and powerless.

When poor people reach this state of voicelessness, powerlessness and helplessness, their sense of happiness and sorrows disappears and they accept their current state of living as ordained by their destiny. The acceptance of this kind of living condition stems from their belief that nothing better can happen to them in their present life. This situation is referred to as their 'Poverty Absorption Capacity' (PAC). If the degree of acceptance by the poor of their state of living in a world of voicelessness and powerlessness is high, then their degree of PAC is also high. When poor people reach this state of mind, it is difficult to bring these people out of poverty without lifting their current state of mind from helplessness to hope and concomitantly without reducing the level of their PAC. But the reduction in PAC level can only be achieved if concerted action is undertaken by the state, NGOs and multilateral agencies to implement genuine programmes for alleviation of economic and social poverty, and thereby to improve their state of mind from the state of hopelessness to that of 'hope'.

Mrinal Dasgupta, in his chapter on poverty alleviation and development in East and South East Asian countries, places strong emphasis on the need for poor countries in sub-Saharan Africa, South Asia and in the Pacific to reduce the level of PAC of the poor. He further stresses the need for rich countries and the World Bank to provide debt relief to the poor countries. He suggests that the impact of economic reform on poverty level in South Asian countries, as well as in Indonesia, has not been favourable. Hence, special attention needs to be given to address the problem of accentuation of the level of poverty resulting from changes in weather, market and investment conditions, as well as in public policy. Thus, along with achieving economic growth and macro-economic stability, the governments of these countries need to facilitate the access of the poor to market opportunities, assets, credit, employment, education, health care, and so on.

Dasgupta further observes that while the impact of reform on the poor in Chile, China, Ghana, Uganda and Vietnam has been favourable by raising the producer prices for small farmers, in Cameroon, India, Bangladesh and a few other countries, after the implementation of reform measures, market forces have reduced implicit subsidies that the farmers used to receive. At the same time, unpredictable behaviour of agricultural credit and marketing activities further worsened the economic condition of the poor farmers.

POVERTY AND ENVIRONMENT RELATIONSHIP ISSUES

In poor countries, lack of income forces a substantial proportion of poor families in rural areas to collect part of their daily requirement of food, fodder, firewood, as well as some income earning inputs such as fallen leaves, from the forest. Due to a high rate of population growth, particularly among the poor families, the number of members in poor families continues to rise and in the absence of any employment opportunities, the number of poor people using the forest and other natural resources, such as 'Village Commons', and the average time spent in forests, continues to rise. As a result, the rate of destruction of forests accelerates, triggering a rapid decline in the capacity of the forest to provide the means of sustenance to the poor people. The capacity of the forest to regenerate itself also weakens further because of illegal conversions of forest land and village commons such as canals, drains and pastures to agriculture land by economically and politically powerful villagers (particularly land holder families) and by large scale clearing of forests illegally (by bribing forest officers, local government leaders and even top level politicians) by timber merchants. The trees acquired illegally are eventually used as inputs for the country's industrial and other development activities. Shifting cultivation has also contributed to environmental degradation in many of these countries. Disappearance of village forests and canals, and their conversion to agriculture plots, increases the frequency and intensity of flooding villages and of agriculture lands, thereby contributing to large scale destruction of agriculture crops. All these, in turn, adversely affect the rate of growth and development of the country which in turn accentuates the level of poverty of the poor. Thus develops a vicious circle of low levels of development activities which, in turn, leads to the degradation and destruction of forests and other natural resources which, in turn, accentuates the level of poverty of the poor. This undermines the country's growth and development outcomes which further increase the poors' reliance on forests and environment for their survival.

However, the persistence of poverty, the destruction of the environment and low growth and development are, to a great extent, the outcome of institutional failures under which appropriate policies for growth promotion, poverty alleviation and environment management are not implemented. Institutional failures provide incentives to groups of individuals to maximise their private gains at the expense of a country's gains. But, it is possible to sharply reduce the adverse effects of growth on the environment and to improve the condition of the poor with effective policies and institutions which will allow the income growth to provide to the countries the resources for improved environmental management and poverty alleviation.

However, formulating effective policies is not as difficult as creating effective institutions. Economists argue that market failures that lead to over exploitation of natural resources stem from external costs that are not borne by producers. Even in a well functioning market economy, externalities require government intervention to reach efficient market outcomes. It is argued that government can confer property rights on private users, regulate access to common resources, impose taxes that reflect external costs, and issue limited access rights.

For example, since forests are a tangible property and exclusive ownership is enforceable, the government can privatise the asset by granting on selling rights to private producers. But the private producer who obtains the ownership rights to a forest will be interested to purchase this right if there is an effective and honest law enforcement institution which will ensure that the intrusion in and encroachment on that private forest by private individuals will be penalised. But, at the same time, the retention of state control over certain proportions of forests alongside tribal villages where extreme poverty is heavily concentrated will be necessary to ensure that the poors' access to forest products are not eliminated.

Thus, the market based solution alone cannot adequately tackle the twin problems of preservation of forests and poverty eradication. The presence of a powerful and honest political institution is crucial to achieving success in meeting these twin objectives.

Dhulasi Vardarajan and Arockia Raj in their chapter on energy, environment and poverty nexus in developing countries, examine the relationship between poverty and environment and the depth of dependence of rural people in poor countries on forest and bio-mass for earning a substantial proportion of their livelihood and fuel. Biomass fuels are used by about 3 million people in the world to cook their food everyday. In India and Nepal, biomass energy contributes 33 percent and 92 percent to the total energy consumption. But, the generation of biomass energy has been significantly contributing to environmental degradation and health hazards. Since the reliance of the poor on natural resources for their food, shelter and energy needs cannot be greatly reduced, it is important to adopt a system of environmental management which will provide all people, particularly the poor, with livelihoods which will be relatively non-polluting and non-resource degrading.

C. Siwar and N. Chamuri in their chapter on poverty and environment in Malaysia and their implications for sustainability, examine the poverty condition in Malaysia and the dependence of the poor on natural resources for their survival. They examine the difficulties experienced by the poor in adopting an environmentally sustainable life style, and analyse some of the programmes implemented by the government to promote environmental sustainability. They also discuss the existing institutional barriers to achieving the twin goals of environmental sustainability and poverty reduction and call for changes in the policy regime for the states and the private sectors cooperation in addressing this issue. However, the authors suggest that the environmental degradation in rural areas in Malaysia has not yet reached such an alarming stage as to threaten the livelihoods of the poor people. Although shifting cultivation is being practised among some indigenous people, this practice is decreasing, as such people are gradually being absorbed in to modern family and in other resettlement schemes. However, it would appear that the environmental degradation has been caused more by inappropriate policy regimes which have promoted large scale agriculture, highway construction, open access to coastal fisheries and so on.

The state in Malaysia is aware of the need to improve the natural resource management by adopting a better land-use planning and sustainable forest management practice, ensuring better use of marine resources and by extending the bio-diversity plan to several provinces.

Apart from framing appropriate laws, the state has begun to use market-based instruments such as pricing of resources, subsidies and taxes, as a means to maintain the quality of the environment. The authors argue that the implementation of a win-win strategy to achieve the goals of poverty alleviation and sustainable environmental management, will require the involvement of poverty stricken indigenous communities, the private sector and the state.

Malaysia and Indonesia are the first and second largest palm oil exporting countries in the world. But, land clearing activities for conversion of forested land for growing oil palm trees in both countries have given rise to recurring haze from forest fires and have caused considerable damage to the Malaysian economy and to human health. While to reduce the adverse impact of haze, both countries have imposed bans on open burnings for land clearance, but the enforcement capacity of Indonesian government is considerably weaker than that of Malaysian government.

Jamal Othman, in his chapter on policy failures and environmental externalities in the oil palm industry in Malaysia and Indonesia, argues that due to Malaysia's commitment towards sustainable forest and environmental management, the rise in export demand for palm oil is likely to produce smaller deforestation impact and to result in less adverse land preparation practices for agriculture expansion. But, in Indonesia, greater use of land for expansion of oil-palm cultivation combined with laxed environmental regulations will continue to give rise to haze externalities, thereby adversely affecting output and human welfare in Malaysia. Hence, he emphasises the need for the Indonesian government to make a genuine effort to develop and implement a better procedure for land procurement, and to implement better environmental regulations.

Importance of Manufacturing, Services and Agricultural Sector for Poverty Alleviation

Since the implementation of poverty alleviation policy in any country requires the creation of employment opportunities in manufacturing, services and agricultural sectors, the availability of credit to producers play an important role in employment creation. In this context, S. Ragothaman has discussed the performance of India's manufacturing and services sector in the post-reform period in chapter seven. Her study shows that despite the abolition in the post-reform period of many controls and regulations which constrained the performance of the manufacturing sector in the pre-reform period, the performance of the manufacturing sector in the post-reform period lagged considerably behind that of the services sector, in terms of growth. But, in terms of the contribution of a sector's growth to the growth of the GDP, the agriculture and manufacturing sectors stand first and second and services comes last. However, because the manufacturing sector depends on the support of the services sector for achieving high growth, measures are needed to ensure robust growth of all three sectors. Also, from the point of view of employment generation, the manufacturing activities both in organised and unorganised sectors play the second most important role after agriculture in the Indian economy. The author suggests that further economic reform measures are needed to facilitate the participation of private sector investment in infrastructure development urgently needed for the growth of the manufacturing and services sectors.

Agriculture plays the most crucial role in poverty alleviation and economic development in most Asian countries, by providing livelihood to the vast majority of population in the country by providing food and raw materials to the industrial and urban sector and by creating a market for domestically produced manufactured goods in the rural sector. However, agriculturists need secured property rights and adequate agriculture finance to enable the agricultural sector to play its role. Lawson Smith and Alfonso Le discuss such issues in Vietnam's agriculture sector in their study of agricultural development and rural finance in Vietnam in chapter eight. The authors argue that during Vietnam's current period of transition from a socialist economy to a market economy, the concept of property is still evolving but ownership rights of property to private individuals is now enforced and accepted by the government. However, an individual can only obtain land under a 50 year lease initially, with the provision that it can be renewed again and the land lease holder will have the immunity from expropriation of land by the government for any redistribution purposes. Nevertheless, the ownership right to land is also enjoyed by the state along with individuals and private families. Hence, in this sense, in the 1980s, while private individuals did not yet seem to have full control over their land, they did have operational control over land, subject to the fulfilment of the condition of transfer of a part of the output to the state. Gradually, in the 1990s, further land reforms enabled households to gain control over their output and cash flow. Controls over agricultural producer prices were lifted and agricultural product markets were liberalised. The system of Land Use Certificates (LUCs), which was implemented to facilitate the establishment, verification and certification of leases and which covered 90 percent of agricultural land, 75 percent of rural residential land, 25 percent of forest land, 20 percent of urban industrial land and 15 percent of urban residential land, produced a strong positive effect on household income, welfare, poverty alleviation and economic development in Vietnam. The market based land reform also acted as a catalyst for the much needed reform in agricultural credit. In Vietnam, rural finance markets need to promote economic growth by mobilizing resources to improve efficiency in resource allocation, to enhance income distribution and reduce poverty and to establish viable financial institutions. Without external finance, households' capability to increase investment and production in agriculture does not rise. Despite difficulties, formal banking facilities are expanding and providing micro-finance to agriculturalists in rural Vietnam. As a result of these important changes in Vietnam's rural economy, the level of poverty declined considerably.

On the other hand, in Chapter Eleven, Taslim Sjah, Donald Cameron and Leon Russell examine the effectiveness of the current system of publicly dispersed agricultural credit in the Lombok region in Indonesia for improving farmers' income, and comment on how to improve the current system as well as to enable farmers to improve their standard of living. It appears from their analysis that due to the perception among the recipient of loans, that a credit is a gift, many loans are not repaid. Also, since loans are perceived as gifts, they are not judiciously used to improve agricultural output and borrowers' income. Their study further reveals that in the distribution, monitoring and repayment collection of credit, such deficiencies as (i) untimely distribution, either too early or too late, to use the credit effectively; (ii) inadequate monitoring of credit distribution, allocation, and of repayment collection, as well as: (iii) untimely collection of credit repayments. Furthermore, attention was not paid to mark adequate provision of extensive education to track farmers to adopt improved agricultural practices and the need to repay loans.

Thus, it appears that in rural Indonesia the agricultural credit system is highly mis-managed and the market for agricultural loans is still not well established, just as in Vietnam where credit is used ineffectively to produce agricultural goods just enough to maintain their subsistence livelihood and not to improve the productivity of land and labour. In such a situation, people living below or just above the poverty line may continue to stay at these levels.

GENDER RELATED POVERTY

So far, our discussion has centred on economic poverty. But discrimination against women in intra family resource allocation, and in social, economic and political interaction outside the confines of their homes on the basis of their gender constitutes social poverty. Even when women do not suffer from economic poverty, they do suffer from some kind of social poverty. But, when their economic poverty is quite acute, their suffering from social discrimination on the basis of customs and prejudices become quite severe.

In Chapter Twelve, Tabitha Kiriti and Kartik Roy discuss the dimensions of poverty of women in Kenya resulting from gender inequality. The authors' research shows that in most indicators of gender empowerment, considerable gender gaps exist in Kenya. The burden of cuts in government expenditure on education, health and other social services has been borne mostly by women and children. Women are mostly engaged in low-paid informal sector employment and their participation in the decision making process within the family and at the institutional level has been extremely low. For Kenyan women and girls, poverty rates have been rising, life expectancy for women falling, the female child mortality rates have been rising, and the burden of providing sustenance to, and caring of, the family have been rising. All of these indicate that the socio-economic status of women in Kenya has been deteriorating and consequently, their poverty level has not been falling.

Since this poverty is economic as well as is deeply rooted in culture, the authors argue that the alleviation of gender poverty in Kenya, as in other developing countries, requires the adoption of a cultural approach.

SOCIAL SECTOR DEVELOPMENT

D. Sinha in Chapter Five places strong emphasis on the need for social sector development to alleviate poverty in India. He argues that since in India, poverty is heavily concentrated in the rural sector where the supply of social sector goods such as communications, education, health, housing, sanitation and so on, is extremely limited, no lasting solution to the problem of poverty can be found unless the state can ensure an adequate supply of these social sector goods to the poor. He further argues that for achieving success in poverty alleviation and human development programmes, participation of the beneficiaries of the programme in the planning and governance of these programmes is essential. Further more, since women bear the major responsibility of providing sustenance and the overall welfare of their families, greater participation of women in economic and political decision making process is necessary.

In developed countries, the state provides the poverty line income in the form of social security benefits to the extremely poor who have no income to maintain even the subsistence level of living. Hence, there is no poverty in developed countries. One factor which has enabled the state in developed countries to make provision for such benefits for the poor is their low level and low rate of growth of population. On the other hand, in low income countries, higher level and higher rate of growth of population than those in developed countries greatly limit the capacity of the state to perform such a task. Sarbeshwar Chaterjee and Sujit Roy, in their chapter on social security and development in India, contend that the aim of 'social security' extends beyond providing doles and other fringe benefits to the poor to sustain their subsistence level livelihood, to enable the poor to participate in and integrate into the major institutions of the society. While the states in South East Asian countries riding on the back of highly successful growth outcomes have been able to achieve significant reduction in poverty level and high level of social sector development, India's record in these areas is poor. The authors observe that while the Indian social security and social welfare system is still at its formative stage of development, the system, quite wrongly, is aiming to include the majority of population as its expected beneficiaries. The social security systems are implemented by many private sector and public sector agencies. There is not a unified approach to implement the social securities programme. The government expenditure (states and central government) on social security as a percentage of total governmental expenditure on all sectors and also as a percentage of GDP remains very low.

Shukla Deb Kanango, in Chapter four, argues that the elimination of poverty and large scale deprivation among the poor in vast rural hinterlands of India necessitate the acceptance by the state of a community development approach as the centre piece of the rural development policy framework. In India, although the state is the major player in implementing community development programmes, it is playing increasing reliance on private sector agencies to carry forward community development works. However, the author argues that since government initiated service programmes are implemented without first consulting with the target groups of beneficiaries, and subsequently involving these groups in the programme implementation, the risk of non-acceptance of such services by the intended beneficiary groups remains high. On the other hand, voluntary agencies usually get intended beneficiaries involved in every stage of the implementation of a community development project as well as in its governance in the post-implementation period. Hence, the acceptance rate of such projects by the target groups of people remains quite high. Over the years, different voluntary organisations have pursued different goals. While some implement their own projects to improve the economic and social conditions of communities at local level, others organise popular participation to improve the performance of government programmes as well as to facilitate the formation of public opinion on many issues of national and international interest.

Commenting on the progress of community development in India, the author notes that for realising the goal of poverty alleviation through community development, the need for honest and efficient democratic government is of paramount importance. However, the corruption in India's political parties and in the government, which pursues the agenda of the political party power instead of genuinely trying to improve the social and economic condition of the poor, have prevented the state sponsored programmes from achieving high rates of success. Nevertheless, she feels that decentralisation of the power of governance at the village level from the provincial government to thousands of local governments will ensure peoples' participation in programmes to improve their own well being.

Finally, R. James Ferguson, in chapter thirteen, discusses the issues in Indonesia's regional interaction with its ASEAN neighbours which is crucial to achieving success in its developmental goals, and of which poverty alleviation is an important component. While each member of the ASEAN accepts that in the absence of political and social stability in the region, more of ASEAN countries can successfully pursue its development programmes, all of them accept Indonesia as a stabilizing factor in the wider region. Nevertheless, Indonesia has faced many problems such as terrorism, inflow of illegal workers, not so friendly relations with Malaysia, cross-boundary environmental damage from forest fires, people smuggling, money laundering, and enormous corruption at all levels of economic and social activities. Despite all these drawbacks, Indonesia has achieved some success in its social development programmes. However, the future success of all countries in this region in preserving the gains they have made in economic and social development depends crucially on deepening the co-operation among all member countries in the East and South East Asian regions in Indonesia.

CONCLUSION

Thus, a number of important lessons that emerge from the discussions presented in this book are outlined below:

Firstly, policy makers in each country need to understand the nature and dimensions of poverty that exist in their country before formulating and implementing poverty alleviation policies.

Secondly, while the re-distribution of income in favour of the poor and direct transfer of income or goods from the state to the poor can alleviate poverty temporarily, these cannot be sustained for a long time by the state unless it achieves high rate of economic growth. Hence, implementing growth-promoting economic policies is crucial to achieving success in poverty alleviation programmes.

Thirdly, the preservation of the environment is necessary to achieve success in poverty alleviation programmes as natural resources provide essential inputs to economic development activities, and also supply to the rural poor a part of their daily needs of food, fuel and fodder. However, increased development activities also contribute to the degradation of the environment. Hence, a win-win strategy of environmental preservation, economic development and poverty alleviation needs to be implemented by all developing countries in the Asia pacific and in other regions.

Fourthly, in any developing country, the growth of manufacturing and service industries is essential for poverty alleviation because these industries can accelerate a country's economic growth rate and can employ a large number of unemployed skilled, semi-skilled and unskilled labourers.

Fifthly, while economic poverty adversely affects both men and women, women suffer from economic as well as cultural poverty. Hence, special attention needs to be paid to the alleviation of poverty of women and girls in each country.

Sixthly, rapid progress made in social sector development in a country can help a country eliminate poverty. The expansion of a social security system in a country can also reduce the level of poverty. But, the successful implementation of any programme of social sector development rests on peoples' co-operation in its design and implementation.

Finally, for any goal of development to be realised, it is necessary for the particular state and other states in the region to maintain co-operation amongst themselves in important political, social, economic and other development issues.

INDEX

A

B

E

F

G

H

N

O

P

T

U